SPIRIT, SCIENCE, AND HEALTH

SPIRIT, SCIENCE, AND HEALTH

HOW THE SPIRITUAL MIND FUELS PHYSICAL WELLNESS

Edited by Thomas G. Plante and Carl E. Thoresen

Foreword by Albert Bandura

4/08

PRAEGER

Westport, Connecticut
London

Library of Congress Cataloging-in-Publication Data

Spirit, science, and health : how the spiritual mind fuels physical wellness /
[edited by] Thomas G. Plante and Carl E. Thoresen ; foreword by Al Bandura.
    p. cm.
    Includes bibliographical references and index.
    ISBN 978–0–275–99506–5 (alk. paper)
    1. Spiritual healing.   2. Medicine—Religious aspects—Christianity.
    3. Health—Religious aspects—Christianity.   4. Mind and body.
    I. Plante, Thomas G.   II. Thoresen, Carl E.
    BT732.5.S665 2007
    201'.7621—dc22   2007016344

British Library Cataloguing in Publication Data is available.

Library of Congress Catalog Card Number: 2007016344
ISBN-13: 978–0–275–99506–5
ISBN-10: 0–275–99506–2

First published in 2007

Praeger Publishers, 88 Post Road West, Westport, CT 06881
An imprint of Greenwood Publishing Group, Inc.
www.praeger.com

Printed in the United States of America

The paper used in this book complies with the
Permanent Paper Standard issued by the National
Information Standards Organization (Z39.48–1984).

10 9 8 7 6 5 4 3 2 1

Contents

Foreword

In this comprehensive volume, Plante and Thoresen provide an insightful overview of issues regarding the influence of spirituality on human health. The recent years have witnessed a major change in the conception of health from a disease model to a health model. It emphasizes health promotion not just disease prevention and disease management. The quality of health is heavily influenced by lifestyle habits. This makes beneficial self-management good medicine.

Health psychology has emerged as a burgeoning field of study. This work is providing new insights into the role of psychosocial factors in human health and the mechanisms through which they produce their effects. Although spirituality, broadly defined, is a significant part of most people's lives, it is rarely included among the traditional psychosocial factors, except in a cursory way. The present volume documents the positive relation of faith and spirituality to health outcomes. Within this context, it addresses a variety of issues, including the conception of spirituality, its development, assessment, and possible ways in which it fosters a healthful life. There is much to be gained by integrating these seemingly divergent paths of theorizing and research.

Social cognitive theory lends itself readily to such an integration because it highlights distinctly human attributes that provide the very capacity for becoming a spiritual being. These attributes include the capacity for symbolization, social modeling, forethought, self-regulation, and self-reflection. Through the power of symbolization, people give structure, meaning, and continuity to their lives. The capacity for forethought enables people to transcend the dictates of their immediate environment. Through exercise of forethought, people motivate themselves and guide their actions anticipatorily. When projected over a long time course on matters of value, a forethoughtful perspective provides direction, coherence, and meaning to one's life. One cannot sit back and wait for faith and spirituality to do the work. It requires a lot of self-regulative effort to turn faith and spiritual beliefs into a life one considers worth living. Through the capacity for self-reflectiveness, people reflect on the meaning of their pursuits, their personal efficacy, and the soundness and functional value of their styles of thinking and behaving. Self-reflection extends beyond self-management of everyday activities. People reflect on the life they have led and the legacy they want to leave. With foreknowledge of their passing, people's self-reflection turns to transcendental and spiritual issues.

The initial efforts by Oman and Thoresen to advance understanding of the development and exercise of spirituality from the perspective of social cognitive theory illustrate the mutual benefits of an integrative approach. Their conceptual analysis offers fresh insights into a variety of linkages of basic knowledge about the determinants and mechanisms of observational learning to spiritual beliefs and practices. Research on spiritual modeling, in turn, extends the scope of modeling to scriptural, transcendent, and inspirational exemplars that have received little attention in traditional psychological theorizing and research.

This edited volume provides an in depth analysis of how faith and spirituality contribute to human health. This is the type of formative analysis that lays the foundation for clarifying how spirituality operates in concert with other psychosocial influences in fostering lifestyles that promote health and those that impair. It will serve as a valuable resource to a wide spectrum of readers.

Albert Bandura, PhD
David Starr Professor of Social Sciences in Psychology
Stanford University
Stanford, California

Preface

Relationships between religion and health outcomes have existed for thousands of years. Regardless of the many different religious or spiritual traditions, many have turned to these wisdom traditions for help in understanding many of life's major concerns: Why am I here? What is the meaning of life? What happens after I die? What is good or bad, right or wrong? What should I believe about myself and other people? How do I best cope with physical, mental, and social stressors? Answers to these universal questions can be found in varying degrees in the major religious traditions of the world.

While these fundamental questions about life may appear quite diverse, they all in some way seem to relate to the overall health and well-being of the person. We now know, for example, that many so-called mental health problems, such as depression, anxiety, and hostility, often have physical health facets to them. Depression influences, sometimes in very serious ways, a variety of physical health processes in the body. The same is true of anxiety and hostility. Similarly, those suffering from major chronic diseases, such as cardiovascular diseases, various cancers, and HIV/AIDS, often struggle with many mental and social emotional health problems as well. Scientific studies continue to confirm an ancient truism that human beings are highly complex organisms with countless networks that connect what we often think of as separate psychological, physiological, and behavioral systems. Thus, for example, the heart itself has been found in research studies to be connected neurologically with the emotional sectors of the brain, something that ancient scriptures proclaimed. In addition, the consistent practice of meditation—where attention is focused on compassionate thought and feelings—has been shown to alter how the brain functions. That is, the controlled study of long-term mediators have yielded dramatic results showing that brain functioning has been substantially increased in the area of the brain linked to positive emotions, making plans, and caring for others. Such scientific studies help refute the long-standing belief that consciousness is a by-product of the brain. Instead, these data show for the first time that one's attention—consciousness—influences how the brain works. Such findings support longstanding religious beliefs that what one habitually thinks about, especially the focus of attention, can alter the character and conduct of one's life.

In recent years, the popular press and mass media have highlighted some of these findings and related issues with many news stories examining relationships between science and religion. Of particular interest has been the role of faith and spirituality in health. Furthermore, scientists from many different academic disciplines have conducted hundreds of empirical research studies on religion and health. While many of these research studies have suffered from weaknesses in how they were designed and conducted, making firm conclusions impossible, more recent research has been conducted with much higher quality of methodological and statistical rigor. Increasingly these quality studies now appear in major scientific professional publications.

The evidence now available suggests, but does not prove, that spiritual and religious practices are often associated with healthier living and positive health outcomes. This includes positive health behaviors and practices, enhanced ability to cope with stressors, including many illnesses, and even with lower rates of all-cause mortality among reasonably healthy adults. Religiously involved people tend to avoid major risk factors for disease, such as cigarette smoking, alcohol abuse, and unsafe sexual practices. Scientists have also found that spiritual and religious involvement is closely associated with better social, emotional, and mental health, such as lower levels of depression, anxiety, as well as better self-esteem, marital stability and life satisfaction, happiness, and perceived well-being. Importantly, studies are also reporting that spirituality and religious engagement relates to positive qualities and personal strengths and character factors, including positive emotions and behaviors, such as forgiveness, hope, and volunteering to serve others. These positive factors are also associated with positive mental and physical health outcomes.

Currently, as with any scientific area of study, the more we come to know, the more we realize what we do not know. An increasing number of issues and questions have been emerging about how we can better clarify how spiritual and religious factors may influence health and how to use current scientific understanding of the spirituality and health relationship to assist the general population. For example, questions such as: How are spiritual models developed? How do models influence spiritual beliefs and practices? Does having a greater sense of purpose, meaning, and vocation in life result in better physical and mental health? How can mindfulness-based meditation and similar techniques be used to improve health outcomes? What are feasible ways to incorporate spiritual practices into a multicultural, multireligious/multispiritual, chronically stressful and hurried, and often quasisecular, highly individualistic culture and environment? These kinds of questions, and many others, are addressed in this book project.

While there are a growing number of empirical studies and several books that have examined relationships between faith and health, no contemporary comprehensive book currently exists that provides state-of-the-art thinking and findings from experts in this area of research and practice from multidisciplinary perspectives. The purpose of this book project is to publish a scholarly and multidisciplinary edited book on the topic of spirituality and health that includes state-of-the-art science and practice written for an educated lay readership and professional audience. The chapters articulate current findings and practice in spirituality and health from the perspectives of psychology, medicine, religious studies, public health, nursing, and pastoral care.

In order to avoid some of the disadvantages of edited books, which sometimes feel fragmented, and to increase the flow between chapters, most of the contributors participated in a conference at Santa Clara University during March 2006 to present their research to each other and to the local professional healthcare community. The conference was cosponsored by the Spirituality and Health Special Interest Group, chaired by Carl E. Thoresen, which is part of the Society of Behavioral Medicine (SBM) as well as the Santa Clara University Spirituality and Health Institute (SHI) directed by Thomas G. Plante. Furthermore, many of the contributors are members of the Santa Clara University SHI who meet regularly to discuss multidisciplinary research and practice in the area of spirituality and health. We hope that the conference and ongoing research institute activities has resulted in a more cohesive and seamless book.

Acknowledgments

Numerous people other than the author(s) or editor (s) assist in the development and completion of a book project. Some provide help in a direct and concrete manner, while others provide help in less direct and more supportive ways. We would like to acknowledge the assistance of the many people who have helped in both ways and have contributed to the development of this project.

First, we would like to thank the many wonderful people at Greenwood/Praeger who have enthusiastically worked to publish this book. We'd especially like to thank editor, Debora Carvalko for her strong interest in the project and her high level of professionalism and vision.

Second, we would like to thank the Santa Clara University Ignatian Center for Jesuit Education and Christian Values (recent directors include Drs. William Spohn, Dennis Moberg, and Fr. Kevin Quinn, S.J., for funding and supporting our research institute and activities on campus.

Finally, we would like to thank friends, colleagues, mentors, and families who have been supportive and instructive in a variety of diverse ways over the years. For Thomas Plante these include mentor Fr. Sonny Manuel, S.J., and family members Lori and Zachary Plante, Eli and Marilyn Goldfarb, Marcia Plante, Mary Beauchemin, Lee Sperduti, Henry and Anna McCormick, and Margaret Condon. For Carl Thoresen, these include mentors Al Bandura, Meyer Friedman, and James Gill, S.J. especially colleagues Alex Sox-Harris and Doug Oman, and family and other colleagues and friends, especially Kay Thoresen, along with Ed Bridges, Ed Burling, Ray Cobb, Ken xiv I **Acknowledgments**

Pargament, Lynda Powell, and Dave Wolf, plus several Stanford doctoral
students interested in discussing spirituality, psychology, and health issues.

Thomas G. Plante
Santa Clara, California
and
Carl E. Thoresen
Los Gatos, California

PART 1

Overview, Assessment, and Modeling

CHAPTER 1

Spirituality, Religion, and Health: What's the Deal?

CARL E. THORESEN

Back in the early 1990s while attending the annual meeting of the Society of Behavioral Medicine (SBM), a colleague asked me what I thought about religion and health? "Not much," I answered, mentioning that I'd never given it much thought. Being asked that question, however, reminded me of my earlier work with postcoronary ("heart attack") patients in the 1980s, who were typically very Type A in their behavior (i.e., quickness to anger, hostile attitude, time-urgent/impatient). Thanks to the pioneering work of cardiologists Meyer Friedman, who discovered the Type A behavior pattern with Ray Rosenman at Mt. Zion Medical Center in San Francisco, I was able to learn a great deal about the social and emotional behaviors and beliefs of recovering heart attack patients.

What came to mind, when asked the above question about religion and health, were these coronary patients. It struck me at the time how much we may have missed the spiritual and religious boat in our work with them. Yes, many benefited in avoiding recurrent heart attacks, some fatal, from our psychologically focused small group treatment. Yes, they learned to reduce abrupt explosive anger episodes, curb their "hurry sickness," and take the edge off their highly competitive approaches to life. But no, we failed to even acknowledge any possible role of spiritual or religious factors that might impact their recovery. Could our approach to helping them avoid future heart attacks and other problems been more effective if we had at least inquired about their spiritual and religious beliefs in ways that clearly respected them yet allowed them, if they were interested, to access these beliefs and traditions in coping more effectively with their health problems? More specifically, would some recognition of their religious beliefs and practices have helped them better understand and resolve some of the challenging issues they struggled with: making major changes in their lifestyles address-ing issues of meaning, self-identity, direction in life, as well as their fears and anxieties about death and dying? I suspect that with informed hindsight the answer is probably, yes.

In this brief introduction I will try to clarify why there may be an upsurge in spiritual interest evidenced in the popular press as well as the different meanings of spirituality and religion. Then I will briefly summarize some of the most compelling research evidence to date.

Why the Interest in Spirituality and Health?

Part of the remarkable recent interest in the relationship between spiritu-ality and health has emerged from the surge of publicity about results of recent scientific studies linking various features of spirituality or religion with positive health-related outcomes. The covers of *Time* and *Newsweek*, for example, have frequently featured some facet of spirituality or religion in health, such as findings of Tibetan Buddhist meditation studies on brain functioning. Several studies have reported, for example, that persons at-tending some kind of religious or spiritual service or ceremony regularly (e.g., once weekly or more) compared to nonattenders live longer.[1, 2] Living longer is equated with living roughly 7 years longer than nonattenders when random samples of the general public are used (that is, in mostly healthy people). In one major study, the health benefits for African American males who attended services weekly was associated with living almost 14 years longer than nonattending African American males.

Keep in mind that over 90 percent of Americans believe in God, gener-ally the personal monotheistic God of the Judeo/Christian/Islamic tradition, although that is shifting with growing numbers of Americans involved in other religious traditions such as Hindu and Buddhist traditions. On av-erage approximately 40 percent of all Americans attend religious services weekly, although that number varies widely in different metropolitan areas (e.g., about 20 percent in San Francisco compared to over 60 percent in Atlanta). Perhaps more importantly, a clear majority of Americans report that their religious beliefs and practices provide a primary source of meaning and purpose in their lives.[3, 4] Indeed some note that their religiousness or spirituality offers them a kind of moral compass or framework not other-wise available in the midst of a highly technological and secularized culture. As one colleague who works in community social services recently noted: "... [my spirituality] centers me, it calms me, it gives me peace ... and it gives me energy I didn't know I had." It may not be surprising that some-one might make a comment like this since history provides exemplars of people who have excelled in life, often against all odds, in striving to meet the needs and welfare of others, often above their own needs. Such persons can be considered spiritual or religious models, illustrating for others how they struggled to overcome more individualistic and hedonistic lifestyles encouraged in our contemporary culture. Some might call this downsizing the demands of excessive, "fill the room" egos.

One of the most interesting studies on the prevalence of interest in spirituality and religion comes from the first nationwide study of spirituality and religiousness in 112,232 beginning college students attending 236 diverse colleges and universities.[5] Their interest reflects comments about meaning and purpose. Most (75 percent) report searching for meaning and purpose such as: "What am I going to do with my life? How will I know if I'm going in the right direction? What kind of person do I want to be?" A total of 80 percent reported that they attended religious services at least once in the past year, 67 percent claim they pray regularly, and 67 percent state that they find strength and comfort from their spiritual or religious beliefs. As with their adult counterparts most ranged from very conservative to very liberal in particular beliefs concerning political and social issues. Positive relationships to health were found among students who were not struggling with their religious beliefs nor conflicted about them. Those who endorsed spiritual factors tended to be somewhat more compassionate, accepting of others, and universal in their outlook.

Are Spirituality and Religion/Religiousness the Same Concepts?

Many challenges emerge in trying to define and assess spirituality and religion/religiousness. Both concepts are complex with several facets or features, some of which are latent, that is, not directly observable but are inferable.[1, 6] Such complexity is no stranger to psychology or science in general. Very important concepts remain difficult to articulate and lack complete agreement about how best to define them. Examples include personality, leadership, wisdom, and health. Given this complexity there is no clear consensus on how to best describe, define, or measure spirituality and religion. Both concepts are clearly related to each other and both contain a connection with what is perceived as sacred in life. For example, one definition of spirituality refers to a person's or a group's search for the sacred and defines religiousness as the same but adds that the search is within a traditional sacred context or setting, as offered by a religion, its house of worship such as a church or temple, and its traditions of belief and practice.[6] Sacred often refers to what is divine or holy or most meaningful and significant. Generally, spirituality has come to focus on the individual and religion is seen as the context and setting in which one seeks the sacred. If spirituality is viewed as seeking the sacred, and religion is primarily the context or social institution that seeks to provide spiritual experiences, then it seems that goals or destinations as well as pathways to reach these goals are involved. In many ways the task of religious institutions, or groups outside of a formal religion, is to provide the knowledge, understanding, skills, and motivation needed to help individuals make progress on their spiritual pathways. Some evidence suggests that religious institutions and other community groups are not providing the needed teaching and learning of spiritual skills and practices that can be used in daily life.[7, 8] Some also wonder if too much attention is given to the right religious beliefs at the cost of less spiritual awareness and practice.[9] The lack of skills in using spiritual practices may be the single missing ingredient that inhibits the kind of spiritual growth that leads to better health and well-being.

A rapidly emerging area of interest involves persons who describe themselves as "spiritual but not religious." Such persons now represent between 20 and 35 percent of the American public. Some attend church services but do not become formal members. Others may view organized religion as antispiritual in nature, focused more on creeds, dogma, ritual, and money as well as abusive of power. Currently we know little about this subgroup of individuals, some of whom have become disenchanted with organized religion, often holding the view that religious institutions do more to obstruct rather than facilitate spiritual growth and development. One finding seems robust: those who identify themselves as spiritual but not religious are not a uniform subgroup but seem to be a composite of those ranging from friendly about religion to very antagonistic with most probably in between these two extreme positions. In addition, this category appears relevant mostly among those who are seeking and searching for ways to be more spiritual, while many church members may be called dwellers rather than seekers, those comfortable with traditional religion focused on the attending church as a place of worship.[10]

What's the Evidence Linking Spirituality, Religion, and Health?

From a conservative, scientific perspective, the evidence is highly suggestive that some reliable if not robust relationships exist between some spiritual and religious factors and some health indicators. Is that relationship causal? That is, do we know, for example, that prayer or attending religious services or volunteering to serve others causes better health or less disease? The answer is no because causal evidence is not currently available. True and perfectly conducted scientific studies cannot be accomplished since, for example, you cannot randomly assign newborns to various religious or nonreligious groups and follow their health outcomes over years, while confined to the experimentally manipulated and controlled group assignment. Granted one can choose to believe that such evidence is available based upon their personal experience, religious texts, or the opinion of others, such as religious leaders. But from a scientific perspective, which is inherently cautious and skeptical, the evidence is not there to claim that spiritual or religious beliefs or practices directly cause better health.

What we do know is based mostly, especially the most impressive evidence, connecting spiritual and religious factors to health, on people who are not suffering from serious diseases, that is, who are fairly healthy people. The strongest evidence linking spiritual and religious factors with health outcomes has been from several large sample studies that followed people over several years. Frequent religious service attendance (i.e., once weekly or more) predicted lower mortality rates when compared to those who attended less often or not at all.[2] Overall, the magnitude of this difference was between 25 and 30 percent fewer deaths; in some studies, women benefited more from attendance than men. This evidence was deemed "persuasive" based on using a set of rigorous criteria to identify well-designed and controlled studies. These findings were provided by an Expert Panel of the National Institutes of Health.[2, 7]

Over 1,000 research studies have appeared in various professional publications on this topic. Understandably, there has been a tendency to confuse if not sometimes misrepresent the evidence by people who have an agenda to promote (either pro or con) about spiritual and religious benefits. Given all of these studies, why is there such limited evidence linking spiritual and religious factors with health? Many reasons exist. Most importantly, just because a study is published does not mean that the study was well done or even adequately conducted. Put simply, the vast majority of studies have looked at the relationships between a spiritual or religious factor and a health indicator of some kind (a physical, social, or mental indicator) at one point in time (called cross-sectional studies). Without knowing which came first (e.g., did prayer come before or after the reduction in depression?) or the relationship reported stable once? Would the same relationship be found if the person's spiritual experiences scale score and blood pressure were measured 3 months later compared to just one time? It is difficult to draw any conclusions in a study conducted only at one point in time regarding a spiritual factor and a health outcome.

We do have, however, many promising hunches from these numerous cross-sectional studies worthy of exploration. It is clear that those who are religiously active, such as frequently attending religious services, tend to engage in less unhealthy behaviors, such as less cigarette smoking, alcohol or drug abuse, unsafe sexual behavior, and more use of seat belts. Also some evidence indicates that spiritual or religiously active persons often experience less depression and anxieties, both linked to health problems, such as coronary disease and immune-related disorders.

One way to clarify how spiritual and religious factors might influence health is to consider possible ways in which they could alter health. Oman and Thoresen[1] have suggested dividing possible ways (called mechanisms) that we have reason to believe could influence health. These possible

mechanisms can shed light on ways that spiritual or religious factors influence health indirectly. These include the following:

- Health behaviors (as noted above, such as less smoking, drug abuse,
  more exercise, and less high-risk behaviors).
- Psychological states (religious or spiritual groups could promote more
  positive emotions, behavior, and thoughts, such as hope, optimism,
  compassion for others and oneself, and forgiveness. In doing so, this
  could reduce the overall burden on the body (called allostatic load)
  and on the mind in that the positive can crowd out the negative
  states).
- Coping (use of positive religious or spiritual ways to manage better
  the challenges and stresses in everyday living, especially dealing with
  negative emotions, such as depression, chronic anger, despair, fears,
  and low self-esteem in more effective ways).
- Social and emotional support (one way that spiritual or religious groups
  can impact health and disease risk is by providing a sense of community
  where one is known and cared for by others. Loneliness can greatly
  harm health and support can be vital, especially if one knows that
  others are providing care and concern by their prayers, their fellowship,
  and their tangible acts of helping.

Currently, the search for possible mediators of spiritual and religious factors that link such factors indirectly to health is a hot topic. A mediating
factor can be thought of something that helps explain why one factor, such
as religious attendance, predicts a health factor indirectly, such as changes in
mortality risk. A fascinating example of this mediating relationship is found
in a study of older adults.[11] High religious services attendees (weekly or
more) were found to have much lower mortality (68 percent fewer deaths)
compared to nonattenders. However that relationship was mediated by another factor, Interleukin-6 (IL-6), a cytokine that fosters several disease processes. High attendance by itself did not directly predict fewer deaths. High
attendance did, however, predict fewer deaths indirectly because attendance
was related to lower levels of IL-6, which in turn directly predicted mortality.
Other factors also directly predicted mortality but when these other factors
were controlled, such as depression and gender, attendance still remained a
significant predictor of less IL-6. The search for mediators will foster major improvements in how studies are conducted, in part because they often
require greater controls and broader assessments. In addition, such studies can encourage if not improve the quality of discourse about spiritual
and religious with colleagues since it moves inquiry beyond simple correlational studies that relate variables without much concern for theoretical
issues.

Closing Comments

Some connections do exist between spiritual and religious factors and the health and well-being of people. Just how and in what way these connections function is a challenging problem, but one well worth the effort. Clearly not every person will be influenced by a particular belief or practice. But undeniably matters of the spirit are very important to many people and with persistent and patient effort we will be able to discern ways that spirituality and religion influence health and well-being.

One area remains understudied because it is very sensitive for many and remains somewhat of a taboo topic. This involves spiritual and religious factors and practices that are harmful if not hazardous to health. It may be that in this area of human experience many are reluctant to even raise questions about possible danger to health created by some religious beliefs or practices. The widely publicized cases of clergy abuse as well as religion-based terrorism have opened the doors rather dramatically to acknowledging the downside of religion and some of its institutional practices. We need to be mindful of the possible harm of religious beliefs and practices and explore ways to prevent harm and hazards to health from developing.

The growing collaborations of empirical scientists with professional religious and spiritual scholars and practitioners bode well.[12] All have much to learn from each other yet each has a sphere of theory and practice that merits respect and may remain distinctively different. Hopefully these collaborative efforts will temper at times the dismissive critiques of some who demean any possible value of having scientists and religious and spiritual professionals work together, since the two domains are sometimes perceived as inherently incompatible. This text offers examples of how colleagues have worked together successfully with lots of mutual respect and warm support to tackle challenging yet compelling topics.

References

1. Oman, D. & Thoresen, C.E. (2005). Do religion and spirituality influence health? In R.F. Paloutzian & C.L. Park (Eds.), *Handbook of the psychology of religion and spirituality* (pp. 435–459). New York: Guilford Press.
2. Powell, L.H., Shahabi, L., & Thoresen, C.E. (2003). Religion and spirituality: Linkages to physical health. *American Psychologist, 58*, 36–42.
3. Paloutzian, R.F. & Park, C.L. (2005). Integrative themes in the current science of the psychology of religion. In R. F. Paloutzian & C. L. Park (Eds.), *Handbook of the psychology of religion and spirituality* (pp. 3–20). New York: Guilford Press.
4. Oman, D. & Thoresen, C.E. (2003). Spiritual modeling: A key to spiritual and religious growth? *The International Journal for the Psychology of Religion, 13*, 149–165.

5. Astin, A.W. & Astin, H.S. (2005). The spiritual lives of college students: A national study of college student's search for meaning and purpose. *Executive Summary*. Access: http://www.spirituality.ucla.edu.
6. Zinnbauer, B.J. & Pargament, K.I. (2005). Religiousness and spirituality. In R.F. Paloutzian & C.L. Park (Eds.), *Handbook of the psychology of religion and spirituality* (pp. 21–42). New York: Guilford Press.
7. Miller, W.R. & Thoresen, C.E. (2003). Spirituality, religion and health: An emerging research field. *American Psychologist, 58*, 24–35.
8. Wuthrow, R. (1998). *After heaven: Spirituality in America since the 1950s*. Berkeley, CA: University of California Press.
9. Borg. M. (2003) *The heart of Christianity*. San Francisco, CA: Harper Collins.
10. Fuller, R. C. (2001). *Spiritual but not religious*. New York: Oxford University Press.
11. Lutgendorf, S.K., Russell, D., Ulrich, P., Harris, T.B., & Wallace, R. (2004). Religious participation, interleukin-6, and mortality in older adults. *Health Psychology, 23*, 465–475.
12. Barbour, I. (2000). *When science meets religion*. San Francisco, CA: Harper Collins.

CHAPTER 2

Prayer and Health

KEVIN S. MASTERS

The English word prayer comes from the Latin *precari* meaning to entreat or ask earnestly. Curiously, this is the same root found in the word precarious. Indeed many pray when life seems precarious and it is during times of illness or great need that prayer is perhaps most widely acknowledged and practiced. There seems to be an almost intuitive notion among people of faith in many cultures that prayer and health are related.

Among the religious, prayer has long been considered a central practice. Highly regarded psychology and religion scholar William James, in his oft quoted passage, noted that prayer is "...the very soul and essence of religion" (p. 486).[1] Though seminaries and other institutions of higher learning devoted to religious studies offer academic examinations of prayer, mostly prayer has been and remains the province of the church, synagogue, mosque, and individual devotee. Gallup polls conducted over the last 50 years continue to reveal that Americans largely believe in and practice prayer. Over this time the finding that about nine out of ten people pray has remained relatively constant with three out of four saying they do so on a daily basis.[2] Although the practice of prayer is highly prevalent among the U.S. population, certain groups appear to be both more likely to pray and more likely to pray frequently. Women, African Americans, and older adults all pray more than men, white Americans, and younger persons though in many cases the percentage differences are small.[3]

People pray, of course, for many things but prayers pertaining to health occupy a particular place of significance for believers of many faiths and there is documentation that these prayers were practiced in antiquity. For example, early Christians practiced prayers for divine healing and the Bible records several instances where these prayers were answered in the affirmative (e.g., Matthew 8:1–13; 15:29–31; John 2:1–13). The Qur'an and Hadith describe two kinds of prayer for health said by Muslims, one may be offered anywhere including from a distance whereas the other must be said in person. In addition to regular prayers said five times daily, Muslims are encouraged to offer du'a or prayers of personal supplication in their own words in any language (Qur'an 2:186, 40:60). During services members of the Muslim faith may ask the imam to say a special prayer at the end of daily services for a person who is sick, with the congregation affirming the prayer. In Judaism, prayers for healing of the sick are an ancient practice that continues as a regular part of services. Members of the synagogue may either call out the names of individuals who are ill or ask the rabbi to announce them.

A recent study by the National Center for Complementary and Alternative Medicine, a division of the U.S. National Institutes of Health, noted that of the ten most often used forms of alternative medicine, prayer for self and prayer for others were the two most commonly named therapies and being in a prayer group was fifth.[4] The use of prayer is so common and apparently widely known that some recent studies of alternative medical therapies excluded it from the outset in order to focus on other lesser-known practices or treatments! Practicing prayer is not unique to the United States. A recent study conducted in Malaysia among Malaysian Muslims found that prayer was the help-seeking behavior most strongly endorsed in response to two stories portraying individuals with mental health problems (scores averaged approximately four out of five on a scale where five meant "very, certainly helpful").[5] Reported in the same study, this time among a group of Chinese of whom 85 percent were Buddhist, prayer ranked notably lower than it did among the Malaysians, yet relative to other help-seeking strategies, it still was accorded a relatively high endorsement. Prayer for health is not only practiced by patients, their families, clergy, and members of their faith community but is also common among at least some health care professionals. A 2005 U.S. national survey of critical care nurses noted that 73 percent of the nurses had used prayer in their practice, 81 percent had recommended it to patients, and 79 percent had been requested by patients and families to pray on their behalf.[6]

Academic Study in Prayer

With growing interest in studying alternative forms of medical therapy, and the acknowledgment that prayer is the most common of these practices, a small but developing body of scholarly scientific research on prayer and how it does or does not relate/contribute to health has emerged. But to study prayer in a scientific manner is a complicated task because prayer as typically practiced is not readily amenable to the types of controlled experimentation that scientists seek to employ and observational studies are often difficult to interpret. For example, many studies measure how often people pray and then relate this to some indicator of health, often a verbal or written report from study participants. Upon first reflection this appears to be a straightforward approach that renders useful and interpretable information; for example, if people who pray more often also report better health then evidence for a beneficial effect of prayer on health has potentially been documented. The problem with this interpretation becomes evident when another relationship is observed. What if instead of finding that more prayer relates to better health what is found is more prayer relates to worse health? What then is the interpretation? In point of fact, both relationships have been observed in the scientific literature. One hypothesis to explain the latter finding is that perhaps people who pray more often are prone toward avoidance methods of coping with stress. Thus, they may fail to take proper action to remedy difficult situations and perhaps become more focused on their poor health through their concentration on it during prayers that ask for healing. This combination of behaviors may lead to greater levels of anxiety and greater anxiety predicts a number of negative health outcomes. In this view, prayer may be an indirect cause of poor health. Alternatively, the relationship might be explained by the observation that individuals who are already suffering through poor health tend to pray more often for their health. In this explanation there is a relationship between number of prayers (more) and worse health, but the worse health "caused," or more accurately preceded, more prayers. Investigators that attempt to explain the sometimes disparate findings of studies that draw relationships between amount of prayer and health have used statistical methods to attempt to rule out other factors that could confound interpretations and have tried to determine which came first, the prayer or the poor health. In the end, however, it remains difficult to draw firm conclusions from observational studies alone; they simply do not use adequate methods to convincingly discern the effects of prayer on health and vice verse.

Another limitation of these studies is that they are quite limited in the information they can provide on the dynamic factors or mechanisms that may be operating in the relationship between prayer and health. For example, they tell us nothing about the emotional or spiritual experience of the individual who is praying, the content of the prayer, or the meaning of the prayer to the supplicant. Fortunately, some investigators have explored these aspects of prayer and provide us with additional and important information.

In 1991 Poloma and Pendleton[7] published the results of an interview survey they conducted with over 500 residents of Akron, Ohio. Based on these data they were able to use statistical methods to identify four distinct types of prayer: (1) petitionary prayer—requesting that God meet specific material needs of self and friends; (2) colloquial prayer—a type of conversation with

God that includes petitionary elements but of a less concrete and specific form than in petitionary prayer; (3) ritual prayer—recitation of prepared prayers available from prayer books, other written sources, or memory; and (4) meditative prayer—perhaps the most difficult of the four to define, meditative prayer involves components of intimacy and relationship with God and is described as adoring, reflecting, and communicating. It is described as less active, verbal, and intercessional than the other three types identified above (see Chapters 5, 6, and 7 of this volume for discussions on passage meditation, meditation in general, and mantram or holy name repetition). Many other prayer typologies have been developed but the work of Poloma and Pendleton is notable for its basis in empirical data and the fact that in subsequent analyses they were able to determine that these different types of prayer had different relationships with aspects of well-being. For example, whereas only meditative prayer demonstrated a significant beneficial relationship with existential well-being and religious satisfaction, colloquial prayer was the only type of prayer to relate to happiness. Also notable was that ritual prayer demonstrated a relationship with negative emotions such that more ritual prayer related to greater experience of emotions such as sadness, loneliness, tension, and fear. Beyond the types of prayers, however, these authors found that the subjective experiences of the individuals praying were the most consistent predictors of well-being. That is, persons who during their prayers felt like they were experiencing an interaction with God or had feelings of increased peace were also the ones more likely to report greater levels of general well-being. Although this research is still observational, it furthers our conceptualization of prayer beyond simple numerical counts of prayer occurrences.

Scientific Research on Distant Intercessory Prayer

Building on the pioneering work of Poloma and Pendleton, McCullough and Larson[8] identified a fifth type of prayer, intercessory prayer. Strictly speaking, intercessory prayer is prayer said for someone else, that is, one individual serves as the "intercessor" (i.e., one interceding or intervening) for another by offering up prayers on the other's behalf. Thus, an intercessory prayer could be said in the presence of the other person, as is done during rituals such as laying on of hands for healing, or it may be offered from a distance, that is, without the presence of the person who is the object of the prayers. Further, intercessory prayers may be said for individuals who do not know that they are being prayed for, as in instances when strangers pray for others or when family/friends pray for a loved one without informing the loved one of the prayers. Many major religious traditions (e.g., Christianity, Islam, and Judaism) accept intercessory prayer as a regular demonstration of their faith.

The first recorded instance of scientists turning their attention to the topic of intercessory prayer likely occurred in 1872 when Sir Francis Galton made it an object of study (cited in Poloma and Pendleton).[7] He later stated, "It is asserted by some, that men possess the faculty of obtaining results over which they have little or no direct personal control, by means of devout and earnest prayer, while others doubt the truth of this assertion. The question regards a matter of fact, that has to be determined by observation and not by authority; and it is one that appears to be a very suitable topic for statistical inquiry... Are prayers answered or are they not? ... Do sick persons who pray or are prayed for, recover on the average more rapidly than others?" (cited in Joyce & Welldon).[9] The scientific data collected on intercessory prayer in the interim has been mostly concerned with distant intercessory prayer, that is, prayers said for another person without the person present. In an effort to use rigorous scientific methods, these studies randomly assign patients to either the prayed-for or not-prayed-for groups without allowing the patients to know which group they are in. The researchers are also careful to be sure that the patients' doctors and nurses are unaware of the patients' status relative to the research study. Further, in some studies the patients and their healthcare providers are not even aware that a study that involves the possibility of them receiving prayer is even taking place (scientifically speaking, a type of triple blind study). By taking these steps the researchers attempt to ensure that any differences that may be found to exist between the two groups are due solely to the effects of prayer itself and not due to any type of placebo or psychological effects, such as reduced anxiety, increased optimism, or comfortable feelings of receiving social support, which may be present when individuals know that they are receiving prayer from others.

The most well known study of distant intercessory prayer was conducted by Randolph Byrd and published in 1988.[10] If one enters "Byrd intercessory prayer" into the Google search engine more than 15,000 links to related Web sites are returned (accessed on November 16, 2006). Clearly this study has been widely reported in both scientific and popular literatures, mostly as providing evidence for the effectiveness of distant intercessory prayer. What happened in this very visible study?

Dr. Byrd randomly assigned nearly 400 patients in a coronary care unit to either receive (prayer group) or not receive (control group) distant intercessory prayer. Neither the patients nor their doctors or staff knew which group the individual patients were in. The prayers for each patient were said by three to seven intercessors who were provided the patients' first names, diagnoses, and general medical condition along with updates regarding their medical condition. They prayed for a rapid recovery and for prevention of complications and death. The intercessors themselves were all born-again Christians who maintained an active prayer life. The most widely cited finding from the study was that, on an overall measure of the patients' hospital course, 85 percent of the prayer group had a good hospital course versus

73 percent of the control group and only 14 percent of the prayer group had a bad hospital course versus 22 percent of the control group. These data met the scientific criteria for a statistically significantly difference, that is, the differences in percentages between the two groups were considered reliable and not likely due to chance findings. Dr. Byrd also found that six individual outcome variables (congestive heart failure, need for diuretics, cardiopulmonary arrest, pneumonia, use of antibiotics, and need for intubation-ventilation) produced differences favoring the prayer group whereas twenty-three other measures showed no differences between the groups and none of the measures produced outcomes favoring the control group. It is of interest to note, however, that although the intercessors specifically prayed for a rapid recovery, there were no differences between the two groups in terms of days in the coronary care unit or days in the hospital. Similarly, the intercessors prayed that the patients would avert death but the data revealed that there were no differences in mortality, that is, a patient in the prayer group was just as likely to die during the study as a patient in the control group.

Critics of the study and how it was interpreted seized on the latter findings. They noted that while six measures showed differences favoring the prayer group, twenty-three others did not and on several of the measures that were the specific objects of prayer no differences were found. Critics also noted that there was a lack of adequate statistical control of the analyses (i.e., essentially too many comparisons) and the study was not guided by a particular theory. Many also noted that replication was necessary before anything of certainty could be stated; after all, this study was conducted on one type of patient (coronary care unit) at one hospital.

A response to these challenges can be found in the work of Harris and colleagues[11] who conducted a somewhat more sophisticated replication of the Byrd study. In their investigation, also of coronary care unit admissions, the patients, their physicians, and the hospital staff did not even know that a study was taking place. The study was designed to determine if intercessory prayer would reduce overall adverse events and length of stay in the coronary care unit and it included the specific measure found to produce significant group differences in the Byrd study. Nearly 1,000 patients were randomly assigned to the prayer or control (no prayer) groups. Intercessory prayer teams consisted of five individuals who believed in God and that God is responsive to prayers for healing. For 28 days they prayed for patients to have a "speedy recovery with no complications (pp. 2, 274)." Similar to results from other studies, this study had mixed findings. Though a global measure of general outcome showed differences between the two groups that favored the prayer group, none of the thirty-four individual components of this measure, including death, showed this same difference. Notably, the study specifically failed to replicate the Byrd study as the measure on which Byrd found differences between the groups showed no differences in the Harris research.

Recently the scientific literature on intercessory prayer was significantly enhanced by two studies that are particularly noteworthy for both their scientific methods and the fact that both included multiple centers in their investigations. In the first of these, Krucoff and colleagues[12] not only included 374 patients from nine different centers (an additional 374 received treatments not related to this review) but also included intercessors from many faiths including Jewish, Christian, Muslim, and Buddhist groups. The patients were again cardiac patients but this time they were undergoing either elective catheterization or percutaneous coronary intervention. Comparisons of those receiving prayer with those not assigned to the prayer condition but receiving their usual medical care revealed no differences on any outcome measures. This study did reveal one surprising finding, however, that further complicates how intercessory prayer studies may be interpreted. Eighty-nine percent of the samples indicated that they were aware of prayer on their behalf that was being offered by individuals not connected to the study. In other words, the no-prayer control group believed that they were receiving quite a bit of prayer, just not from the designated intercessors. The authors referred to this phenomenon as "off-protocol prayer" and rightly noted that it is a confound that cannot be controlled. Simply stated, if nearly everyone in intercessory prayer studies is receiving prayer, there is no control or comparison group. This situation is analogous to the placebo group in a drug study actually taking the drug under investigation but getting it from someone other than the research investigators.

The most recent distant intercessory prayer study was led by Herbert Benson and his team of researchers from Harvard Medical School.[13] This investigation included patients at six hospitals in the United States who were undergoing coronary artery bypass graft surgery and were randomly assigned to one of three groups. In this case the groups consisted of those informed that (1) they may or may not receive prayer (but actually received it); (2) they may or may not receive prayer (but actually did not receive it); and (3) those told they would receive prayer and actually received it. Individuals prayed for by the study group received 14 days of prayer. The results demonstrated that prayer itself had no effect on complication-free recovery from the surgery, but, in an interesting twist, the group of patients who were certain that they would receive intercessory prayer from the research team had a higher incidence of complications than did the patients who received prayer but were uncertain about it (group 1 above). The authors offered no explanation for this finding. They did note that most study participants expected to receive prayers from family or friends not associated with the study and that participants may have prayed for themselves.

Each of the studies presented above provides a snapshot of the scientific information on intercessory prayer, but one may wonder what happens if the results of all the existing studies are pooled together. In other words, if we were to summarize the results of all the intercessory prayer studies to date what would we find? Through the use of a technique called meta-analysis this type of information can be obtained. In 2006 Masters and colleagues[14] published a meta-analysis that combined the results of all scientifically published distant intercessory prayer studies. A total of fourteen studies were included in the meta-analysis although one study was eliminated in some calculations because of evidence that the results of the study may have been falsified. Three of the studies detailed above were included; the study by Dr. Benson was not as it had not been published in the scientific literature at the time of the analysis. Across the studies were included patients with cardiac conditions, leukemia, infertility, mental health problems, rheumatoid arthritis, alcoholism, and some receiving kidney dialysis, along with healthy subjects needing intercessory prayer for other reasons. When the results were analyzed, including the one study that had suspicion of false findings, a small effect for intercessory prayer was obtained; however, when this suspect study was excluded no effect for intercessory prayer was found. Also investigated was whether the following study characteristics influenced results: (1) subjects were randomly or nonrandomly assigned to conditions; (2) subjects received daily or less often prayer; or (3) subjects received prayer interventions of longer duration. None of these variables influenced the results. The authors attempted to conduct other analyses pertaining to the types of prayers offered and types of intercessors offering the prayers but due to limitation in the original studies these analyses could not be carried out.

In consideration of the scientific literature, Masters[15] offered a conceptual critique of distant intercessory prayer studies. A major issue that challenges the scientific integrity of this research is the problem, noted earlier, of off-protocol prayer. Receipt of such prayer presents a significant and seemingly insurmountable confound regarding the interpretation of findings. In essence, distant intercessory prayer per se can never be studied, but only the effects of the distant intercessory prayers said by members of a research team can be subjected to scientific scrutiny. If all that can be known, in a scientific sense, is whether the effects of prayers said by members of a research team are effective then surely the study of distant intercessory prayer is severely limited, perhaps trivialized, regarding any information it may shed on the intended object of study. But there remain other conceptual issues that are also troubling. For example, the strongest conclusion favoring prayer interventions that could reasonably be made about the findings of certain of these studies is that they found some evidence supporting the effectiveness of the prayers, that is, on some, not all, of the measures prayer was supported. But in each case this difference was found on a small percentage of the measures. How would one explain findings of, for example, reduced use of antibiotics for the prayer group but no differences in mortality? Does God care more about antibiotic use than mortality? Another way of looking at the data is to compare individual participants in the prayer and control groups. The data that are analyzed in each study consist of grouped findings; the average result for one group is compared with the average result from the other group. But within each group some individuals do better than others and across groups some of those in the control group do better than some in the prayer group. Does this mean that the prayers are more effective for some prayed for persons than others and that, indeed, some people who are not prayed for benefit more than some people who are prayed for? If so, what determines these effects? Finally, there is the question of what has guided the choice of populations to study? For instance, why have individuals who have suffered untreatable paralysis not been studied? No doubt many of these patients would like to recover their ability to ambulate and since there are no medical treatments that are effective they seem to be an ideal population for receipt of distant intercessory prayer. Surely prayer should not be confined to only those patients and conditions for which there is medical treatment; in fact, it would seem that just the opposite would be the case. Or consider prayer studies of individuals who have lost their vision? Both blindness and paralysis seem to provide quintessential examples of the types of conditions that could benefit from prayer and both also have very straightforward measures of outcome, that is, ambulation and sight. Frankly, it seems unpleasantly telling that distant intercessory prayer studies have been largely limited to the study of conditions for which there are at least some medical treatments available or where there may be diagnostic or medical outcome uncertainty.

Another important question, however, has been largely overlooked in the distant intercessory prayer studies; that is, what is the effect of intercessory prayer on the intercessors themselves? Does praying for someone else influence the mental and physical health of the one who is praying? This question is quite appropriate for scientific study as one could hypothesize various psychological processes that could influence outcomes. Both the processes and the outcomes are observable, measurable, and potentially even controllable with proper experimental methods. Data from one of the distant intercessory prayer studies bear on this question. O'Laoire[16] had the intercessors keep a prayer log and also had them complete several measures of various aspects of their psychological (e.g., anxiety, self-esteem, general mood, and depression) and spiritual functioning. He found that the more the intercessors prayed, the better were their reports of spiritual and psychological functioning. Further, over the course of the study the improvement demonstrated by the intercessors in the areas of spiritual health, relationships, and creative expression were greater than those of the individuals who received the prayers. To be clear, this was essentially an observational study and there are numerous viable explanations for the results apart from the interpretation that prayer brought about these positive changes. But this aspect of the study points to a possible new direction in the study of distant intercessory prayer that holds promise for elicitation of better understanding of the effects of prayer on health.

Scientific Study of Prayer Apart from Distant Intercessory Prayer

Below I will present brief, noncomprehensive, overviews of other areas of study that pertain to the question of prayer and health. Each of these areas holds promise for new and groundbreaking research.

Prayer as Coping

Several studies have documented that prayer is often used as a way to cope with stressful events or poor health and this research is not confined to U.S. populations. For example, a 2001 study[17] in Egypt found that 60 percent of patients undergoing a MRI examination spontaneously used prayer to relieve anxiety. The author of the study contends that Egyptian culture supports such practice and recommends that prayer can be a vital support in times of medical crisis. A 1983 study[18] of African Americans found that 44 percent indicated that prayer was the one coping response that was most helpful when dealing with a serious personal problem. This study also determined that prayer was deemed most helpful more often by older individuals who were female and of lower income. Prayer may also be a more effective coping strategy when practiced by those who were already quite religious or had developed what might be called a religious worldview in advance of the stressful event or onset of the illness.

Some investigators, however, have found the use of prayer as a coping strategy to be linked with less effective coping strategies such as trying to avoid the stressor. Lawson and colleagues,[19] for example, studied prayer among chronic pain patients using a scale they developed and initially found that increased use of prayer was correlated with generally less effective coping strategies. However, later examination of the wording of the scale items revealed that they were constructed in such a way that by virtue of the phrases used they linked prayer with wishing or hoping, that is, less active and generally less effective coping strategies. Other investigators[20] noted that prayer may indeed be part of a passive or deferring coping style, however, it may alternately be part of what has been called a collaborative coping strategy, one in which the individual beseeches God's help with the situation but also recognizes that she/he must be an active partner in solving the problem. Prayer as part of this coping style has been found to relate positively with indicators of better health. This area of research demonstrates that it is important to understand the practice of prayer as it interacts with other aspects of the individual's personality and functioning.

Prayer Content

Does the content of one's prayers bear a relationship with health? The findings of Poloma and Pendleton mentioned earlier, suggest this might be the case. More recent evidence comes from studies conducted by Dr. Neal Krause. Investigating the data collected during a nationwide survey of approximately 1,500 older adults, Krause found that the deleterious effects of chronic financial problems on self-rated physical health were significantly reduced (though not eliminated) among those who often prayed for others, however, praying for material things did *not* reduce these harmful effects.[21] Further, the findings remained even when statistical controls for age, sex, education, marital status, race, and church attendance were enacted. Though this study has many strengths including the use of a nationwide sample and statistical controls, it remains observational in nature. As Dr. Krause notes other factors, for example compassion or intrinsic religious orientation, could lead individuals to both greater frequency of prayer for others and better self-rated health.

In a separate analysis of the same sample, Krause[22] found that feelings of self-worth were highest when individuals believed that only God knows when and how to best answer prayer. In contrast, self-esteem was lower among individuals who believed that prayers were answered immediately and believed that they get what they ask for. Taken together these studies suggest that the content and expectancies that prayers hold may well be important in determining how prayer relates to functional health but clearly more research is needed.

Future Directions

By now two things should be clear: (1) many people consider prayer to be important to their health, and (2) more work needs to be done by the research community to offer scientific data on important aspects of the prayer-health relationship. I do not recommend more studies that focus on the effects of distant intercessory prayer on patients; however, studies of effects on the intercessors themselves may prove quite illuminating. A major weakness in all but the distant prayer studies is the reliance on observational data. Though it is difficult in the area of prayer to conduct experimentally designed research complete with control groups and random assignment of participants to groups, it is not impossible. Greater efforts to implement these types of studies could help clarify the importance of factors such as the content of prayer or type of prayer in regard to health outcomes. Studies utilizing prayer as an intervention are an obvious candidate in this area. In a recent uncontrolled intervention study by Dr. Julie Exline and colleagues[23] the use of prayer was found to predict better mood among posttraumatic stress disorder patients. Follow-up on this intriguing finding is needed. Experimental studies could also allow us to learn more about the physiological processes that accompany prayer. For example, are there different physiological responses that accompany meditative vs. petitionary prayer and could these provide plausible explanations for how type of prayer may link to health outcomes of the supplicant?

Though experimental research is sorely needed, significant advances in technology allow for improvements in observational research designs as well. For example, ambulatory measures of variables such as blood pressure or blood glucose can now be incorporated in research that uses handheld computers in ways that can shed greater light on relationships between prayer and health relevant variables as they exist in individuals' daily lives. These handheld computers, used in a method that researchers term ecological momentary assessment, provide access to real-time data. Study participants carry these devices with them and respond to queries. The responses are recorded on the computer and are time and date stamped so that temporal relationships may be observed. This method would allow investigators to study, for example, whether blood pressure measures are lower on days where several prayers are offered versus days that are essentially void of prayer with further analysis of the contents and experience of prayer possible.

We have only scratched the surface in our understanding of prayer and health. Stronger research designs, better uses of more powerful technologies, and greater attention to the topic that is beginning to now entice capable researchers into the area should all lead to better information on the role of prayer as it pertains to health. Clearly prayer will remain important in terms of how people understand and try to influence their health and lead their lives. Correspondingly, I hope that scientists will recognize the lack of a constitutional guarantee for the separation of science and religion and will in greater numbers pursue research on prayer with both eagerness and an even hand. Amen.

References

1. James, W. (1902–1997). *William James: Selected writings.* New York: Book-of-the-Month Club.
2. Gallup, G. (May 1999). As nation observes national day of prayer, 9 in 10 pray—3 in 4 daily. Retrieved on November 21, 2006, from http://www.galluppoll.com/content/?ci=3874&pg=1.
3. Pargament, K.I. & Brant, C.R. (1998). Religion and coping. In H.G. Koenig (Ed.), *Handbook of religion and mental health* (pp. 111–128). San Diego, CA: Academic Press.
4. Barnes, P., Powell-Griner, E., McFann, K., & Nahin, R. (2002). *CDC advance data report #343: Complementary and alternative medicine use among adults:*

United States, 2002. Washington, DC: National Center for Complementary and Alternative Medicine.

5. Edman, J.L. & Koon, T.Y. (2000). Mental illness beliefs in Malaysia: Ethnic and intergenerational comparisons. *International Journal of Social Psychiatry, 46,* 101–109.

6. Tracy, M.F., Lindquist, R., Savik, K., Watanuki, S., Sendelbach, S., Kreitzer, M.J., et al. (2005). Use of complementary and alternative therapies: A national survey of critical care nurses. *American Journal of Critical Care, 14,* 404–414.

7. Poloma, M.M. & Pendleton, B.F. (1991). The effects of prayer and prayer experiences on measures of general well-being. *Journal of Psychology and Theology, 19,* 71–83.

8. McCullough, M.E. & Larson, D.B. Prayer. In W.R. Miller (Ed), *Integrating spirituality into treatment* (pp. 85–110). Washington, DC: American Psychological Association.

9. Joyce, C.R.B. & Welldon, R.M.C. (1965). The objective efficacy of prayer: A double-blind clinical trial. *Journal of Chronic Diseases, 18,* 367–377.

10. Byrd, R.C. (1988). Positive therapeutic effects of intercessory prayer in a coronary care unit population. *Southern Medical Journal, 81,* 826–829.

11. Harris, W.S., Gowda, M., Kolb, J.W., Strychacz, C.P., Vacek, J.L., Jones, P.G., et al. (1999). A randomized, controlled trial of the effects of remote, intercessory prayer on outcomes in patients admitted to the coronary care unit. *Archives of Internal Medicine, 159,* 2273–2278.

12. Krucoff, M.W., Crater, S.W., Gallup, D., Blankenship, J.C., Cuffe, M., Guarneri, M., et al. (2005). Music, imagery, touch, and prayer as adjuncts to interventional cardiac care: The monitoring and actualisation of noetic trainings (MANTRA) II randomized study. *Lancet, 366,* 211–217.

13. Benson, H., Dusek, J.A., Sherwood, J.B., Lam, P., Bethea, C.F., Carpenter, W., et al. (2006). Study of the therapeutic effects of intercessory prayer (STEP) in cardiac bypass patients: A multicenter randomized trial of uncertainty and certainty of receiving intercessory prayer. *American Heart Journal, 151,* 934–942.

14. Masters, K.S., Spielmans, G.I., & Goodson, J.T. (2006). Are there demonstrable effects of distant intercessory prayer? A meta-analytic review. *Annals of Behavioral Medicine, 32,* 337–342.

15. Masters, K.S. (2005). Research on the healing power of distant intercessory prayer: Disconnect between science and faith. *Journal of Psychology and Theology, 33,* 268–277.

16. O'Laoire, S. (1996). An experimental study of the effects of distant, intercessory prayer on self-esteem, anxiety, and depression. *Alternative Therapies in Health & Medicine, 3,* 38–53.

17. Selim, M.A. (2001). Effect of pre-instruction on anxiety levels of patients undergoing magnetic resonance imaging examination. *Eastern Mediterranean Health Journal, 7,* 519–525.

18. Neighbors, H.W., Jackson, J.S., Bowman, P.J., & Gurin, G. (1983). Stress, coping, and black mental health: preliminary findings from a national study. In

R. Hess & J. Hermalin (Eds.), *Innovation in Prevention* (pp. 5–29). New York: Haworth Press.

19. Lawson, K., Reesor, K.A., Keefe, F.J., & Turner, J.A. (1990). Dimensions of pain-related cognitive coping: Cross-validation of the factor structure of the coping strategy questionnaire. *Pain, 43,* 195–204.

20. McIntosh, D.N. & Spilka, B. (1990). Religion and physical health: The role of personal faith and control. In M.L. Lynn & D.O. Moberg (Eds.), *Research in the social scientific study of religion* (Vol. 2, pp. 167–194). Greenwich, CT: JAI Press.

21. Krause, N. (2003). Praying for others, financial strain, and physical health status in late life. *Journal for the Scientific Study of Religion, 42,* 377–391.

22. Krause, N. (2004). Assessing the relationships among prayer expectancies, race, and self-esteem in late life. *Journal for the Scientific Study of Religion, 43,* 395–408.

23. Exline, J.J., Smyth, J.M., Gregory, J., Hockemeyer, J., & Tulloch, H. (2005). Religious framing by individuals with PTSD when writing about traumatic experiences. *The International Journal for the Psychology of Religion, 15,* 17–33.

CHAPTER 3

A Few Good Measures: Assessing Religion and Spirituality in Relation to Health

PETER C. HILL, KATIE J. KOPP, AND RICHARD A. BOLLINGER

In 2005, participants in Chicago's Lakeshore Marathon were shocked to find out when reading the newspaper the next day that instead of running the traditional 26.2 miles in the marathon—certainly grueling enough for any of the competitors—the course was charted wrong and they actually ran about 27.2 miles. As a result, runners were initially discouraged by their "slow" times, people trying to pace themselves ended up confused, and muscles were perhaps even a bit more sore than normal. One lesson learned that day by runners and marathon officials was that *measurement is very important.*

In research too, measurement is very important. Without good measurement, the data that are collected in the process of doing a research study are of little, if any, value. When empirically studying religiousness and spirituality (RS), most measures employed are self-report scales. Participants, in such measures, are asked to respond to multiple items designed to assess such aspects of the total RS experience as beliefs, attitudes, feelings, values, or behavior. This chapter will discuss four measurement-related topics relevant to conducting research and doing applied professional work on the RS-health connection: (1) general measurement issues; (2) RS variables and related measures of importance to health researchers; (3) alternatives to self-report measures; and (4) guidance for choosing a measure.

General Measurement Issues

Who should be concerned about good measurement? Everyone interested in the RS variable should. Though measurement issues are inherently important to empirical researchers, they are also relevant to healthcare providers, social workers, clinical psychologists, and virtually any applied professional in the helping disciplines, which, in the case of the RS variable, would include religious leaders such as clergy, youth leaders, spiritual directors, chaplains, and the like. Just as K-12 teachers should understand and be able to properly interpret the results of academic achievement tests to help delineate student strengths and weaknesses, so too should RS professionals other than researchers be knowledgeable about basic measurement issues, at least to the point of being able to discriminate between good valid measures and measures of less merit.

With that said, most measures discussed in this Chapter were initially developed as research tools and that continues to be their major purpose. Because researchers rarely care to diagnose individual cases, one important implication is that normative data are generally not available. For example, with the current state of measurement, you cannot determine that someone is the 58th percentile on spiritual maturity, like you can determine one's math achievement score. Furthermore, although some applied religious professionals have attempted to develop RS measures for specific purposes, often for ministry in churches (such as acknowledging "spiritual gifts"), none of such measures that we are aware of meet the following criteria for high quality measurement. Our recommendation for the person with applied RS interests is to use the measures represented in this chapter (though what is covered here is only a sampling of the many good measures that are available).

Given the importance of using "good" measurement tools, the question then arises, "What makes one scale better than another?" There are both theoretical and technical considerations in determining the best measure for a given research study.

Theoretical Considerations

The importance of theory in choosing a measure cannot be overemphasized, for no single scale is best for every study. Ideally, the researcher has designed a study with a solid theoretical base; that is, predictable relationships between variables of interest should be rooted in a theoretically coherent framework that will yield testable hypotheses. This is not to say that hypotheses need to be supported for success of a research program; theoretical progress can also be achieved by developing new ideas in response to empirical anomalies. The researcher must then choose a measure that is best suited for the research question at hand.

Any attempt to measure a concept such as religiousness or spirituality requires that the concept be specified in measurable terms. Such an *operational definition* is especially important when applied to religiousness and spirituality because little agreement appears to exist as to the meaning of these terms or even if these terms represent identical, overlapping, or unique constructs[1] (for a thorough analysis on the relationship between religious-ness and spirituality, see Hill et al.)[2] Therefore, when beginning the search for RS measures, theoretical clarity is imperative. Consumers of research should also be well versed on the various dimensions of RS experience to help determine the appropriateness of potential measures. Section II of this chapter will include a discussion of the major dimensions of RS, particularly those that have been associated with physical and mental health, and will highlight scales for each dimension that are considered *reliable* and *valid*. It is to such technical issues that we now turn.

Technical Considerations

The two most important technical issues to consider are the scale's reli-ability and validity. The more reliable and valid a measure is, the more useful it is for conducting scientific research. Though brief scales (some-times just one-item scales) may be appealing because of timesaving and convenience qualities, they also tend to be less reliable and perhaps less valid. This is but another reason why most RS measures consist of multiple items, sometimes broken down by statistical analysis into multiple factors or subscales.

Reliability refers to the consistency of a measure and is usually assessed in terms of either (1) *internal consistency* or (2) *consistency across time*. If a scale item, for example, did not fit particularly well with the other items or was measuring a different construct than the rest of the items of a scale (easily identified with an appropriate statistical package), the internal consistency would be lowered. Internal consistency is most often measured by a statistic called Cronbach's *alpha*, which ranges from 0 to 1.0 with a higher value indicating greater consistency. Alpha levels of RS constructs preferably are above 0.80 but frequently are acceptable around 0.70.[3] When assessing consistency of a measure over time, better known as *test-retest reliability*, the reliability coefficient is a correlation between the test scores of a group of individuals who are administered the scale on two different occasions (usually between 2 weeks and 6 months apart). Internal consistency reliability indicators (i.e., Cronbach's alpha) are used far more frequently when developing RS measures than test-retest reliability.

Consideration of the scale's *validity*, generally defined as the extent to which a test measures what it purports to measure, is also crucial. Simply determining whether or not the scale looks like it is measuring what it is supposed to be measuring, referred to as *face validity*, is too subjective and therefore not scientifically useful. *Content validity* refers to whether or not a representative sample of the domain is being covered. For example, perhaps you are working with a measure of spiritual disciplines. If your measure inquires about prayer, fasting, and tithing, but does not address reading sacred texts, service, or fellowship, the entire behavioral domain has not been sampled and your scale would lack content validity. *Construct validity* examines the agreement between a specific theoretical construct and a measurement device and may rely heavily on what is already known about a construct. *Convergent* and *discriminant* validity are both subdomains of construct validity and can be considered together. Convergent validity asks the question, "How well does this measure correspond to similar measures of the same or similar constructs?" while discriminate validity asks the question, "How is this test unrelated to measures of different constructs?"

These general measurement issues apply to virtually all forms of assessment in psychology, not just to issues involving the RS variable. Now our attention will focus on issues unique to RS study.

Measurement in Specific Religious and Spiritual Domains Related to Health

Religion and spirituality are complex multidimensional phenomena. Following the format developed by Hill,[3] we will consider 8 dimensions of the RS construct organized under two broad categories first suggested by Tsang and McCullough:[4] dispositional and functional RS. The *dispositional* RS level is the broader, superordinate level where the measure might identify how religious or spiritual a person is at basically a trait level. RS dispositions may describe highly internalized processes that are difficult to ascertain by simply asking a participant to report religious activity. The *functional* level of RS is the more focused, subordinate level, which often assesses subdimensions of the broader dispositional factor. This second organizational level tries to measure how RS perceived realities function in people's lives: their RS motivations, how they deploy RS to cope with everyday demands, and so forth. Tsang and McCullough wisely recommend that researchers interested in the functional level also statistically control for dispositional RS, so that any effects attributed to a functional RS characteristic are disentangled from a more general RS disposition. However, the distinction between the two levels is not always clear; what may be considered a disposition from one perspective may be more accurately analyzed at a functional level from another perspective.

Before we look specifically at both dispositional and functional RS measures, we should point out that some scales have tried to assess the multifaceted nature of the RS experience by having a few items each on several dimensions. Though numerous multidimensional measures exist (Hill & Hood[5] devote an entire section of their compendium to multidimensional measures), one deserves special mention here. The Fetzer Institute/National Institute of Aging Working Group[6] created a 38-item Multidimensional Measure of Religion and Spirituality that includes items from 10 different RS domains (8 of which are the domains around which this section is later structured). The Fetzer-NIA scale has adequate reliability and validity and has been included in the 1997–1998 General Social Survey (GSS), a random annual survey of Americans conducted by the National Opinion Research Center, where the generalizability of the measure—at least to the U.S. population—was established. If a comprehensive instrument is desired, the Fetzer-NIA scale deserves serious consideration. However, it should be noted that the instrument includes several items that may assess mental health (e.g., feelings of peace and harmony) rather than simply RS; therefore a relationship between mental health and the RS is almost guaranteed, a potential artifact that should be considered if this measure is used in mental health research.

The following measures are only a sample of a large number of available RS measures (See Hill & Hood[5] for a comprehensive list of RS measures published prior to 1996 and Hill,[3] pages 55–57, for a less comprehensive—but more updated—list of measures categorized by 12 RS dimensions, including the 8 dimensions discussed in this chapter). All of the scales discussed in the following sections are well designed, have good psychometric properties, and have been used in numerous studies.

Dispositional Religiousness or Spirituality

Tsang and McCullough[4] present a cogent case for an inherent or dispositional aspect of general religiousness or spirituality. They build their case upon three points: first, indicators of different aspects of religiousness (e.g., church attendance, prayer) are meaningfully correlated; second, in factor analyses of multi-item measures of religiousness, emerging factors tend to be correlated, indicating a higher order factor of general religiousness; and finally, recent research has suggested that religiousness may be partially heritable. Inherent RS has not been studied at great length in relationship to health, likely due to the difficulty of measuring such a general construct. However, understanding the possible unique contribution of a general, dispositional religiousness or spirituality to health, apart from any functional aspects of religiousness, would undeniably be beneficial.

Scales assessing general RS. Scales attempting to measure general religiousness or spirituality tend to use language broad enough to encompass most religious or spiritual traditions. Paloutzian and Ellison's[7] Spiritual Well-Being scale is one of the most utilized and well-validated scales for measuring both spiritual well-being and general religiousness. Plante and Boccaccini[8] designed the Santa Clara Strength of Religious Faith Questionnaire, which utilizes language open enough to be applicable for the general public, not simply the "religious." A short form of the Santa Clara measure has also been developed.[9] Similarly, Piedmont's[10] Spiritual Transcendence Scale and Hood's[11] Mysticism Scale measure a general spiritual orientation that is not limited to any specific religious tradition.

Religious or spiritual commitment. RS commitment scales attempt to measure how internally invested a person is in their spiritual or religious beliefs. RS commitment includes the extent to which an individual has developed a spiritual lens and framework through which the world is perceived and understood.

Hill and Pargament[1] suggested that those who see the world in largely spiritual terms will likely have a greater appreciation for the sacred and will see the sacred as encompassing the totality of life. Less of a distinction will be made between aspects of the world that are sacred and those that are not (e.g., one's body or psyche may be considered sacred, leading to greater physical and mental care). Also, an internal RS commitment provides people with a purpose and destination for living, admonishing strivings toward religious and spiritual goals that have been linked to better health and well-being. The Religious Commitment Inventory-10 should be given serious consideration as a measure of religious commitment.[12] It has been tested and has demonstrated good reliability and validity on individuals from a variety of religious traditions, including Christians, Buddhists, Muslims, and Hindus, something rare among RS measures.

Religious and spiritual developmental maturity. It may well be that the RS-health connection is mediated by the degree of RS maturity. One who approaches religion in an anxiety-driven manner may not experience the same benefits as one whose religion is a source of peace and comfort. Several measures have been developed to tap into this construct.

Since conception of RS maturity is often defined through a particular tradition, measures are frequently tradition specific. The Faith Maturity Scale is designed to measure the extent that a person displays the characteristics that would be expected of someone with a faith in accordance with mainline Protestant denominations.[13] Ellison[14] developed the Spiritual Maturity Index, an instrument designed to measure spiritual maturity from a Christian perspective. The operational definition of spiritual maturity has included an avoidance of narrow-minded adherence to laws or rules, spontaneity of Christian practices in everyday life, and closeness of relationship to God.

Several scales have been designed to measure one's perceived closeness to the divine—an important component of RS maturity in many traditions. Perceived closeness to God can theoretically be linked to health through attachment theory. Some attachment theorists have claimed that God can be perceived as (and related to) as an attachment figure. Therefore, people who experience a secure attachment to God may also experience greater security in stressful situations and therefore lower levels of psychological stress. Hall and Edwards[15] developed the Spiritual Assessment Inventory (SAI) to measure spiritual maturity from an object-relations perspective. Higher scores on the SAI have been related to relational maturity in religious college students. Though not from an attachment perspective, Underwood[16] created the Daily Spiritual Experiences Scale (DSES) to measure an individual's perceived interaction with the transcendent on a daily basis. The DSES attempts to be more universally applicable than the more explicitly Christian-based SAI.

Functional Religiousness or Spirituality

Religious motivation. Somewhat related to RS commitment is the question of motivation. What is the motivating force behind a person's religiousness or spirituality? Does an internal RS conviction or commitment serve as the basis of one's motivation, or does one's RS motivation lie in the form of personal or social gains?

Gordon Allport[17] laid the groundwork for studying internal religious motivation. He later created the Religious Orientation Scale (ROS), which attempts to measure both intrinsic and extrinsic religious motivations. Though extensively used, the ROS has been subjected to much criticism, including the ideas that it may be confounded with social desirability and have both methodological and theoretical shortcomings.[18] Gorsuch and McPherson[19] applied several decades worth of research on the ROS to create the 14-item Revised Religious Orientation Scale (what they called I-E/R), which is perhaps the best measure of intrinsic and extrinsic religious orientation available.

Batson and colleagues have long argued that measures of religious orientation emphasizing only intrinsic and extrinsic motivations have overlooked important considerations of RS maturity claimed by Allport himself; that is, one must also consider the positive role of doubt and an appreciation of the complexities of the human drama. This willingness to enter into "an open-ended, responsive dialogue with existential questions raised by the contradictions and tragedies of life"[18] exemplifies what they refer to as a *quest* religious orientation for which they have developed a specific measure.

Religious or spiritual social participation. An individual's religiousness or spirituality has often been assessed in health studies by a single item centering on the frequency of one's attendance at a place of religious worship. In a recent report, Weaver and Koenig[20] summarized recent findings between attending religious services once a week and health. The studies included a 28-year study of 5,000 adults, which found that even after removing the effects of social support and health practices, attending services reduced risk of dying by 23 percent. A similar study with 4,000 older adults replicated the same findings. Although a single question or item can measure religious attendance, several measures have been developed that provide a more comprehensive examination of organized religious involvement. The Religious Involvement Inventory (RII)[21] includes a 14-item church involvement subscale and has reasonably good psychometric qualities. The RII goes beyond Sunday attendance to also address the extent of time invested in a church. The Springfield Religiosity Scale[22] assesses organizational religiosity by also differentiating between attendance in religious services and involvement in other religious group activities such as Bible study groups or Sunday school.

Spiritual private practices. Private spiritual activities or behaviors such as prayer, meditation, scripture reading, and other potential solitary activities are often measured using one or two items. The Duke Religious Index (DUREL) has a "nonorganizational or private religious expression" scale consisting of one item.[23] The entire DUREL consists of five items, measures organizational and intrinsic religiousness in addition to nonorganizational religiousness, and has good psychometric properties. The Religious Background and Behavior Scale[24] measures private religious and spiritual practices and was developed for use with a clinical population. This scale is pluralistic in its religious focus.

Religious or spiritual support. The quality of relationships (both divine and human) is of extreme importance in many world religions where a variant of the Golden Rule (be compassionate and loving toward others) is either explicitly articulated or implicitly understood. Therefore, religious groups have often been places where members seek out care, support, and connectedness. RS support provides similar health benefits as general social support in that RS support serves as a source of self-esteem, companionship, and protection against the harmful effects of life's stressors. In addition, though, religious support may have other benefits that extend beyond the bounds of traditional social support. Kahn and Antonucci speak of a *support convoy*,[25] which consists of a group of like-minded people who share a similar worldview and values and who will walk through life together. Religious congregations may serve as this support convoy, walking with, praying, and supporting one another through difficult times. This coupled social and religious encouragement may be particularly beneficial because of the interaction between two significant life domains. Fiala, Bjorck, and Gorsuch[26] developed the Perceived Religious Support Scale and found that religious support as measured by the scale was associated with lower levels of depression and more positive life satisfaction.

Religious/spiritual coping. Defined by one researcher as "a search for significance in times of stress"[27] RS coping strategies may be particularly useful when people are pushed beyond their limits by situations involving uncontrollable circumstances. RS coping, understood as the extent to which individuals use their religious or spiritual beliefs to help them adjust during difficult times, is usually positively associated with mental health including improved psychological adjustment and decreased stress in patients and significant others (even after controlling for nonreligious coping), lower mortality in older adults, and even, among grieving parents, finding meaning in the death of their children.

The RCOPE,[28] the most comprehensive RS coping scale to date, has been validated on both physically healthy and medically ill patients and the results have been encouraging. Recognizing that not all religious coping is beneficial, the same team of researchers also developed the Negative Religious Coping Scale to measure maladaptive religious coping.[29]

Alternatives to Self-Report Measures

Every measure mentioned to this point is a paper-and-pencil self-report scale and such measures have their limitations. The core issue, ultimately, is that the accuracy of self-report measures depend on both subjects' willingness and ability to report private knowledge without either intentional or unintentional distortion. Specifically, some of the factors that bias self-reports include demand characteristics, evaluation apprehension, and impression management. RS beliefs, attitudes, and behavior may be especially vulnerable to such biasing factors due either to (1) the sheer importance of RS beliefs and practices to RS committed people, or (2) the power of an RS social context whereby people may feel compelled or socially expected to hold certain beliefs or values.[30] Other problems with self-report measures include the possibility of a required reading and comprehension level that may be higher than the ability level of some respondents. Furthermore, some paper-and-pencil measures may not engage the interest of the respondent, which, in turn, may foster response sets (i.e., answering all questions with the same response).

To further advance our understanding of the psychological underpinnings of RS experience, alternative RS measures are needed. Some alternative measures include using qualitative research (e.g., interviews, discussions with focus groups) as a complement to quantitative research, thereby helping to help unpack the richness of the RS experience that self-report measures frequently miss; employing others' (e.g., friends, family members, and professional staff) reports on both RS practices and health, an approach especially useful for clinical populations; utilizing nonverbal measures such as picture drawing of RS objects or concepts, a technique frequently used in research with children; and making better use of physiological indicators (e.g., immunological functioning, fMRI) of RS experiences.

Furthermore, not all RS experience is of the type that is easily reportable. People may have implicit RS beliefs, attitudes, or values that are "introspectively unidentified (or inaccurately identified) traces of past experience that mediate favorable or unfavorable feeling, thought, or action toward social objects" (p. 8).[31] Recent methodological advances of implicit measures of social cognition could be applied to the study of RS beliefs, values, and practices. For example, Hill[32] noted that response time, a measure of attitude accessibility in the social psychology literature, could be used as a measure of the centrality or importance of the RS factor, a recommendation recently applied to empirical research by Wenger.[33]

Other implicit measures of RS experience may use variants of the Implicit Attitude Test (IAT) such as that recently reported,[34] semantic decision tasks, or measures of judgment speed, and amount of material recalled. Though implicit measures of cognition are not without controversy and usually require computer software and some technological expertise, such methodologies are becoming easier to use and are increasingly available to researchers. However, for the RS professional other than researchers, it is likely that the self-report measures reviewed in this chapter will be the most useful and, for the foreseeable future, perhaps the only measurement tool available. And so, as we draw this chapter to a close, we will review some general principles that might help in deciding which, among a few good measures, one should choose.

Guidance for Choosing a Measure

Choosing a measure requires consideration of several criteria. *First*, one must consider the purpose of the research. Is the purpose to scientifically advance our understanding of RS experience or is it to apply already existing knowledge to some sort of applied phenomena. Much research on the RS-health connection is of the applied category. If one is trying to advance knowledge within the RS domain (what is sometimes referred to as "basic" research), then research questions and hypotheses should intentionally be guided by a broad theoretical framework (though frequently this is not the case) and measures chosen should be conceptually compatible with that framework. Theory is also important to the applied researcher, but often the research is focused on specific empirical questions (e.g., whether social support provided by fellow church congregants contributes to mental health) where guidance by a broad theoretical framework is perhaps less essential. For the applied professional who wants to use an instrument for purposes other than research, concern about underlying theory is important to the extent that one can decide whether or not the measure under consideration is a good match for one's purposes. *Second*, whether one is interested in doing research (whether basic or applied) or utilizing a measure for some other purpose, one must have a clear conception of what specific aspect of the RS experience is of research interest. Often one approaches a research or applied issue thinking that he or she has a broad and clear understanding of the RS construct at hand, but in reality that individual may be thinking only in terms of some limited RS dimension. Nothing is wrong with conceptualizing the RS variable along certain dimensions and, in terms of disaggregating the constructs, particularly as they are perhaps functionally related to physical and mental health, such dimensional focus is helpful and necessary. But the RS variable is complex and experientially rich, so measures and resulting findings along single dimensional lines must be interpreted with great caution.

Third, it is important to use measures with established reliability and validity. Some scales may *appear* valid but, as already noted, face validity by itself is not scientifically acceptable. *Fourth*, consider your population of interest (and, of course, for the researcher your sample should represent your population well) and consider whether the scale at hand works with your population. If you are working with a pluralistic population and a particular scale was developed for a specific religious population, then that scale may not be useful. *Fifth*, be flexible and creative, but not too creative. Research itself and the application of research for other purposes require that you approach your topic *conceptually*. Many people approach their work looking for measures designed for very specific populations (e.g., a measure on religious coping designed for people who are terminally ill, a measure for people with specific forms of disability, a measure for a very particular religious grouping) and then are discouraged when they cannot find such a measure. It is important to look for measures that are conceptually related (e.g., general religious coping measures, a nonverbal measure such as picture drawing for people who are illiterate, a well-established general measure that can be adapted to a specific group) to your topic of interest. This approach may require modification of another measure, but you are further ahead if you first explore the existing measurement literature. You'll be surprised at what you can find!

Conclusion

Research can offer many insights into the relationship between RS and health. This relationship, although interesting, can be difficult to understand as it is full of complexities and paradoxes. For example, attendance at church services is related to good health outcomes, but only if that attendance is not driven by anxiety. In the movie *A Few Good Men*, Jack Nicholson's character, Colonel Jessep, famously said, "You want answers? You can't handle the truth!" We believe though that a few good reliable and valid measurement tools will help researchers find answers that can lead to truth, which not only can be handled, but also welcomed in research endeavors.

References

1. Hill, P.C. & Pargament, K.I. (2003). Advances in the conceptualization and measurement of religion and spirituality. *American Psychologist*, *58*, 64–76.
2. Hill, P.C., Pargament, K.I., Hood, R.W., Jr., McCullough, M.E., Swyers, J.P., Larson, D.B., et al. (2000). Conceptualizing religion and spirituality: Points of commonality, points of departure. *Journal of Theory and Social Behavior*, *30*, 51–77.

3. Hill, P.C. (2005). Measurement assessment and issues in the psychology of religion and spirituality. In R.F. Paloutzian & C. L. Park (Eds.), *Handbook of the psychology of religion and spirituality* (pp. 43–61). New York: Guilford Press.
4. Tsang, J. & McCullough, M.E. (2003). Measuring religious constructs: A hierarchical approach to construct organization and scale selection. In S.J. Lopez & C.R. Snyder (Eds.), *Positive psychological assessment: A handbook of models and measures* (pp. 345–360). Washington, DC: American Psychological Association.
5. Hill, P.C. & Hood, R.W., Jr. (Eds.) (1999). *Measures of religiosity.* Birmingham, AL: Religious Education Press.
6. Fetzer Institute/National Institute of Aging Working Group (1999). *Multidimensional measurement of religiousness/spirituality for use in health research: A report of the Fetzer Institute/National Institute on Aging Working Group.* Kalamazoo, MI: John E. Fetzer Institute.
7. Paloutzian, R.F. & Ellison, C.W. (1982). Loneliness, spiritual well-being, and quality of life. In L.A. Peplau & D. Perlman (Eds.), *Loneliness: A sourcebook of current theory, research and therapy* (pp. 224–237). New York: Wiley Interscience.
8. Plante, T.G., & Boccaccini, B.F. (1997). The Santa Clara strength of religious faith questionnaire. *Pastoral Psychology, 45,* 375–387.
9. Plante, T.G., Vallaeys, C.L., Sherman, A.C., & Wallston, K.A. (2002). The development of a brief version of the Santa Clara strength of religious faith questionnaire. *Pastoral Psychology, 48,* 11–21.
10. Piedmont, R.L. (1999). Does spirituality represent the sixth factor of personality? Spiritual transcendence and the five-factor model. *Journal of Personality, 67,* 985–1013.
11. Hood, R.W., Jr. (1975). The construction and preliminary validation of a measure of reported mystical experience. *Journal of the Scientific Study of Religion, 14,* 29–41.
12. Worthington, E.L., Jr., Wade, N.G., Hight, T.L., Ripley, J.S., McCullough, M.E., Berry, et al. (2003). The religious commitment inventory-10: Development, refinement, and validation of a brief for research and counseling. *Journal of Counseling Psychology, 50,* 84–96.
13. Benson, P.L., Donahue, M.J., & Erickson, J.A. (1993). The faith maturity scale: Conceptualization, measurement, and empirical validation. In M.L. Lynn & D. O. Moberg (Eds.), *Research in the social science study of religion*, Vol. 5 (pp. 1–26). Greenwich, CT: JAI Press.
14. Ellison, C.G. (1983). Spiritual well-being: Conceptualization and measurement. *Journal of Psychology and Theology, 11,* 330–340.
15. Hall, T.W. & Edwards, K.J. (1996). The initial development and factor analysis of the spiritual assessment inventory. *Journal of Psychology and Theology, 24,* 233–246.
16. Underwood, L.G. & Teresi, J.A. (2002). The daily spiritual experience scale: Development, theoretical description, reliability, exploratory factor analysis, and

preliminary construct validity using health-related data. *Annals of Behavioral Medicine, 24,* 22–33.

17. Allport, G.W. (1950). *The individual and his religion: A psychological interpretation.* New York: Macmillan.

18. Batson, C.D., Schoenrade, P., & Ventis, W.L. (1993). *Religion and the individual: A social-psychological perspective.* New York: Oxford University Press, p. 169.

19. Gorsuch, R.L. & McPherson, S.E. (1989). Intrinsic/extrinsic measurement: I/E-revised and single-item scales. *Journal of the Scientific Study of Religion, 28,* 348–354.

20. Weaver, A.J. & Koenig, H.G. (2006). Religion, spirituality, and their relevance to medicine: An update. *American Family Physician, 73,* 1336–1337.

21. Hilty, D.M. & Morgan, R.L. (1985). Construct validation for the religious involvement inventory: Replication. *Journal of the Scientific Study of Religion, 24,* 75–86.

22. Koenig, H.G., Smiley, M., & Gonzales, J.A.P. (1988). *Religion, health, and aging: A review and theoretical integration.* Westport, CT: Greenwood.

23. Koenig, H.G., Meador, K., & Parkerson, G. (1997). Religion index for psychiatric research: A 5-item measure for use in health outcomes studies [Letter to the editor]. *American Journal of Psychiatry, 154,* 885–886.

24. Connors, G.J., Tonigan, J.S., & Miller, W.R. (1996). A measure of religious background and behavior for use in behavior change research. *Psychology of Addictive Behaviors, 10,* 90–96.

25. Kahn, R.L. & Antonucci, T.C. (1980). Convoys over the life course: attachment, roles, and social support. In P. B. Baltes & O.G. Brim (Eds.), *Life Span Development and Behavior* (pp. 253–286). New York: Academic Press.

26. Fiala, W.E., Bjorck, J.P., & Gorsuch R.L. (2002). The religious support scale: Construction, validation, and cross-validation. *American Journal of Community Psychology, 30,* 761–786.

27. Pargament, K.I. (1997). *The psychology of religion and coping: Theory, research, practice.* New York: Guilford Press, p. 90.

28. Pargament, K.I., Koenig, H.G., & Perez, L.M. (2000). The many methods of religious coping: Development and initial validation of the RCOPE. *Journal of Clinical Psychology, 56,* 519–543.

29. Pargament, K.I., Smith, B.W., Koenig, H.G., & Perez, L. (1998). Patterns of positive and negative religious coping with major life stressors. *Journal of the Scientific Study of Religion, 37,* 711–725.

30. Burris, C.T. & Navara, G.S. (2002). Morality play—or playing morality: Intrinsic religious orientation and socially desirable responding. *Self Identity, 1,* 67–76.

31. Greenwald, A.G. & Banaji, M.R. (1995). Implicit social cognition: Attitudes, self-esteem, and stereotypes. *Journal of Personality and Social Psychology, 102,* 4–27.

32. Hill, P.C. (1994). Toward an attitude process model of religious experience. *Journal of the Scientific Study of Religion, 33,* 303–314.

33. Wenger, J.L. (2004). The automatic activation of religious concepts: Implications for religious orientations. *International Journal of Psychology and Religion, 14,* 109–123.

34. Bassett, R.L., Smith, A., Thrower, J., Tindall, M., Barclay, J., Tiuch, K., et al. (2005). One effort to measure implicit attitudes toward spirituality and religion. *Journal of Psychology and Christianity, 24,* 210–218.

CHAPTER 4

How Does One Learn to Be Spiritual? The Neglected Role of Spiritual Modeling in Health

DOUG OMAN AND CARL E. THORESEN

"Jesus replied, 'A Samaritan...was moved with pity...bandaged his wounds...and took care of him.... Go and do likewise.'"

—(Luke 10:30–37)

When religions are sifted.... They begin to look like data banks that house the winnowed wisdom of the human race.

—(Huston Smith)[1] (p. 5)

A penchant for storytelling is a striking feature of all cultures, especially of religious and spiritual traditions. A common concern of many traditional stories—whether historically derived or parables—is to transmit the words and deeds of *spiritual models*, persons who exemplify positive spiritual qualities. For example, 2,000 years ago, Jesus used the parable of the Good Samaritan to illustrate authentic love of one's neighbor. After recounting the Samaritan's rescue of an injured man abandoned beside a road, Jesus told his listener to follow the Samaritan's compassionate example (see epigram above).

Learning about spiritual models may have health effects—that is our theme in this chapter. Of course, spiritual models are often encountered in the flesh, not only in stories. We may have one or more family members who demonstrate spiritual qualities (perhaps a favorite grandmother). We may know someone at our school, workplace, or religious organization. When their lives agree with their uplifting message, we may be inspired by a prominent preacher, social activist, or spiritually oriented musician. For many Oprah Winfrey may serve as a spiritual example of redemptive hope and optimism. Or, as has happened to millions, we may be deeply impressed by figures such as Mother Teresa, the Dalai Lama, or Nelson Mandela, seen in person, on television, or read about in newspapers or books. In all these ways, as well as through histories and parables, we are likely to encounter potential spiritual models who may influence our overall health and well-being, including our physical health.

How might health effects arise from spiritual models? And might these effects be used beneficially by ordinary people and by religious professionals, as well as by physicians, psychologists, and other health professionals? We will first briefly describe scientific perspectives on the importance of learning from social models about life in general, as well as about spirituality. Then we examine scientific perspectives on how spirituality affects health, and describe what is gained by considering spiritual models. Several applications of this *spiritual modeling perspective* to healthcare and healthy living are then considered. We conclude by suggesting some possible long-term implications for healthcare systems. We do not discuss the different ways the term spirituality has been used, from being seen as synonymous with organized religion to completely independent of religion. Readers interested in these definitional issues are encouraged to consult discussions available elsewhere.[2; 3]

How Do We Learn?

There is now a great deal of scientific evidence that *social learning*—learning by observing the actions and attitudes of other people—is a predominant form of human learning. Learning from models is distinct from didactic instruction, which usually involves *telling* a person information that he or she should learn. The most complete scientific account of social learning is provided by psychologist Albert Bandura, whose Social Cognitive Theory has been productively applied to education, physical and mental health, athletic achievement, organizational functioning, and many other important domains of human activity. Over the past three decades, Bandura's Social Cognitive Theory has been the single most influential and highly cited theory in psychology.

Much social learning occurs through face-to-face observation of the behaviors of other persons in one's home or community setting, and observing the consequences brought by those behaviors. Parents of young children come to realize that their actions often are reenacted, sometimes unintended, by their very observant children. The apprenticeship model used down through the ages relies largely on social modeling. However, Bandura notes that "a special virtue of modeling is that it can transmit simultaneously knowledge of wide applicability to vast numbers of people . . . by drawing on conceptions of behavior portrayed in words and images"[4] (p. 47). Potentially influential models include not only family and community, but also people encountered through the electronic media, reading, and storytelling.

Social models are powerfully influential. Indeed, past research shows that

[T]he power of example to activate and channel behavior has been abundantly documented.... One can get people to behave altruistically, to volunteer their services, to delay or to seek gratification, to show affection, to behave punitively, to prefer certain foods and apparel, to converse on particular topics, to be inquisitive or passive, to think innovatively or conventionally, and to engage in almost any course or action by having such conduct exemplified.[4] (p. 206)

Four main psychological processes underlie observational learning: attention, retention, reproduction in behavior, and motivation. Learning from models requires *attention* to a model's actions, *retention* in memory of what was observed, and attempts at *reproduction in behavior*. Finally, unless adequate *motivation* is present, a learned behavior may never be practiced or implemented. The same four processes are involved in learning from contemporary models, as well as from historical models that may be encountered through reading, storytelling, or other media.

How We Learn Spirituality

Spiritual learning can take place in any context, and is not confined to religious organizations, as affirmed by the fact that one-third of U.S. adults describe themselves as "spiritual but not religious."[5] However, major religious traditions have long recognized the importance of spiritual modeling, and attempted to facilitate it. In Christianity, for example, spiritual modeling is affirmed in the title of *The Imitation of Christ*, a fifteenth-century devotional book widely read by Protestants, Catholics, and Orthodox alike. Islam celebrates Muhammad as a "beautiful exemplar" (*uswa hasana*, Qur'an 33:21). Hindu scriptures affirm that "What the outstanding person does, others will try to do. The standards such people create will be followed by the whole world" (Bhagavad Gita 3:21).

The four social learning processes described above have long been recognized by all major religious traditions. In numerous ways, each tradition has tried to harness systematically these above processes to teach spiritual attitudes and behaviors. For example, worship services often include scriptural readings that direct *attention* to the words and deeds of major spiritual figures such as Jesus, Moses, or the Buddha; Over time many scriptural passages are read repeatedly, fostering *retention*. Religious traditions encourage supportive communal fellowship with others who can function as positive spiritual models, and emphasize important spiritual qualities such as charity, truthfulness, and humility, to be *reproduced* in daily life; Finally, *motivation* to persist in growing spiritually over time is supported by worshipping together regularly, rituals, music, encouraging testimonials, and celebrating benefits obtained in this life and after death. Religious figures, especially the founders and mystics within major traditions, offer repeated testimony to the great peace ("which passeth all understanding," Philippians 4:7) and happiness ("that never leaves," Dhammapada 1:2) that come to persons who persist in the spiritual quest.

What Is Learned from Spiritual Models?

Through social learning processes, people may acquire almost any spiritually relevant attitude, belief, or behavior. They may also learn about the *identities* and life stories of revered spiritual models deemed most worthy of emulation. Each religious tradition—as well as many "spiritual but not religious" individuals—possesses a perspective about which attributes and behaviors are viewed as most important for spiritual growth. Although differences exist, scholars note that major religious traditions recommend similar spiritual pathways. Ultimately, all seek to foster sanctifying, far-reaching transformations of "character, conduct and consciousness"[6] (p. 29). Shared practices include efforts to reduce material or sensory cravings, to calm the mind, and to develop concentration, generosity, and wisdom.[7] Recent research by psychologists reveals similarities in recognizing virtues and character strengths in several broad areas that include wisdom, courage, compassion, and transcendence.[8] Huston Smith, an eminent scholar of religion, reports that all major religious traditions recommend cultivating virtues analogous to charity, veracity, and humility[1] (p. 387).

Such spiritual qualities, virtues, and strengths often require prolonged cultivation, analogous to high-level "human capital" skills acquired through secular education or training. This has led some scholars to refer to skill in spiritual practices and behaviors as "spiritual capital."[9] Similarly, Smith has noted (see epigram, above) that religious traditions at their best "look like data banks that house...winnowed wisdom"[1] (p. 5). Minimally, the human "data banks" of spiritual and religious traditions contain teachings and information about:

- Beliefs (e.g., the nature of human beings and higher powers)
- Practices (e.g., virtues, rituals, and exercises for spiritual growth)
- Models (e.g., identities and biographies of saints, sages, and religious founders who vividly exemplify beliefs, practices, and wisdom)

Importantly, most religious traditions rely heavily on *narratives* for transmitting spiritual "data." If we succumb, however, to a scholastic preoccupation with beliefs and doctrines, then we risk missing a great deal of the spiritual capital that is available and transmitted every day within religious traditions. Indeed, by relying heavily on narratives, traditions may have chosen a very effective strategy. Scientific research demonstrates that people create stories to make more sense of their lives.[10] Furthermore, a story may not be factual but still be true for the storyteller. "These evolving stories—or *narrative identities*—provide our lives with some semblance of meaning, unity, and purpose.... Our stories are implicated in determining what we do and how we make sense of what we do"[10] (p. 14). One recent ethnically and politically diverse interview study of the lives of eighty-four highly nominated moral exemplars in American society found that religious faith was central to the vast majority's life calling. "This faith ... is what held the exemplars together during all the trials ... in short, what made the center hold throughout all the decades of the exemplars' uniquely consequential lives"[11] (p. 311).

The Spiritual Modeling Perspective

The universal importance of spiritual modeling suggests a new perspective on health, which we shall call a *spiritual modeling perspective*. This perspective is based on two scientifically supported principles: (1) spiritual models influence spiritual growth, and (2) spiritual involvement influences health.

A spiritual modeling perspective seeks to understand the combined implications of these two principles. It directs our attention to how health is shaped in part by what people learn from spiritual models. More specifically, a spiritual modeling perspective holds that factors affecting learning from spiritual models have *consequences*.

This spiritual modeling perspective does not conflict with other models of how spirituality or religion relate to health. It may, however, alert us to new ways to foster health, and perhaps new ways to support people in their efforts to grow spiritually.

Spiritual Models and Health

How Spirituality Affects Health

Empirical evidence suggests that spirituality and religion are generally associated with better health and longer life. [2; 3; 12] Negative health effects have been observed for some types of religion (e.g., views of God as highly vengeful, or refusals to accept blood transfusions by some groups). Unhealthy behaviors may also be acquired through emulation from persons unwisely regarded as spiritual models.[13] Because positive influences on physical and mental health predominate, recent scientific work has focused on understanding and explaining such benefits.

Improved health behaviors, social support, and psychological factors are commonly cited as pathways by which spirituality affects health.[3; 12] These pathways, rather than the internal workings of religion and spirituality, are the focus of most models for how religious and spiritual involvement affect health. These internal workings are often left unspecified not because religion and spirituality are seen as simple processes, but because there are many different ways that their internal workings can be conceptualized and described.

How Spiritual Modeling Works

The spiritual modeling perspective suggests an approach to conceptualizing the internal workings of spirituality. Beliefs, practices, and spiritual models are three main components of religion and spirituality that we noted earlier. Over time these components influence each other and mutually interact. For example, one's beliefs (e.g., Catholic versus Protestant) influence who one is likely to view as a spiritual model (e.g., Ignatius of Loyola versus Martin Luther), as well as how strongly one may be motivated to engage in various spiritual practices (e.g., confession versus scriptural reading). Similarly, one's spiritual practices (e.g., prayer, meditation, or spiritual reading) may influence one's beliefs (e.g., belief in God) as well as facilitate identifying and learning from spiritual models. Finally, even though major faiths revere similar character strengths and virtues,[1; 8] the precise identities of an individual's primary spiritual models (e.g., the Pope versus Mohammed) may powerfully shape a multitude of details about beliefs and practices that are worthy of emulation (e.g., attending confession versus praying toward Mecca). These dynamic reciprocal influences are illustrated in Figure 4.1.

The Spiritual Modeling Health Framework

When we insert the dynamic interactions suggested by the spiritual modeling perspective (see Figure 4.1) into a conventional health effects model, we obtain the Spiritual Modeling Health Framework (SMHF). The SMHF explicitly connects a person's engagement with learning from spiritual models to multiple physical and mental health outcomes. It also recognizes that effects of spiritual or religious involvement are shaped by social and cultural context (e.g., demographics and personal history). In line with the conventional approach, the SMHF framework holds that learning from spiritual models fosters health through mechanisms that include social support and health behaviors, as well as variables related to mental health, such as character strengths and virtues.

Figure 4.1
How Spiritual Models Reciprocally Interact with Other Components of Spirituality

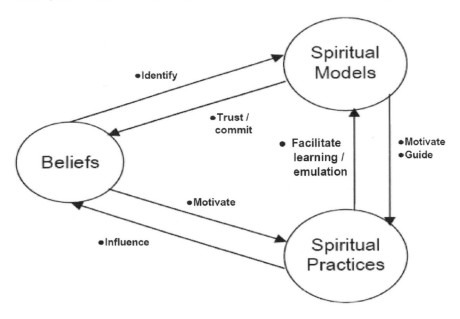

In the SMHF framework, effects from spiritual models are not seen as arising totally independently of a person's spiritual beliefs and practices. Rather, spiritual models, beliefs, and practices are seen as interacting and mutually supportive, perhaps akin to different food groups within a balanced diet. In food science, proteins, vitamins, and other nutrients act synergistically rather than fostering health in isolation. Nevertheless, an individual's recommended program of dietary improvement may target specific food groups as especially needing improvements in quality or quantity. Similarly, the SMHF envisions synergistic effects from spiritual models, practices, and beliefs. Implicitly, the SMHF highlights the fact that some individuals may benefit from receiving tools or other supports that help them learn more effectively from spiritual models that inspire them.

Preliminary Empirical Support

The SMHF framework is still in its preliminary stages of validation, but some supporting evidence is available. One task of scientific validation is demonstrating that the components of the model can be measured. For the SMHF, one challenge is showing that an individual's access to spiritual models can be measured. Our work on this task has relied on self-report questionnaires, by far the most common and convenient strategy to measure religious and spiritual constructs (see Hill, Kopp, and Bollinger, this volume). We developed a questionnaire termed the Spiritual Modeling Inventory of Life Environments (SMILE) questionnaire. The SMILE assesses perceptions of spiritual models across a variety of life domains (family, school, religious or spiritual organizations, traditional and contemporary famous people). These responses can be used to compute a summary measure of spiritual model availability across all domains. When the SMILE was administered on two occasions about 7 weeks apart to the same group of sixty-six college students, we found that summary scores for each individual were highly correlated across time responses, indicating a stable and "reliable" measurement instrument (the correlation was 82 percent, or $r = 0.82$). Such summary scores, of course, do not capture the details of individual experience. But they provide a rough sense of the degree to which individuals perceive that spiritual models are available to them.

Second, we have found that this summary measures demonstrated the expected relationships with health factors. We administered the SMILE measure to a group of 964 students at four public and private colleges in California, Tennessee, and Connecticut. We found that spiritual models predicted life satisfaction, a variable measuring the mental health pathway. We also found that spiritual models were associated with positive health behaviors such as exercise, diet, adequate sleep, wearing seat belts, and refraining from smoking, and that many of these associations were independent of other spiritual variables.[14] Overall, the protectiveness of spiritual models was similar to that of attending religious services, which several previous studies have confirmed is associated with better health behaviors among both adults and adolescents (see Cotton, Grossoehme, and Tsevat, this volume).

Practical Application to Health

In our postmodern culture, perhaps especially in the United States, many people are not satisfied with their opportunities to learn from spiritual models. For example, a recent study reported that U.S. high school students perceived a "dearth of contemporary role models—parental or otherwise"[15] (p. 7). When asked to cite exemplars of various character strengths, students were "more likely to name biblical figures or civil rights leaders from the 1960s rather than exemplars from contemporary society"[15] (p. 11). One student observed: "We just don't see many people today who are wise or honest or whatever because those sorts of things aren't valued as much in our society"[15] (p. 11).

Another important area of popular discontent relates to medical care. Many patients experience a discomforting compartmentalization. One survey of more than 900 family practice patients found that two-thirds wanted discussions of spiritual issues for the sake of improving physician-patient understanding. Yet between 80 and 90 percent of patients reported that a physician had never inquired about their spiritual or religious beliefs.[16] Such de facto compartmentalization of health and spirituality appears historically unprecedented. A major medical education journal notes that modern Western medicine, "shorn of every vestige of mystery, faith, or moral portent, is actually an aberration in the world scene"[17] (p. 807). Historians tell us that modern civilization is characterized by increasingly refined differentiation among diverse spheres of culture and society, such as the economy, science, the arts, and religious organizations. Such differentiation is often very valuable and useful, but it can evolve to the extreme of a destructive *dissociation*, "with little or no discourse between these spheres"[18] (p. 55). Suppression or absence of discourse risks fostering an overly reductionistic science and medicine inclined to believe that "there is no reality save that revealed by science, and no truth save that which science delivers"[18] (p. 56).

Besides direct health benefits arising from spiritual models, we suggest that a spiritual modeling perspective can reveal and clarify approaches to redressing healthcare compartmentalization and imbalance. In this section, we describe several empirical intervention studies that suggest how spiritual models might be more fully integrated into healthcare systems. These examples illustrate strategies that support several of the spiritual modeling processes described earlier (attention, retention, reproduction in behavior, and motivation). Some of these interventions offer resources for augmenting knowledge about spiritual models. Others support deeper assimilation and stronger connections to spiritual models that are *already known*. In different ways, they all provide tools for overcoming compartmentalization. They help reintegrate spirituality in part by supplying tools for *retaining* memory of spiritual models throughout multiple spheres of daily activity, thereby facilitating *reproduction* of similar spiritual behaviors at various times throughout the day.

Importantly, none of these applications rely solely on strengthening connections to spiritual models. Each also supplies other health-supportive factors. But a spiritual modeling perspective shows how these interventions may draw some of their power from oft-neglected spiritual modeling processes.

Example 1: Spiritual Meditation

Our first example shows that a minor spiritual modification of a well-known healthcare intervention may produce worthwhile benefits. Amy Wachholtz and Ken Pargament compared the consequences of meditating on a spiritual focus with a secular focus. They examined college students ($n = 68$), most of whom described themselves as slightly or moderately spiritual and religious. After random assignment to secular or spiritual meditation, participants were asked to meditate daily for 20 minutes over 2 weeks. In comparison with a secular focus such as "I am joyful," meditating on a spiritual focus, such as "God is joy," led to reduced anxiety, improved mood, and substantial increases in pain tolerance.[19]

Why might these benefits occur for only the spiritually focused group? The precise causes or "mechanisms" have not yet been clarified scientifically. But a spiritual modeling perspective suggests psychological processes that could have contributed to the greater benefits from a spiritual focus. Because of its mental associations, a spiritual focus might facilitate remembering spiritual models and enacting the ideals, beliefs, and practices that they represent (helping to reproduce behavior). This might happen in at least two ways. First, with inspiration from spiritual models more mentally available at the time of meditation, spiritual-focus meditators may have meditated more deeply, and received correspondingly greater health benefit from the *psychophysical process of meditation itself*. Second, steeping the mind for 20 minutes in a spiritual phrase might make spiritual thoughts more *generally mentally accessible* during the remainder of the day. With spiritual ideals and models more mentally available, spiritual-focus meditators could have been more able to enact specific spiritual coping methods, character strengths, and other spiritual practices that foster health.

Wachholz and Pargament's remarkable study shows clearly that health outcomes can be affected not only by physical behaviors, but also by spiritual meanings, as predicted by a spiritual modeling perspective.

Example 2: Spiritual Cue Words

The principle that a spiritual phrase can activate spiritual associations is also relevant to an intervention studied by Jill Bormann of the San Diego Veteran's Administration. As described by Bormann and Oman (this volume), this intervention was similar to Wachholz' spiritual meditation in that a variety of short words or phrases were used that could elicit spiritual associations. Recommended phrases are drawn from a range of distinct spiritual and religious traditions, and include "Jesus," "Barukh attah Adonai" (Jewish), and "Om mani padme hum" (Buddhist). Like Wachholtz's intervention, Bormann's spiritual phrases—often called mantrams or holy names—are too short to contain substantial amounts of information about spiritual models.

A distinguishing feature of Bormann's mantram intervention is *when during the day* the spiritual phrase is repeated. Whereas Wachholtz's spiritual meditators repeated their spiritual phrase during sitting meditation, Bormann trained participants to mentally repeat a mantram or other spiritual phrase at *opportune moments throughout the day or night*: for example, while walking, waiting in line, when sitting in a dentist's chair, or falling asleep.

Research described by Bormann and Oman (this volume) suggests that mantram repetition is helpful to general and patient populations for managing stress, anxiety, and anger, and for improving quality of life and spiritual well-being.

Why might these benefits occur? A spiritual modeling perspective alerts us to how the mantram may elicit mental associations related to spiritual models, beliefs, practices, and narratives. Just as with spiritual meditators, such mental associations may help those who repeat a spiritual cue word, mantram, or holy name to overcome compartmentalization, and to enact healthy spiritual attitudes and behaviors throughout daily living.

Example 3: Supportive Assessment

A different method of connecting participants with spiritual models and other spiritual resources has been studied at Indiana State University by Jean Kristeller and her colleagues.[20] This intervention focused on how physicians might address spiritual concerns of patients facing life-threatening illnesses. Like spiritual meditation and mantram repetition, Kristeller's intervention may have strengthened the ability of patients to draw on spiritual models and other spiritual resources. Here, the link is provided not by repeating a spiritual phrase, but by the physician demonstrating respect for possible spiritual resources. Such behavior, we suspect, may have reassured patients that they will be supported, rather than opposed, in drawing upon spiritual resources in managing their illnesses.

Kristeller's intervention helped physicians overcome several obstacles to discussing spiritual concerns. It offered them a flexible yet structured 7-step protocol that guides discussions of spiritual and religious issues in a manageable time period (5–7 minutes). Physicians open the discussion in a neutral and inquiring manner ("When dealing with a serious illness, many people draw on religious or spiritual beliefs to help cope. It would be helpful to me to know how you feel about this"[20] (p. 331)). Further inquiries are adjusted to the patients' initial responses (positive, neutral, or rejecting). For patients with positive or neutral responses, the sixth step involves offers of assistance as appropriate or available (e.g., "there is a support group ... "). Initial research with 118 cancer patients revealed that after 3 weeks, patients randomized to this intervention experienced reduced depressive symptoms, improved quality of life, and perceived higher levels of interpersonal caring from their physician.

Attitudes toward the role of spiritual resources, whether intended or not, are modeled every day by physicians and other health professionals. For example, not asking about a patient's spiritual resources conveys an attitude about such possible resources. Kristeller's approach reminds us of the need for all health professionals to understand how they can model attitudes of mutual understanding and respect for spiritual resources of patients. In doing so, they often can help patients utilize their spiritual resources effectively in coping with health problems. Physicians and other health professionals can demonstrate by their example that spiritual and medical goals can be in harmony. In addition such demonstrations can foster increased motivation for patients to adhere to medical regimens. Technically, this process has been called *motivational goal alignment*.[21]

Example 4: Meditation Plus Inspiration

A fourth intervention that supports learning from spiritual models is a well-studied form of meditation called Mindfulness Based Stress Reduction (MBSR), or Mindfulness Training, developed by Jon Kabat-Zinn at the University of Massachusetts Medical School.[22] MBSR teaches a type of sitting meditation, which involves focusing the mind on the breath. Considerable evidence now suggests that MBSR fosters better health outcomes among patient groups. Some evidence also demonstrates increases in perceived spirituality among college students from MBSR training.[23]

Importantly, as it is usually taught, MBSR supports learning from spiritual models. For example, MBSR is taught in a group setting, allowing fellow participants to draw on each other as models. Furthermore, texts from spiritually oriented poets such as Jalaluddin Rumi, Walt Whitman, or others, are commonly used in MBSR sessions to illustrate, inspire, and support meditative states of mind. A poem by Rainer Rilke, for example, supports an attitude of trust in a higher power: "Life has not forgotten you, it holds you in its hands and will not let you fall"[24] (p. 506). The specific poetic texts used in MBSR sessions are not standardized, but are selected by MBSR teachers, depending on the background or interests of trainees. It seems clear that the MBSR intervention surpasses our three earlier examples by *augmenting* participants' knowledge of spiritual models. This is done by exposing participants to well-developed expressions of spiritual perspectives—perspectives that may become more intelligible and meaningful in view of participants' own experiences with meditation.

Example 5: Integrated Passage Meditation

A final intervention that supports learning from spiritual models involves an integrated set of practices, called the Eight Point Program (EPP). The EPP provides many opportunities to learn from spiritual models, as described in detail by Flinders, Oman, and Flinders (this volume). The core of the EPP is a form of sitting meditation, termed passage meditation. Typically a person memorizes a text, such as the 23rd Psalm, and focuses the mind on repeating the passage silently and slowly. In this way, attention is given to key attitudes and behaviors of eminent spiritual models such as Jesus, the Buddha, the Psalmist, Teresa of Avila, or Mahatma Gandhi. Other practices or "points" include slowing down, putting others first, and frequent repetition of a mantram or holy name at opportune moments (described earlier in Example #2). Well-controlled studies suggest that the EPP can produce large reductions in stress[25] (see Flinders, Oman, and Flinders, this volume, for a review).

The EPP supplies spiritual modeling information using a sourcebook of meditation passages drawn from all major spiritual wisdom traditions.[26] Like MBSR, the EPP is commonly taught in a group setting, allowing participants to function as models for each other. Furthermore, as a comprehensive program, the EPP appears to support each of the four spiritual modeling processes with regard to eminent models from wisdom traditions. For example, memorizing and meditating on an inspirational passage, as noted, gives focused *attention* to the modeling information contained in the passage. Repeatedly meditating on the words builds *retention*. This, in turn, enhances the *reproduction* of the ideals in the passages during the day. Many passages also recount positive experiences that come to those who persist in spiritual practice, thereby supporting *motivation* to practice.

An empirical study of forty-four college students found that the EPP increased learning from spiritual models in comparison to a control group, and also in comparison to MBSR, the type of meditation described in Example #4.[23] This finding is consistent with an analysis of the spiritual modeling content in empirically studied forms of meditation, which found support for spiritual modeling by MBSR, but the highest level of support by the EPP.[27]

Conclusion

We have presented a spiritual modeling perspective and suggested its connection to improving health. Evidence was reviewed briefly and a framework was presented showing how learning from spiritual exemplars could plausibly influence health. We presented five examples of how a spiritual modeling perspective suggests or reinforces some new directions for health practice. Examples included three spiritually supportive forms of meditation, a brief assessment of patient spiritual resources, and use of mantrams and holy names. Each employs slightly different methods for fostering learning from spiritual models, and seeks to reduce the sharp separation of health from spirituality. This list of spiritual modeling applications, of course, is far from complete—additional examples include Dreher and Plante (this volume), and a recent study of Centering Prayer.[28]

We encourage healthcare and religious organizations, professionals, and laypersons to consider their health- and spirituality-related activities in light of a spiritual modeling perspective. Questions to consider include: Are adequate opportunities available for learning from spiritual models—both from the local community and from spiritual wisdom traditions? Do the interventions presented earlier suggest possible ways to support learning from spiritual models that could be more fully integrated into daily routines? How might such changes be implemented soon? What are the potential costs? Potential benefits? In light of potential costs and benefits, is the currently available evidence enough to justify developing and conducting a program to foster learning from spiritual models?

It is also possible that a spiritual modeling perspective, appropriately implemented, may have wider relevance—for example, in college education, where large majorities of U.S. college students report having an interest in spirituality (80 percent) or searching for meaning/purpose in life (76 percent).[29] Eminent opinion researcher and trend analyst Daniel Yankelovich recently observed that Americans hunger for spiritual ways of truth seeking. He suggested that higher education, "As the home base of specialized knowledge ... may have to do a great deal more in coming decades to recognize, respect, codify, and clarify the strengths and limitations of nonscientific ways of knowing vis-à-vis scientific knowledge."[30] Conceivably, the study of spiritual models could help clarify the diverse paths to truth and wisdom that have been discovered by the human family.[31]

On global, organizational, professional, and personal levels, relations between spirituality and health are a topic of increasing public and professional interest, one that is here to stay. We hope that a spiritual modeling perspective can help clarify these relations not only theoretically, but also lead to fruitful applications that foster health and well-being.

Acknowledgments

We wish to thank the many people who have helped us to develop the spiritual modeling perspective, including especially Albert Bandura and Eknath Easwaran. Some of this material was presented by the first author as a keynote address at the Society of Behavioral Medicine's Spirituality and Health Special Interest Group Pre-Conference, "Spirituality, Science and Health: What's Going On and Why?" held at Santa Clara University, Santa Clara, CA, March 22, 2006.

References

1. Smith, H. (1991). *The world's religions: Our great wisdom traditions*. San Francisco, CA: Harper San Francisco.
2. Miller, W. R. & Thoresen, C. E. (2003). Spirituality, religion, and health: An emerging research field. *American Psychologist, 58*, 24–35.

3. Oman, D. & Thoresen, C. E. (2005). Do religion and spirituality influence health? In: R.F. Paloutzian & C. Park (Eds.), *Handbook of the psychology of religion and spirituality* (pp. 435–459). New York: Guilford.

4. Bandura, A. (1986). *Social foundations of thought and action.* New Jersey: Prentice Hall, Englewood Cliffs.

5. Gallup Poll. (2002). Gallup poll, January 14, 2002, question qn45, http://institution.gallup.com/documents/question.aspx?QUESTION=134971, accessed October 31, 2006.

6. Easwaran, E. (1991/1978). *Meditation: A simple eight-point program for trans-lating spiritual ideals into daily life.* Tomales, CA: Nilgiri Press, full text also at, http://www.easwaran.org.

7. Walsh, R. N. (1999). *Essential spirituality: The 7 central practices to awaken heart and mind.* New York: Wiley.

8. Peterson, C. & Seligman, M. E. P. (2004). *Character strengths and virtues: A handbook and classification.* Washington, DC and New York: American Psy-chological Association and Oxford University Press.

9. Finke, R. (2003). Spiritual capital: Definitions, applications, and new fron-tiers. Paper for Spiritual Capital Research Program Planning Meeting, Philadel-phia, PA, October 10, 2003, accessed May 6, 2006, http://www.metanexus.net/spiritual_capital/research_articles.asp.

10. McAdams, D. P. (2006). *The redemptive self: Stories Americans live by.* New York: Oxford University Press.

11. Colby, A. & Damon, W. (1992). *Some do care: Contemporary lives of moral commitment.* New York: Free Press.

12. Koenig, H. G., McCullough, M. E., & Larson, D. B. (2001). *Handbook of religion and health.* New York: Oxford University Press.

13. Silberman, I. (2003). Spiritual role modeling: The teaching of meaning sys-tems. *The International Journal for the Psychology of Religion, 13,* 175–195.

14. Oman, D., Thoresen, C. E., Park, C. L., Shaver, P. R., Plante, T. G., & Hood, R. W. (2005). Spiritual models predict health behaviors in college undergradu-ates. *Poster presented at the 26th Annual Meeting of The Society of Behavioral Medicine, Boston, MA: April 15, 2005.*

15. Steen, T. A., Kachorek, L. V., & Peterson, C. (2003). Character strengths among youth. *Journal of Youth & Adolescence, 32,* 5–16.

16. McCord, G., Gilchrist, V. J., Grossman, S. D., King, B. D., McCormick, K. E., Oprandi, A. M., et al. (2004). Discussing spirituality with patients: A rational and ethical approach. *Annals of Family Medicine, 2,* 356–361.

17. Barnard, D., Dayringer, R., & Cassel, C. K. (1995). Toward a person-centered medicine: Religious studies in the medical curriculum. *Academic Medicine, 70,* 806–813.

18. Wilber, K. (1998). *The marriage of sense and soul: Integrating science and religion.* New York: Random House.

19. Wachholtz, A. B. & Pargament, K. I. (2005). Is spirituality a critical ingredient of meditation? Comparing the effects of spiritual meditation, secular meditation, and relaxation on spiritual, psychological, cardiac, and pain outcomes. *Journal of Behavioral Medicine, 28*, 369–384.
20. Kristeller, J. L., Rhodes, M., Cripe, L. D., & Sheets, V. (2005). Oncologist assisted spiritual intervention study (OASIS): Patient acceptability and initial evidence of effects. *International Journal of Psychiatry in Medicine, 35*, 329–347.
21. Ford, M. E. (1992). *Motivating humans: Goals, emotions, and personal agency beliefs.* Newbury Park, CA: Sage.
22. Kabat-Zinn, J. (1991). *Full catastrophe living: Using the wisdom of your body and mind to face stress, pain, and illness.* New York: Dell.
23. Oman, D., Shapiro, S., Thoresen, C. E., Flinders, T., Driskill, J. D., and Plante, T. G. (2007). Learning from spiritual models and meditation: A randomized evaluation of a college course. *Pastoral Psychology, 55*, 473–493.
24. Shapiro, S. L. (2001). Poetry, mindfulness, and medicine. *Family Medicine, 33*, 505–506.
25. Oman, D., Hedberg, J., & Thoresen, C. E. (2006). Passage meditation reduces perceived stress in health professionals: A randomized, controlled trial. *Journal of Consulting and Clinical Psychology, 74*, 714–719.
26. Easwaran, E. (2003/1982). *God makes the rivers to flow: Sacred literature of the world.* Tomales, CA: Nilgiri Press, large parts also online: http://www.easwaran. org.
27. Oman, D. & Beddoe, A. E. (2005). Health interventions combining meditation with learning from spiritual exemplars: Conceptualization and review. *Annals of Behavioral Medicine, 29*, S126.
28. Ferguson, J. (2006). Centering Prayer as a healing response to everyday stress at a Roman Catholic parish in Silicon Valley [dissertation]. Berkeley, CA: Graduate Theological Union.
29. Astin, A. W., Astin, H. S., Lindholm, J. A., Bryant, A. N., Calderone, S., & Szelenyi, K. (2005). The spiritual life of college students: A national study of college students' search for meaning and purpose. Los Angeles, CA: Higher Education Research Institute, University of California, full text online: http://spirituality.ucla.edu/reports/index.html.
30. Yankelovich, D. (2005). Ferment and change: Higher education in 2015, *The Chronicle of Higher Education/Chronicle Review*, Vol. 52, B6+.
31. Oman, D., Flinders, T., & Thoresen, C. E. (in press). Integrating spiritual modeling into education: A college course for stress management and spiritual growth. *The International Journal for the Psychology of Religion.*

PART 2

MEDITATION

CHAPTER 5

Meditation: Exploring the Farther Reaches*

SHAUNA L. SHAPIRO AND ROGER WALSH

Meditation has been practiced in many forms and in many cultures over many centuries. Historically, it has been practiced for at least 3,000 years since the dawn of Indian yoga and is a central discipline at the contemplative core of each of the world's great religions. It is most often associated with the Indian traditions of yoga and Buddhism, but has also been crucial to the Chinese Taoist and neo-Confucian traditions. The great monotheisms—Judaism, Christianity, and Islam—have also offered a variety of meditative techniques, although they never obtained the popularity and centrality accorded them in India.

The Perennial Philosophy

The importance accorded meditation by the perennial philosophy—the common core of wisdom and worldview that lies at the heart of each of the great religions—is based on three crucial assumptions; assumptions that speak to vital aspects of our nature and potential as human beings. Yet, with the exception psychologies such as transpersonal and integral, these assumptions lie outside most mainstream Western psychology and thought.

1. Our usual psychological state is suboptimal and immature.

---

*Portions of this chapter have been presented elsewhere and most especially in Shapiro, S.L., & Walsh, R. (2003). An analysis of recent meditation research and suggestions for future directions. *The Humanistic Psychologist, 31*, 86–114.

William James provided a pithy and poetic summary stating that "most people live, whether physically, intellectually, or morally, in a very restricted circle of their potential being. They make use of a very small portion of their possible consciousness. We all have reservoirs of life to draw upon, of which we do not dream."

2. Higher states and stages are available as developmental potentials.

What we call "normality" and have regarded as the ceiling of human possibilities is increasingly coming to look like a form of arbitrary, culturally determined, developmental arrest.[1] Mainstream developmental psychology itself is coming to a similar conclusion. Beyond Piaget's formal operational thinking lies postformal operational cognition, beyond Kohlberg's conventional morality are postconventional stages, beyond Fowler's synthetic-conventional faith lie conjunctive and universalizing faith, beyond Maslow's self-esteem needs await self-actualization and self-transcendence, and beyond Loevinger's conformist ego lie the possibilities of the autonomous and integrated ego.[2–7] In short, beyond conventional, personal stages of development await postconventional, transpersonal stages and potentials.

3. Psychological development to transpersonal states and stages can be catalyzed by a variety of psychological and spiritual practices.

Indeed, the contemplative core of the world's religions consists of a set of practices to do just this. Comparison across traditions suggests that there are seven practices that are widely regarded as central and essential for effective transpersonal development. These seven are an ethical lifestyle, redirecting motivation, transforming emotions, training attention, refining awareness, fostering wisdom, and practicing service to others.[8] Contemplative traditions posit that meditation is crucial to this developmental process because it facilitates several of these processes.

Defining Meditation

For all of the above reasons, meditation is of great interest to researchers and clinicians interested in positive psychological, transpersonal, and spiritual qualities. This leads to the important question, "what is meditation?" Meditation can be defined as a family of practices that train attention and awareness, usually with the aim of fostering psychological and spiritual well-being and maturity. Meditation does this by training and bringing mental processes under greater voluntary control, and directing them in beneficial ways. This control is used to cultivate specific mental qualities such as concentration and calm, and emotions such as joy, love, and compassion. Through greater awareness, a clearer understanding of oneself and one's relationship to the world develops. Additionally, it is held that a deeper and more accurate knowledge of consciousness and reality manifests.

A common division is into concentration and awareness types of meditation. Concentration practices attempt to focus awareness on a single object such as the breath or a mantra (internal sound). By contrast, awareness practices allow attention to move to a variety of objects, and investigate them all. And yet, there are many varieties of meditation and no adequate taxonomy has been devised. For simplicity and the purposes of this paper, we need simply point out that meditations vary in:

1. The type of attention: *Concentration* meditations aim for continuous focus primarily on one object, such as the breath or an inner sound. *Awareness* or *open* meditations aim for fluid attention to multiple or successively chosen objects.

2. The relationship to cognitive processes: Some practices simply observe cognitions such as thoughts or images, while others deliberately modify them.

3. The goal: Some practices aim to foster general mental development and well-being, while others focus primarily on developing specific mental qualities, such as concentration, love, or wisdom.

Meditation is most often associated with India but is actually a worldwide practice found in every major religion and most cultures. Examples include Taoist and Hindu yogas, Jewish Hassidic and Kabalistic *dillug* and *tzeruf*, Islamic Sufism's *zikr*, Confucian quiet-sitting, Christian contemplations, and Buddhist meditations.[1,8,9] In their traditional settings they are usually embedded in supportive lifestyles (such as ethics) and practices (such as the body postures of yoga) designed to optimize development.

By far the most researched and practiced types of meditation are mindfulness and Transcendental Meditation (TM). Mindfulness is an open focus or awareness practice usually identified with Buddhist mindfulness or *vipassana* (literally "clear seeing") insight meditation, but also central to Taoist "internal observation" practice.[10] TM is a mantra (inner sound) practice that researchers sometimes describe as concentrative, but in advanced stages awareness becomes increasingly panoramic. Hundreds of other meditation practices await research.

Contemplative traditions posit that through the process of meditation, physical, psychological, and spiritual health are cultivated. Contemporary research offers preliminary yet growing support to some of these claims. Below, we briefly summarize the general findings of meditation on reducing physical and psychological symptoms. We then review studies that explore the effects of meditation on positive psychological and transpersonal health, and offer a case study of meditation's applications to this domain.

Foundational Research Studies

Researchers primarily have examined meditation's effects as a self-regulation strategy for stress management and symptom reduction. Over the past three decades, there has been considerable research examining the psychological and physiological effects of meditation. Meditative practices are now being utilized in a variety of health care settings. This is understandable because research suggests that meditation may be an effective intervention for cardiovascular disease, chronic pain, anxiety and panic disorder, substance abuse, dermatological disorders, reduction of psychological distress and symptoms of distress for cancer patients; and reduction of medical symptoms in both clinical and nonclinical populations (for reviews see[11,12,13]).

A Return to the Original Intentions of Meditation

Abraham Maslow stated, "... what we call 'normal' in psychology is really a psychopathology of the average, so undramatic and so widely spread that we don't even notice it ordinarily."[14] Meditation has been suggesting this for over 2,500 years. The intention behind meditation is to "wake up" from a suboptimal state of consciousness; wake up to our true nature.

Walsh[15] identified traditional aims of meditation practice as including "the development of deep insight into the nature of mental processes, consciousness, identity, and reality, and the development of optimal states of psychological well-being and consciousness" (p. 19). From a growth perspective, it is essential to learn ways to free ourselves from the artificial and unnecessary limits we impose, as well as to learn to expand our worldviews. This liberation involves recognizing and letting go of old structures and boundaries and evolving to more complex worldviews. Meditation provides roadmaps to develop empathy, compassion, awareness, and insight.

And yet, research exploring the effects of meditation to attain these goals has been scarce. With few exceptions, research has not measured the deeper levels of meditation's original intent, but instead has focused on traditional psychological variables. Rosch[16] succinctly put it, "Yes, research on the meditation traditions can provide data to crunch with the old mindset. But they have much more to offer, a new way of looking."

Consciously examining the original intentions of meditation to cultivate positive qualities and spiritual development will help us uncover, Maslow[5] famously called "the farther reaches of human nature." While continuing basic research, we can also examine the foci and goals of the meditative traditions themselves, assess their accompanying psychologies and philosophies, and explore their many implications for our understanding of human nature, pathology, therapy, and potentials. Such a research program may offer far-reaching benefits. These include facilitating emerging movements such as positive psychology and the psychology of spirituality and health, as well as integrative movements such as cross-cultural psychology, integral psychology, and integrative psychotherapy.[17,18]

To this end, a small number of pioneering studies provide a valuable foundation. These studies suggest meditation can produce improvements in: self-actualization, empathy, sense of meaning, happiness, a positive sense of control, increased moral maturity, and increased spirituality (for review see[19]). Positive behavioral effects include: heightened perception (visual sensitivity, auditory acuity); improvements in reaction time and responsive motor skill; increased field independence; increased concentration and attention.[12] In addition, meditation appears to result in improvements in aspects of intelligence, school grades, learning ability, and short- and long-term recall.[20]

The studies provided a solid beginning upon which recent research has been building. Below we review a sample of recent, well-designed studies on the effects of meditation on positive psychological variables and spirituality.

Analysis of Recent Research

Psychological Findings

Cognition and Creativity. Three recent studies examined the effects of TM meditation on cognition. One hundred and fifty-four Chinese high school students were randomized into a TM group or a napping group.[21] The TM technique and napping were practiced for approximately 20 minutes twice a day. At 6-month follow-up, the TM group demonstrated significantly increased practical intelligence, field independence, creativity, and speed of information processing, as well as significantly decreased anxiety compared to the control group. The authors suggest that these findings indicate that TM's effects extend beyond those of ordinary rest.

The findings of this study were replicated in a sample of 118 junior high Chinese students who were randomly assigned to a TM group, a contemplative meditation group, or a no treatment control group. All students practiced their respective meditation techniques for 20 minutes twice a day. At 6-month follow-up the TM group showed improvement on creativity, anxiety, information processing time, and practical intelligence as compared to the contemplation group. The contemplation group improved on information processing time as compared to the control group.

These general findings were replicated in a third study examining the effects of TM compared to a no treatment control group on ninety-nine male vocational students from Taiwan. At 12 months follow-up, the TM group significantly increased practical intelligence, field independence, whole-brained creativity, and speed of information processing, and significantly decreased anxiety as compared to the control group. In summarizing the implications of these three studies, the authors suggest that the findings strongly support the hypothesis that TM improves performance on a number of cognitive and affective measures. However, for a critical review that attributes much of the cognitive benefits claimed for TM to expectancy and design factors, see Canter & Ernst's review.[22]

Interpersonal relationships. Practices for cultivation of love, compassion, empathetic joy, and equanimity have a long tradition in the meditative disciplines.[8] Most notable are the Brahma Vihara practices, which involve four distinct meditation practices focusing respectively on the cultivation of loving kindness, compassion, empathic joy, and equanimity.[23] A recent[24] incorporated the meditative practice of loving kindness (metta), one of the Brahma Viharas, into a mindfulness-based intervention for couples. Forty-four couples that were in well-adjusted relationships and had been married an average of 11 years were randomly assigned to a waiting-list control or the meditation intervention. The program consisted of eight $2^1/_2$-hour sessions and a 6-hour retreat. In addition to components modeled on the Mindfulness-Based Stress Reduction Program,[25] a number of elements related to enhancing the relationship were added, including loving kindness meditation, partner yoga exercises, focused application of mindfulness to relationship issues, and group discussions. Results demonstrated that the couples in the meditation intervention significantly improved relationship satisfaction as well as relatedness to and acceptance of the partner. In addition, individuals reported significant increases in optimism, engagement in exciting self-expanding activities, spirituality, and relaxation. Interestingly, increases in engagement in exciting self-expanding activities significantly mediated improvements in relationship quality.[26]

The above study supports earlier research, which examined the effects of Zen breath meditation as compared to relaxation on college adjustment.[27] Seventy-five undergraduates, matched on initial anxiety, were randomized into meditation, relaxation, and control groups. The students received only 1 hour of instruction in either technique and were instructed to practice it once daily for at least 20 minutes. Anxiety and depression scores significantly decreased in both meditation and relaxation groups as compared to the control group; however only the meditation group had a significant positive effect on interpersonal relationships.

Long-term Retreats. Page and colleagues[28] performed a largely exploratory qualitative analysis of the written self-perceptions of retreatants after a 6-month period of isolation and silent meditation during the third year of a 4-year Tibetan Buddhist retreat. Retreatants were forty-six self-reported Tibetan Buddhists from internationally distributed locations. Three independent raters broke down the subjects' written responses into their smaller units of independently meaningful content, divided them into "internal" or "external" categories, and then grouped internal units into emergent themes.

Five themes of internal self-perception were identified: (1) happiness/satisfaction; (2) struggle leading to insight; (3) practice/meditation; (4) sense of time and; (5) goals/expectations. Females tended to write more about satisfaction while males wrote more about struggle leading to insight. Sense of time was reported to be absent or distorted, and future goals tended to be generalized toward maintaining the conscious self-awareness acquired during isolation. These preliminary findings suggest that a long-term retreat, including 6 months of isolation, may enhance personal awareness to a level that supports increased life satisfaction. And yet these findings should be considered with caution. Only twenty-three of forty-six original participants remained by the third year of the retreat, an attrition rate that could signify a high potential for self-selection bias in terms of motivation, happiness, and expectation. With such a unique population, more comprehensive measures, quantitative analysis, and a more developed and delineated description of self-awareness would be of great benefit.

Self-Concept. Using a cross-section study design, Hamierl and Valentine[29] investigated the effect of Buddhist meditation on intrapersonal (self-directedness), interpersonal (cooperativeness), and transpersonal (self-transcendence) levels of the self-concept. Subjects included prospective meditators ($n = 28$) with no experience, beginners ($n = 58$) with less than 2-years of experience, and advanced meditators ($n = 73$) with more that 2-years of experience. Advanced meditators scored significantly higher than prospective meditators on all three subscales, advanced meditators scored significantly higher than beginners on the interpersonal subscale, and beginners scored significantly higher than prospective meditators on the transpersonal subscale. Only the advanced meditators scored higher on the transpersonal than on the intrapersonal subscale. The authors concluded that scores on the intrapersonal, interpersonal, and transpersonal levels were a positive function of meditation experience, suggesting that progress in Buddhist meditation leads to significant growth in these components of personality.

Empathy. All schools of meditation have emphasized concern for the condition of others and an intention to "promote an empathy with created things that leads toward oneness with them." Twelve recent researches demonstrate that meditation practice does indeed lead to greater levels of empathy.

In a randomized controlled study Shapiro and colleagues[30] examined the effects of a mindfulness meditation-based program on seventy-eight medical and premedical students. Results indicated increased levels of empathy and decreased levels of anxiety and depression in the meditation group as compared to the wait-list control group. Furthermore, these results held during the students' stressful exam period. The findings were replicated when participants in the wait-list control group received the mindfulness intervention.

The findings of this study are supported by a recent study examining the effects of MBSR on counseling psychology students' empathy. Counseling students who participated in an 8-week MBSR course demonstrated significant prepost increases in empathic concern for others as compared to a matched control group.[19]

Spirituality. Spirituality is difficult and complex to measure. It means different things to different people, is experience, and is talked about in unique ways. However, across all traditions, there is agreement that spirituality involves movement toward transpersonal experiences and reduced egocentricity. Meditative disciplines particularly value and cultivate transpersonal states in which the sense of identity extends beyond (trans) the individual person or personality to encompass wider aspects of humankind, life, and even cosmos. Western psychologists periodically rediscover some of these transpersonal states. Examples include Maslow's "peak" and "plateau" experiences, Jung's "numinous experience," Grof's "holotropic experience," Fromm's "at-onement," and James' "cosmic consciousness."[1] Such experiences are often referred to as "spiritual moments" and may lead to an overall enhanced sense of spirituality. Current research demonstrates that meditation disciplines offer practices and frameworks to help cultivate transpersonal and spiritual experiences.

In the study by Carson and colleagues[26] noted previously, the couples who received the mindfulness meditation relationship enhancement intervention reported significantly increased spirituality compared to the control group. This supports earlier findings that MBSR intervention significantly increased spiritual experience in medical students as compared to wait-list controls.[30] These results were replicated when the control group received the same mindfulness intervention. Further, Astin[31] demonstrated significant increases in spiritual experience in a randomized controlled study comparing a mindfulness meditation intervention to a control group of undergraduate students.

A Case Study

Above we summarized current research demonstrating the potential of meditation to help cultivate positive psychological and spiritual qualities. We now describe a case study of a woman who is recovering from breast cancer, illustrating how meditative techniques assisted this client in coming to terms will her illness, as well as addressing existential, psychospiritual, and even transcendent issues.

Mrs. X was 58 years old when she was diagnosed with Stage II breast cancer. She received chemotherapy and radiation treatment and was currently in remission when she entered the Mindfulness-Based Stress Reduction (MBSR) program. She had been vital and active throughout her life; a successful lawyer as well as mother of three children (all of whom were adults and out of the home when she received her cancer diagnosis). Although her cancer was in remission Mrs. X continued to have deep anxiety about recurrence. She reported feeling that her life was on hold and that every day she experienced intrusive thoughts about recurrence. She described a sense of hopelessness and claustrophobia—reporting that she felt trapped in this new and "damaged" body. She reported that she was unable to live freely because the fear weighed her down.

During the MBSR intervention, Mrs. X, along with the other twenty women in the program, learned meditative techniques including sitting meditation, body scan meditation, and mindful movement. She also learned about mindfulness, defined as present moment nonjudgmental awareness, and its applications to daily life. During the meditation practices, Mrs. X began to slowly and gently bring awareness to her anxiety; giving it space and close attention. She began to see how crippling her fear of recurrence was, how it was preventing her from actually living right now in this moment. And yet, her fear remained. As she continued to observe it over the days and weeks of meditation, she began to notice that the fear was not only a fear of recurrence but also a fear that she could no longer trust life. She discovered anger mixed in with the fear, a sense of "why me? Why did I get cancer?"

Mrs. X was invited to simply observe her emotions and thoughts and then to let them go and return to her breath and her body as anchors to the present moment. Through this continuous practice of attending to her direct experience with a degree of equanimity and clarity she began to shift her relationship to her fear, her anxiety, and her anger. She began to see things from a less personal perspective, and to see them with greater objectivity and clarity. She understood that she was not her thoughts or her emotions and did not have to believe them. Mrs. X realized that she could actually observe her thoughts without getting caught in their drama and without buying into the story. With this greater objectivity and equanimity Mrs. X was able to allow her fears to arise and to give them space. She was able to see them more clearly and to deepen her understanding of them.

Mrs. X described one sitting meditation where she was attending to the fear and as she sustained her nonjudgmental attention the fear began to dissolve and was replaced by a sense of ease and trust. She felt her body sitting, stable, supporting her. She felt herself expanding and realized that she was not simply this small body sitting, but part of an infinitely larger whole. She realized she was not alone and that she could let go and trust that God and the universe would support her. Mrs. X reported a sense of relief and comfort after this experience.

As the 8-week MBSR program drew to a close, Mrs. X shared that she felt much freer and more present. She reported feeling a sense of gratitude and appreciation for each moment of life, as opposed to living each moment with fear. She said her children and husband noticed the change. They felt her joy and her ease and a renewed connection and vitality emerged in their relationships. She shared that most importantly she had a renewed trust in herself and in life. Mrs. X left the MBSR programs with meditation tapes and a commitment to continue her formal meditation practice as well as informally applying mindfulness to daily life. At a 6-month follow-up interview, she reported she was still feeling the same sense of trust, gratitude, and ease that she had found 6 months earlier in the MBSR program. She said that although it was difficult to continue the formal meditation practice, she was able to meditate 1 day a week for 30 minutes (instead of her intended 3 days a week). She also shared that the awareness of the breath helped keep her anchored to the present moment and to a connection with a larger whole.

This case study demonstrated that meditation techniques could have a healing effect by allowing the practitioner to experience transpersonal and spiritual states. These transformational experiences are thought to occur due to a profound shift in relationship to experience. This shift involves a rotation from subject to object, which enables one to see with greater clarity and objectivity. This shift, often referred to as reperceiving[32] or disidentification,[33] creates greater space and clarity around one's experience. As this shift deepens, one is able to let go of the small egoist self. When these shifts occur, participants often report a sense of transcending the smaller self, a sense of spiritual connection, and a sense of liberation. As seen in the case of Mrs. X, this shift helped promote a healing of her fear of recurrence and a reconnection with her sense of trust and the sacred in life.

Discussion

As the above summary of the research and case study support, meditation appears not only to decrease pathology, but can have profound effects on positive qualities and spirituality. With the emergence of the field of positive psychology and a host of new measures, research, and theories, the time is ripe to refocus research and clinical work on the original intentions of meditation practice. It is time to expand the paradigm from pathology to positivity and the transpersonal. As noted, most meditation research has used the traditional biomedical paradigm in which the focus is on symptom reduction. Future research could expand this model by examining the effects of meditation on variables consistent with the classical goals of meditation, such as the development of spirituality, exceptional maturity, love, and compassion, and lifestyles of service and generosity.

Questions for Future Research

As we expand our paradigm of meditation practice, exciting and novel questions emerge. Below we outline seven important directions for future study.

1. *Differentiation between types of meditation.* There are many types of meditation. This is crucial to recognize for theoretical, practical, and research reasons. Yet researchers often implicitly assume that different meditations have equivalent effects. This is an assumption to be empirically tested. Most likely, different techniques have overlapping but by no means equal effects. In general, we anticipate that there will be both general and specific effects of different types of meditation. Many meditations may foster psychological and spiritual well-being and development on multiple dimensions. However, specific meditations may also produce very specific effects (e.g., Tibetan dreams yoga for developing lucid dreams, and a variety of practices that cultivate emotions of love or compassion). Therefore, it is essential that researchers clearly define the type of meditation being studied.

2. *Temporal effects.* Frequency and duration of meditation practice must be recorded (e.g., meditation journals) to determine if greater meditation induces greater effects and if so, is the relationship linear, curvilinear, or some other more intricate pattern. Interesting questions that emerge include how much meditation practice is required to enhance spirituality? Empathy? Moral development?

3. *Follow-up assessment.* Follow-up should include long-term as well as short-term assessment. It will be interesting to explore if spiritual development carries on and to examine in what ways people continue to progress as they continue their meditation practice.

4. *Inclusion of experienced meditators.* Researchers should include long-term, experienced meditators as well as beginning meditators. Also,

when matching control subjects to long-term meditators in retrospective studies, in addition to age, gender, and education, it would be important to consider matching subjects on the dimension of an alternative attentional practice (e.g., playing a musical instrument). The inclusion of long-term meditators, for example Tibetan yogis with more than 10,000 hours of meditation practice, would help elucidate the profound effects on spiritual development and well-being that arise with intensive and continuous meditation practice.

5. *Examination of interaction effects.* The practice of meditation may interact with a variety of relevant psychological, spiritual, and clinical factors. Factors of current interest include other health and self-management strategies, psychotherapy, and especially already established religious and spiritual practices.

6. *Qualitative data.* The subtlety and depth of meditation experiences do not easily lend themselves to quantification. Further, the interplay between subjective and objective is essential to understanding meditation. Qualitative data provides a means to access the subjective experience of the meditator.

7. *The value of practice for clinicians and researchers.* Several lines of evidence suggest that personal practice of meditation may enhance one's understanding of meditative and transpersonal experiences, states, and stages. This is a specific example of a general principle. Without direct experience, concepts (and especially transpersonal concepts) remain what Immanuel Kant calls "empty" and devoid of experiential grounding. Without this grounding we lack *adequatio:* the capacity to comprehend the deeper "grades of significance" of phenomena,[34] which,[35] summarized in *The Perennial Philosophy*, as "knowledge is a function of being." As the philosopher[36] pointed out, in meditation the "deepest insights are available to the intellect, and powerfully so, but it is only when those insights are discovered and absorbed by a psyche made especially keen and receptive by long coursing in meditative discipline that they begin to find their fullest realization and effectiveness." There are several good books for beginners. [37, 38]

Therefore, for research to progress, optimally it may be helpful for researchers and clinicians themselves to have a personal meditation practice. Without direct practice and experience we may be in part blind to the deeper grades of significance of meditation experiences, and blind to our blindness.

Conclusion

During the past four decades, research in meditation has developed a strong foundation, demonstrating significant psychological, physiological, and therapeutic effects. However, the original intentions of meditation reach far beyond our current paradigm of symptom reduction. As we expand our models to include positive psychological, transpersonal, and spiritual variables, we will begin to understand the farther reaches of human potential. The exploration of meditation requires great sensitivity and a range of methodological glasses. Future research could benefit by looking through all of them, thereby illuminating the richness and complexity of meditation.

References

1. Walsh, R. & Vaughan, F.E. (Eds.) (1993). *Paths beyond ego: The transpersonal vision.* New York: Tarcher/Putnam.
2. Fowler, J. (1981). *Stages of faith: The psychology of human development and the quest for meaning.* San Francisco, CA: Harper & Row.
3. Kohlberg, L. (1981). *Essays on moral development. Vol. I. The philosophy of moral development.* New York: Harper and Row.
4. Loevinger, J. (1997). Stages of personality development. In R. Hogan, J. Johnson, & S. Briggs (Eds.), *Handbook of Personality Psychology* (pp. 199–208). San Diego, CA: Academic Press.
5. Maslow, A. (1971). *The farther reaches of human nature.* New York: Viking.
6. Wilber, K. (1999). Eye to eye. In *The collected works of Ken Wilber* (5 Vols.). Boston, MA: Shambhala.
7. Wilber, K. (2000a). *Integral psychology: Consciousness, spirit, psychology, therapy.* Boston, MA: Shambhala.
8. Walsh, R. (1999). *Essential spirituality: The seven central practices.* New York: Wiley & Sons.
9. Goleman, D. (1988). *The meditation mind.* Los Angeles, CA: Tarcher.
10. Wong, E. (1997). *The Shambhala guide to Taoism.* Boston, CA: Shambhala.
11. Andresen, J. (2000). Meditation meets behavioral medicine. *Journal of Consciousness Studies, 7,* 17–74.
12. Murphy, M., Donovan, S., & Taylor, E. (1997). *The physical and psychological effects of meditation: A review of contemporary research with a comprehensive bibliography* (2nd ed.). Petaluma, CA: Institute of Noetic Sciences.
13. Walsh R. & Shapiro, S.L. (2006). The meeting of meditative disciplines and western psychology: A mutually enriching dialogue. *American Psychologist, 61,* 227–239.
14. Maslow, A.H. (1968). *Toward a psychology of being* (2nd ed.). New York: Van Nostrand Reinhold.
15. Walsh, R.N. (1983). Meditation practice and research. *Journal of Humanistic Psychology, 23,* 18–50.
16. Rosch, E. (1999). Is wisdom in the brain? *Psychological Science, 10,* 222–224.

17. Arkowitz, H. & Mannon, B. (2002). A cognitive-behavioral assimilative integration. In F. Kaslow & J. Lebow (Eds.), *Comprehensive Handbook of Psychotherapy* (Vol. 4, pp. 317–337). New York: John Wiley.

18. Snyder, C. & Lopez, S. (Eds.) (2002). *Handbook of positive psychology.* New York: Oxford Press.

19. Shapiro, S.L. (2006). Paper presentation. *Annual Mindfulness in Medicine, Health Care and Society.* Worcester, MA. March 2006.

20. Cranson, R.W., Orme-Johnson, D.W., Gackenbach, J., Dillbeck, M.C., Jones, C.H., & Alexander, C.N. (1991). Transcendental meditation and improved performance on intelligence-related measures: A longitudinal study. *Personality & Individual Differences, 12,* 1105–1116.

21. So, K. & Orme-Johnson, D. (2001). Three randomized experiments on the longitudinal effects of the transcendental meditation technique on cognition. *Intelligence, 29,* 419–440.

22. Canter, P. & Ernst, E. (2003). The cumulative effects of transcendental meditation on cognitive function: A systematic review of randomized controlled trials. *Wien.Klin Wochenschr, 115,* 758–766.

23. Kornfield, J. (1993). Even the best meditators have old wounds to heal: Combining meditation and psychotherapy. In R. Walsh & F. Vaughan (Eds.), *Paths Beyond Ego* (pp. 67–68). New York: Tarcher/Putnam.

24. Carson, J., Carson K., Gil K., & Baucom D. (2004). Mindfulness based relationship enhancement. *Behavior Therapy, 35,* 471–494.

25. Kabat-Zinn, J. (1990). *Full catastrophe living.* New York: Delacourte Press.

26. Carson, J., Carson, K., Gil, K., & Baucom, D. (in press). Mindfulness-based relationship enhancement. *Behavior Therapy.*

27. Tloczynski, J. & Tantriella, M. (1998). A comparison of the effects of Zen breath meditation or relaxation on college adjustment. *Psychologia: An International Journal of Psychology in the Orient, 41,* 32–43.

28. Page, R.C., McAuliffe, E., Weiss, J., Ugyan, J., Stowers-Wright, L., & MacLachlan, M. (1997). Self-awareness of participants in a long-term Tibetan Buddhist retreat. *Journal of Transpersonal Psychology, 29,* 85–98.

29. Haimerl, C.J. & Valentine, E. (2001). The effect of contemplative practice on interpersonal, and transpersonal dimensions of the self-concept. *Journal of Transpersonal Psychology, 33,* 37–52.

30. Shapiro, S.L., Schwartz, G.E.R., & Bonner, G. (1998). The effects of mindfulness-based stress reduction on medical and pre-medical students. *Journal of Behavioral Medicine, 21,* 581–599.

31. Astin, J.A. (1997). Stress reduction through mindfulness meditation: Effects on psychological symptomatology, sense of control, and spiritual experiences. *Psychotherapy & Psychosomatics, 66,* 97–106.

32. Shapiro S.L., Carlson, L., Astin J., & Freedman, B. (2006). Mechanisms of Mindfulness. *Journal of Clinical Psychology, 62,* 1–14.

33. Segal, Z., William, J.M., & Teasdale, J. (2002). *Mindfulness-based cognitive therapy for depression.* New York: Guilford Press.

34. Schumacher, E. (1977). *A guide for the perplexed.* New York: Harper and Row.
35. Novak, P. (1989). Buddhist meditation and the great chain of being: Some misgivings. *Listening, 24,* 67–78.
36. Huxley, A. (1945). *The perennial philosophy.* New York: Harper & Row.
37. Bodian, S. (1999). *Meditation for dummies.* Foster City, CA: IDG Books.
38. Tart, C. (Ed.) (1992). *Transpersonal psychologies* (3rd ed.). New York: Harper-Collins.

CHAPTER 6

The Eight-Point Program of Passage Meditation: Health Effects of a Comprehensive Program

TIM FLINDERS, DOUG OMAN, AND CAROL LEE FLINDERS

When the Christian monk, John Cassian, brought the spiritual wisdom of the desert fathers to Gaul in the fifth century—laying the foundation for Catholic contemplative practice for the next 1,500 years—it was understood that these practices were meant primarily for monks and nuns leading monastic lives. This strict demarcation between religious and laity, or "householders," remains a fixture of Christian contemplative practice until the present day, and has been a cornerstone of most contemplative traditions in the East.

These distinctions have become blurred recently, at least in the United States, partly as a result of the proliferation of Eastern spiritual practices in this country during the past few decades. Millions of Americans report a daily meditation practice—estimates range as high as 50 million (23 percent of U.S. adults)[1]—and the great majority are not cloistered monks or nuns but upwardly mobile professionals busying themselves with careers and families in the cities and suburbs of middle America. Yet most of the contemplative disciplines they practice—Zen, Mindfulness, Dzogchen, Vipassana (Insight), and Transcendental Meditation, to name the more popular—are adaptations of historically monastic practices brought here from the East by monks.

The Eight-Point Program

The Eight Point Program (EPP) is a widely used contemplative practice that emerged in its present form during the 1960s. Eknath Easwaran (1910–1999) systematized the EPP at the University of California, Berkeley, for students preparing to enter the professional workforce and lead active, family and career-centered lives. A teacher, writer, and householder himself, Easwaran taught what was perhaps the first accredited course offered on meditation at a major Western university, "Theory and Practice of Meditation" (1967–1968).[2]

The EPP enlists classical contemplative practices like meditation and mantram repetition to support laypeople as they address the daily challenges of today's time-pressured, multitasking, relentlessly competitive workplace. Passage Meditation, the EPP's most distinctive feature, enables a practitioner to receive guidance from the attitudes and insights of sages, saints, and scriptures of all the world's great wisdom traditions.[3] In this way, more effectively than any other program that we know, the EPP blends a deep engagement with wisdom traditions that has been, historically, the prerogative of religious professionals and monastics, with the comprehensive supports needed by practicing laity. Moreover, the EPP is universal, accessible to individuals without religious beliefs who seek health or spiritual benefits, as well as to mainstream religious seekers that include Christians, Jews, Muslims, Buddhists, and Hindus.[4]

These special features of the EPP—universality, comprehensiveness, and deep engagement with wisdom traditions—are summarized in Table 6.1.

The next section describes Passage Meditation and other components or "points" of the EPP. We then outline processes through which the EPP may foster health and spiritual growth, reviewing relevant empirical findings from randomized, controlled trials and other studies that document such benefit. We conclude with reflections on implications for healthcare organizations, professionals, and laypersons.

The Eight-Point Program and Passage Meditation

Easwaran's book *Meditation*[2] remains the definitive description of the EPP. Table 6.2 summarizes the EPP's eight points and places them alongside some major modern lifestyle challenges that each addresses.

The first and foundational EPP point is *Passage Meditation*.

> *Point 1—Passage Meditation*—Among contemporary forms of concentrative meditation, Passage Meditation is unique in focusing attention on the words of inspirational passages, rather than on the breath (Vipassana), sounds (TM/Transcendental Meditation), or very short spiritual phrases (Centering Prayer). Practitioners memorize a text, usually from a scripture or a major spiritual figure (see Figure 6.1). Atheistic or agnostic practitioners may avoid deistic or theistic references by selecting Buddhist, Taoist, or other passages that emphasize qualities such as compassion and equanimity.[5] Each practitioner sits, with eyes closed, and mentally recites the words of the passage for 30

Table 6.1
Distinctive Features of the Eight-Point Program (EPP)

Distinctive Feature	Explanation
Universal	The EPP follows a nonsectarian approach, and EPP practices can be used comfortably by individuals practicing any major world religion, as well as by those adhering to no religion at all. Analogues to EPP practices already exist in all the major religions—the EPP's contribution is to organize and present them in a form readily accessible to people living ordinary lives in the modern world.
Comprehensive	The EPP provides a comprehensive program for spiritual living, lending support and assistance to the struggles and choices a person faces in all aspects of life. (For example: while the first point, Passage Meditation, helps a person to develop focused attention, the other seven points help to integrate that focus and poise into daily living).
Wisdom-based	Using the EPP brings a person into direct daily contact with the words of the world's great wisdom traditions. The EPP is based on Passage Meditation: meditating daily upon the memorized words of a great saint or sage such as Francis of Assisi, Mahatma Gandhi, or Teresa of Avila, or upon passages from scripture including the 23rd Psalm, the Sermon on the Mount, or the Buddha's Dhammapada.

minutes as slowly as possible, giving complete attention to each word. As distractions arise, they are not so much resisted, as ignored; attention is gently returned to the words of the passage each time it wanders. Practitioners do not follow *any* associations of ideas, even beneficial ones.

The second EPP point is mantram repetition (also sometimes called holy name repetition, or using a spiritual cue word). Variants can be found in all major religious traditions. Mantram repetition is a primary tool or bridge for integrating the calm and clarity gained from sitting meditation into the remainder of the day.

Table 6.2
The Eight-Point Program (EPP) and Contemporary
Challenges

EPP Point	Modern Challenges It Addresses
1. Passage Meditation	Distraction; spiritual alienation
2. Mantram Repetition	Negative thinking; chronic, obtrusive thoughts
3. Slowing Down	Chronic Hurry/"Hurry Sickness"[a]
4. One Pointed Attention	Compulsive multitasking/"Polyphasic thinking"[a]
5. Training the Senses	Sensory overload; over-consumption
6. Putting Others First	Self-absorption; egocentricity
7. Spiritual Association	Social and spiritual isolation
8. Inspirational Reading	Disillusion; pessimism
Total EPP program	Chronic stress; lack of meaning; lack of spiritual growth

[a]Quotations show how this challenge was characterized in research on Type A Behavior Pattern.

Point 2—Mantram Repetition—A mantram (mantra) is a short word or phrase that is repeated over and over silently or out loud. Popular mantrams include the "Jesus Prayer" of Eastern Orthodox Christianity, the name of Jesus (Roman Catholicism), and *Rama* (Hindu: Mahatma Gandhi's mantram). In the EPP, practitioners choose a mantram and repeat it (*"Rama, Rama, Rama"* ... *"Jesus, Jesus, Jesus"*) as opportunities arise: while walking, waiting in line, stopped at a traffic light, while falling asleep. Mantram repetition is also used in times of stress, to calm the mind when pressured, or to interrupt negative thinking when angry or afraid. Repetition of a word or short spiritual phrase is a widespread contemporary practice made popular by Herbert Benson's *Relaxation Response* and Transcendental Meditation, both of

Figure 6.1

Sample Inspirational Passages. *Note:* Passages are drawn from *God makes the rivers to flow: Sacred literature of the world*, a sourcebook containing passages drawn from all major spiritual traditions. (See reference #5) Many passages from Buddhist and Taoist traditions do not contain theistic references, and are of particular appeal to agnostics or other nonreligious individuals.

Source	Passage	Tradition
Psalm 23	The Lord is my shepherd, I shall not want. He maketh me to lie down in green pastures: He leadeth me beside still waters...	
Prayer of St. Francis of Assisi	Lord, Make me an instrument of Thy Peace, Where there is hatred, let me sow love; Where there is injury, pardon...	
Discourse on Good Will	May all beings be filled with joy and peace. May all beings everywhere, the strong and the Weak, the great and the small...	
Baba Kuhi of Shiraz	In the market, in the cloister, only God I saw. In the valley, on the mountain, only God I saw...	

which use them as the focus of their meditative practice. Unlike these, EPP mantram repetition is *not* used during sitting meditation and is therefore more available for use during the day. (See also Bormann and Oman's Chapter in this volume.)

The third and fourth points might be termed "mindfulness" points:

Point 3—Slowing Down is the practice of moving with care and deliberation through the day so as to minimize the stress caused by hurry and time pressures. It does not necessarily mean going slowly, but requires setting priorities and limiting activities so as not to live with the constant sense of time-urgency that characterizes contemporary life and has been linked to coronary illness.

Point 4—One-Pointed Attention invites the EPP practitioner to do only one thing at a time, and to give it full attention. While this practice may appear counterintuitive in a culture where multitasking is endemic, it offers a way to remain centered in the midst of the continuous assault of interruptions that characterize the modern workplace. One-pointedness is a common feature of Buddhist Mindfulness meditation and of Indian yoga systems.

The final four points foster freedom from narrowing and sometimes addictive habits, and provide support.

Point 5—*Training the Senses* directs practitioners to discriminate in lifestyle choices. It is not presented as a moral injunction, but as a discipline to gain freedom from habits like smoking, excessive drinking, and overeating. These compulsive behaviors are strongly implicated in chronic conditions such as cancer and coronary illness. Some form of sense discrimination can be found in all major religious and contemplative systems, both East and West.

Point 6—*Putting Others First* asks practitioners to move their focus of concern and attention to the needs of others—family, colleagues, community, and the world—and away from serving only private self-interest. Putting Others First recasts into a contemporary formulation the early Christian concept of *agape*, universal love, as well as Buddhist *metta*, compassion.

Point 7—*Spiritual Association*—Like Christian Fellowship or the Buddhist Sangha, Spiritual Association emphasizes the importance of coming together with like-minded practitioners as a way to offer and receive support.

Point 8—*Inspirational Reading*—Daily spiritual reading is recommended as a source of inspiration and motivation for EPP practitioners. *Lectio Divina* is a traditional Christian devotional practice centered on reading and reflecting on scripture.

The EPP is structurally integrative. That is, the eight points reinforce each other in a web of supportive strategies that draw on the calm and vitality of meditation to help deepen wisdom and meet the challenges of the day. For example, Passage Meditation trains the mind to slow down and focus thoughts, while the repetition of the mantram helps the mind focus while under stress. Similarly, Slowing Down and One Pointed Attention replicate during the rest of the day, *in vivo*, a person's effort in meditation to slow down and focus attention.

Widespread Cross-Cultural Appeal

Perhaps because the appeal of the EPP cuts across and transcends the most common categories of religious and sectarian identity, it rarely appears on lists of popular meditation practices such as TM, Vipassana, and Zen. However, the EPP in its present form has been used by thousands of practitioners over several generations since its introduction in the 1960s. In the past decade, the EPP has found a worldwide audience as the pressures of a globalized economy move seeking individuals to turn to contemplative practices like the EPP. Translations of EPP instructional materials by independent publishers appear in more than twenty languages in two dozen countries in North and South America, Europe, and Asia.[6]

How the EPP Fosters Health

How might the EPP affect physical and mental health? It is now well recognized that mental and physical health are closely related. A mentally healthy person is likely to cope more effectively with stress and experience lower levels of distress. Chronic stress is now a well recognized adverse influence on physical health.[7] Mentally healthy individuals are also less likely to resort in times of distress to smoking, heavy drinking, overeating, or other detrimental health behaviors. EPP effects on physical health are likely to arise in part through EPP effects on mental health.

The EPP may affect mental health through several interrelated processes that include training attention, strengthening the will, fostering character strengths and virtues, supporting better social relationships, more effective coping with stressors, more satisfying personal strivings and life commitments, and a more reliable capacity for wise living. The EPP may also affect physical health directly through some practices, such as Meditation and Training of the Senses. Since a comprehensive taxonomy of plausible processes is beyond the scope of this chapter, in what follows we highlight several of the more scientifically important and plausible processes of health benefit from the EPP.

> *Overall healthy lifestyle and effective coping.* As noted in Table 6.2, each EPP point helps address one or more modern lifestyle challenges. Thus, analogues to each EPP point have been independently studied in previous health research, and corresponding scientific mechanisms of benefit have been postulated.[8] For example, Training the Senses can foster improved health behaviors, and Mantram Repetition supports freedom from rumination (chronic, obtrusive thoughts), as well as from chronic hostility and other forms of compulsive negative thinking.

> *Effects from sitting meditation.* Decades of scientific research have documented health benefits from meditative practices, especially sitting meditation. Most meditation research has focused on physiological outcomes, linking meditation to better immune system functioning and salutary reductions in physiological arousal, including reduced blood pressure, heart rate, and other telltale markers of chronic stress overload.[9] A recent National Institutes of Health expert panel found

"persuasive" evidence that meditation interventions are associated with better health outcomes among clinical populations.[10] Randomized studies link meditation to reduced stress, recovery from clinical depression, and greater longevity. Behavioral benefits from meditation have also been reported, including reduced anxiety, lessened chemical dependency, and enhanced empathy, memory, and intelligence.[9]

Training attention is often cited as a defining feature of concentrative meditative practices,[9, 11] and is a direct goal of the EPP. As noted earlier, when practitioners of Passage Meditation find that their attention has wandered, they return it to the words of the passage. Repeating this exercise appears to build a sort of "bring back muscle" that strengthens the will for making wiser lifestyle choices during the day. Indeed, evidence suggests that self-control "can best be understood as conforming to a strength or muscle model"[12] and that "attention is the first and often most effective line of defense in nearly every sphere of self-control."[12] Over long periods of time, a meditator may not only experience health benefits, but also develop a "[p]owerful concentration [which] amplifies the effectiveness of any kind of activity."[11]

Character strengths and virtues. By training attention, and helping a person assimilate attitudes embodied in meditation passages (e.g., the Prayer of Saint Francis), the EPP may foster growth in a variety of virtues and character strengths. Classical human virtues such as forgiveness and compassion are encouraged by spiritual traditions, and increasing evidence supports their beneficial effects on mental health.[13]

Spiritual and religious coping. By helping a person assimilate attitudes embodied in meditation passages (e.g., the 23rd Psalm), the EPP may foster increased or more beneficial profiles of using distinctively religious and spiritual methods of coping with stress (examples will be discussed later).[14] *Adaptive goals and strivings.* By helping a person assimilate values and goals represented in meditation passages (e.g., the Discourse on Good Will), the EPP may free a person from excessively materialistic aspirations. Evidence suggests that spiritual strivings foster personality integration, and help reduce internal conflicts and distress.[15]

Wisdom. More generally, the EPP may foster wiser choices in all spheres of daily living. "When religions are sifted" for their best qualities, writes eminent scholar Huston Smith, "they begin to look like data banks that house the winnowed wisdom of the human race."[3] By helping a person assimilate the wisdom embodied in meditation passages, the EPP may foster wiser coping, striving, and habitual daily living.

Spiritual modeling. Even more generally, the EPP appears to foster enhanced learning from spiritual wisdom figures, such as the Psalmist, Saint Francis, and the Buddha. Meditating on a spiritual wisdom figure's words fosters assimilation of the attitudes and wisdom embedded in those words. Scientifically, this process is termed spiritual modeling[16] (see also Oman and Thoresen, this volume). Later, we offer a fuller analysis of how the EPP supports spiritual modeling processes.

Summary of Pathways to Health

Is there a simple and memorable way to summarize all these potential pathways through which the EPP might affect health and well-being? Perhaps not. But *transformation of consciousness* is a metaphor that highlights several of the more noteworthy pathways. Selecting passages from the world's wisdom traditions and focusing attention on their words in meditation, practitioners imprint these ideals on their mind and imagination. The process of meditation also builds concentrated attention and the mental capacity to translate these ideals into practice, into "character, conduct and consciousness."[2]

Empirical Research on the EPP

The EPP was developed primarily as a spiritual path, but several studies have now documented positive relations of the EPP with human health and well-being. Of special interest are two recent randomized, controlled studies that provide the strongest empirical evidence of EPP benefits. Because they eliminate most forms of bias, randomized studies are regarded in health research as providing the most compelling evidence for an intervention's effectiveness. These randomized studies showed that beginning to practice the EPP produced measurable change in two important populations: health professionals[17, 18] and college students.[19, 20] Changes were observed in stress, well-being, spirituality, and self-confidence (self-efficacy) for specific skills. Findings of several EPP studies (conducted primarily by our colleagues and us), are summarized in Table 6.3.

Health Professionals

The first randomized study of the EPP examined fifty-eight healthcare workers in a large urban hospital in the western United States. Study participants included nurses, physicians, chaplains, and other healthcare professionals. The study was advertised as offering potential stress management benefits, and only professionals with regular patient contact were eligible. Participants were randomly assigned either to a treatment group

Table 6.3

Selected Published Studies of the Eight-Point Program of Passage Meditation

Study No.	Population and Design	Main Findings	Reference[a]
#1	58 Healthcare workers randomized to • EPP ($n = 27$) • Control ($n = 31$) and assessed at pre- and postintervention and 8- and 19-week follow-up	⇨ Stress reductions were large, sustained at 19 weeks, highly statistically significant, and mediated by adherence to EPP practices. ⇨ Mental health improvements were significant. ⇨ Favorable changes also seen after 8 weeks in vitality, job satisfaction, personal accomplishment, and reduced emotional exhaustion.	17
		⌘	
#2	The design and participants from Study #1, plus in-depth interviews of 24 participants after EPP training	⇨ Caregiving self-efficacy gains sustained at 19 weeks, significant, and mediated most strongly by One Pointed Attention. ⇨ Interviews revealed that One Pointed Attention was in turn fostered by Mantram, Meditation, and Slowing Down.	18
		⌘	

(continued)

Table 6.3
(continued)

Study No.	Population and Design	Main Findings	Reference[a]
#3	12 nurses from Study #1 interviewed following EPP training	⇨ Most (92 percent) found that EPP enhanced personal capacities essential to workplace performance. ⇨ Workplace self-management was fostered by Passage Meditation plus four EPP points that were directly usable during the workday: Mantram, Slowing Down, One Pointed Attention, and Putting Others First.	22
		⌘	
#4	44 college students randomized to • EPP (*n* = 14) • MBSR (*n* = 15) • Control (*n* = 15) and assessed at pre- and postintervention and 8-week follow-up	⇨ EPP but not MBSR led to increases in self-efficacy for learning from famous/traditional spiritual models, the availability of pre-1900 spiritual models, and the influence of famous/traditional spiritual models. ⇨ Both EPP and MBSR led to large reductions in imagery of God as primarily controlling, and decrease in negative religious coping.	19
		⌘	

| #5 | The same design and participants as Study #4 | ⇨ Perceived stress reductions and forgiveness increases were significant (no differences found between EPP and MBSR). | 20 |

Note: EPP = Eight-Point Program of Passage Meditation; MBSR = Mindfulness Based Stress Reduction. [a]Number in reference list of article containing study results.

that received 8 weekly 2-hour classes in the EPP, or to a control group that did not receive instruction until after the completion of the study. The classes emphasized using Passage Meditation and EPP mantram repetition as a means to build concentration and gain control over intrusive thoughts, both in meditation and during the day. Study participants described themselves primarily as Protestant Christian (38 percent), Roman Catholic Christian (29 percent), or of no religious affiliation (21 percent). Questionnaire self-report measures of several outcomes of interest were given to all participants prior to the beginning of the course. All participants were reassessed on these variables three more times: immediately after the course, 8-weeks later, and again 19 weeks after the end of the course.

Stress and Mental Health. At the end of the course, tests showed that caregivers who received EPP training had lower levels of perceived stress than caregivers who had been enrolled in the control group (see Table 6.3, Study #1). These differences were statistically significant, indicating that they could not easily have occurred by chance. They relied on a measure of stress that has been correlated with numerous health variables including accelerated cellular aging, depression, health services utilization, and the common cold.[21]

Over the following 8 weeks, stress reductions remained large and statistically significant. Despite the lack of social support from the weekly classes during this follow-up period, stress reductions were actually slightly larger after 8 weeks than at postintervention. And at the 19-week follow-up assessment, nearly 5 months after classes ended, EPP group reductions in perceived stress relative to the control group remained statistically significant.[17] Figure 6.2 shows the changes over time in the stress levels of the treatment and control groups.

These stress reductions are quite large when compared with the effects seen in most intervention studies. Their meaning can be interpreted by comparisons with percentile distributions in the general population. Our average study participant began with stress levels in approximately the

Figure 6.2

Perceived Stress Changes over Time in Health Professionals for EPP versus a Control Group. *Note:* Group differences in change since pretest were significant at all Exams ($p < 0.05$). Horizontal lines represent perceived stress changes of one half pretest SD. Graph based on results in Oman, Hedberg, and Thoresen (2006) (#17 in references)

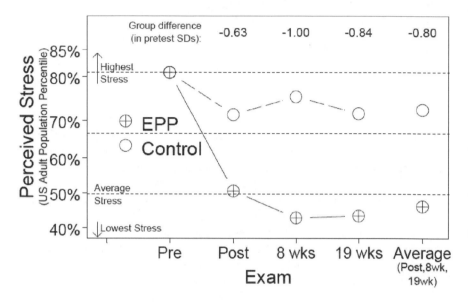

highest 20 percent of the population (in technical terms, elevated by about one standard deviation, or "+1 SD"). After treatment, the average EPP participant's stress was reduced to slightly below the population mean (see Figure 6.2). Some participants began with even higher stress levels—for example, about one-sixth (16 percent) of our participants would have been in the top 4 percent of the general population with the highest stress. After treatment, an expected average of only 3.5 percent, rather than 16 percent, would suffer from these extreme levels of stress. Analyses showed that these stress reductions were mediated (i.e., could be explained) by the degree to which they adhered, on average, to the eight EPP practices.[17]

These perceived stress changes were the most dramatic changes that we observed. But other measures of well-being also changed. Mental health, assessed with a widely used scale, also showed statistically significant improvement. At 8-week follow-up, we found reduced levels of emotional exhaustion as well as increased vitality, job satisfaction, and sense of personal accomplishment (see Table 6.3, Study #1).

Caregiving self-efficacy. We also thought that EPP training might improve these health professionals' abilities to do their jobs, especially in skills involving human relationships. Through reduced stress, higher mindfulness, and increased equanimity, compassion, and other character strengths, EPP participants might become more able to carry out the relational features of their jobs. Assessments therefore included a published 34-item scale to measure participants' self-efficacy (self-confidence) in relational skills. Scale items emphasized skills involving (1) managing relationships with patients and coworkers; (2) managing boundaries between work and the rest of life; and (3) helping patients deal with suffering, mortality, and other ultimate concerns.[6]

Results (see Table 6.3, Study #2) showed that participants trained in the EPP increased in self-efficacy in comparison with controls, and these gains were nearly fully retained at the final 19-week follow-up assessment. These gains were most clearly mediated by reductions in stress and practice of One Pointed Attention. These findings were corroborated by telephone interviews with twenty-four of the participants (five physicians, twelve nurses, and seven others), an average of 3 months after the intervention. The interviews revealed that most participants could recount specific ways in which program points had helped them to be more effective in their work. The interviews also showed that EPP points work synergistically: although self-efficacy gains were most clearly a consequence of more focused attention, One Pointed Attention was itself viewed by participants as the result of other EPP points, especially Mantram, Meditation, and Slowing Down.[18] For example, one participant said:

> The mantram calms me down, slows me down and I feel that I can deal with whatever the situation is that got me upset.[18]

Nurses study. A more intensive analysis of interviews with the twelve nurses corroborated these findings (see Table 6.3, Study #3). In addition, many nurses found the practice of Putting Others First, as presented in the EPP, helpful for improved workplace self-management. Overall reported gains included an increased ability to focus on the task at hand, a renewed sense of enjoyment in their work, and maintaining better emotional balance with less frustration and anger. Several of the nurses referenced the benefits of Slowing Down and One Pointed Attention in their work:

> I found [that] what works is a one-pointed focusing, one-pointed attention. If I can stay with that I slow down ... If I try to keep that in mind I do so much better.

Others expressed an increased ability to experience compassion and empathy.

> One thing I learned since [the program] is to really first try to take a look at how everybody else is looking at it and understand where they're coming

from. That doesn't necessarily change where I'm coming from or what I'm thinking is right, but I can approach it with them just a little bit differently.[22]

College Undergraduates

A second randomized study examined EPP effects on stress and mental and spiritual well-being on college students.[20] Undergraduates at a Catholic university in California were invited to enroll if they were interested in meditation-based practices that could help them manage stress and foster well-being. Participants ($n = 44$) were randomly assigned to one of three groups: one group received EPP training, a second group received training in Mindfulness Based Stress Reduction (MBSR; see Oman and Thoresen, this volume), and a control group did not receive training until after the completion of the study. The EPP and MBSR groups were conducted concurrently, and each met over 8 weeks for 90 minutes every week. Study participants described themselves primarily as Roman Catholic (49 percent) or of no religious affiliation (42 percent). Questionnaire self-report measures were administered immediately before and after the interventions, and 8 weeks later. For several outcomes, changes in the EPP and MBSR groups did not significantly differ from each other, suggesting very similar effects, and were pooled together in analyses of how they differed from controls.

> *Stress, rumination, and forgiveness.* Compared to controls, the intervention groups showed significantly reduced perceived stress and increased ability to forgive others. They also showed marginal reductions in rumination, but did not differ from controls in a measure of hope (see Table 6.3, Study #5).
>
> *Spiritual well-being.* Compared to controls, each intervention group showed reduced tendencies to use negative forms of religious coping (e.g., "I feel God is punishing me for my sins or lack of spirituality"). They were also less likely to view God negatively as highly controlling (e.g., seeing God as "restricting" rather than "freeing"). Each of these changes was quite large and highly significant, roughly equal in magnitude to the stress reductions noted among health professionals. Interestingly, participants remained unchanged in related but distinct measures assessing their views of God as mainly loving, and in using positive forms of religious coping (e.g., "I think about how my life is part of a larger spiritual force"). Perhaps increases in these qualities require greater time to cultivate (see Table 6.3, Study #4).
>
> *Spiritual models.* The EPP and MBSR significantly *differed* from each other in their impact on participants' spiritual models. Compared to

controls, EPP participants showed significant increases in self-efficacy for learning from famous/traditional spiritual models, the availability of pre-1900 spiritual models, and the influence of famous/traditional spiritual models. Changes in MBSR and control participants did not differ (Study #4).[19] These findings were expected because of the higher support offered by the EPP for learning from spiritual models, especially traditional models. They give preliminary confirmation that the EPP indeed helps a person absorb models available in the "data banks" of the wisdom traditions.

Other Studies

HIV/AIDS patients. Measurable effects from EPP-based interventions have also been found in other populations. A randomized intervention sponsored by the U.S. Centers for Disease Control found that an adaptation of the EPP was more effective than psychotherapy, stress management, community service, or a control condition in reducing risky sexual behaviors among gay men.[23] A second study of the same cohort found that participants randomly assigned to the EPP adaptation showed improvements in distress and general well-being, and consistent improvement across all scales of depression, hostility, anxiety, phobic anxiety, and paranoia, while those assigned to traditional psychotherapy, traditional stress management, or a control condition had improvement on only some of the scales.[24]

Teachers in Training. A small randomized intervention ($n = 21$) conducted at Stanford University found that beginning schoolteachers who were trained in an EPP adaptation experienced significantly reduced perceived stress compared to controls.[25]

Summary of Evidence

Together, these studies suggest that the EPP holds considerable promise for fostering health and spiritual benefits. Improvements, sometimes quite dramatic, have been documented using randomized designs. Gains have been found in measures of well-being, personal effectiveness, and spirituality, and corroborated in subjective reports. EPP practices have statistically mediated (explained) larger benefits. One study confirmed that the EPP does foster drawing upon "data banks" of spiritual models. Yet it must be remembered that most findings to date involve individuals who chose to enroll in studies offering potential stress-management benefits. Would similar gains be enjoyed by college students or health professionals who were less interested in stress management? Or by members of other groups who may have difficulty concentrating, such as victims of Post Traumatic Stress Disorder? Findings so far are very encouraging, but science and common sense urge caution in generalizing. To date, evidence is clearest in documenting gains in well-being, effectiveness, and spirituality among self-selected members of groups that are primarily healthy, but experience high levels of challenge and stress.

Implications

The Eight-Point Program of Passage Meditation, we have suggested, offers an unusual combination of special features (see Table 6.1). Perhaps most unusual among nonsectarian programs is the EPP's systematic support for deep assimilation of key elements of spiritual wisdom traditions, especially through meditation passages (see Figure 6.1). A recent review presented at the Society for Behavioral Medicine confirmed that among nonsectarian meditation-based health interventions, the EPP offered the highest level of support for learning from exemplars from spiritual wisdom traditions.[26] Indeed, the EPP is evidently "particularly sophisticated in its organized use of spiritual modeling strategies."[16] Because of its compatibility with all major religious faiths, the EPP might potentially help many individuals in the United States and elsewhere to draw more deeply and effectively on the riches of their own traditions. Would such strengthened spiritual engagement foster health benefits?

Empirical research, reviewed earlier, clearly links the EPP to health-related benefits, sometimes quite dramatic. Potential health applications of the EPP include formal health promotion efforts (e.g., offering organized classes) as well as integration into individual recommendations by physicians, nurses, psychologists, social workers, and clergy. Self-care is also an important application—for example, many individuals have integrated systematic, committed EPP practice into their daily living after becoming acquainted with it through popular books or word of mouth.

How Passages Contribute to Health and Spiritual Growth

Less clear is the precise contribution to health of the EPP's special features concerning spiritual content (e.g., meditation passages). Using inspired passages might foster health even if its only contribution was to provide extra motivation to engage in a salutary practice of daily meditation. But recent research does demonstrate that compared to a secular focus, meditating on a spiritual focus can be more effective for reducing anxiety and improving mood and pain tolerance.[27] Such differences may arise because a spiritual focus fosters a different set of associations, attitudes, and behaviors throughout the day. Similarly, the EPP's special spiritual content may well produce benefits that accumulate over time. Persuasive empirical evidence now documents that spiritual and religious involvement offers health and longevity gains that cannot be explained by other well-established secular risk factors.[28] Through mechanisms described earlier—absorbing through meditation the words, attitudes, wisdom, strivings, character strengths, and coping methods of spiritual models—EPP practitioners may also plausibly be hypothesized to reap long-term health benefits.

Of particular interest are findings that the EPP enhanced self-efficacy for learning from spiritual models (see Table 6.3, Study #4). Self-efficacy is a central construct in Albert Bandura's Social Cognitive Theory (SCT), for many years the most highly cited and widely applied modern psychological theory.[29] Self-efficacy is a technical term for a person's self-confidence for carrying out tasks in a particular skill domain. Self-efficacy is typically among the strongest predictors of objective performance for any type of activity, and is increasingly used to evaluate programs for education, training, and behavioral modification. Documented gains in self-efficacy support the EPP's theorized capacity to foster learning from spiritual models, a finding that represents a pioneering application of Bandura's theory to spirituality.[30]

Bandura's SCT also helps illuminate from a scientific perspective how the EPP may foster spiritual growth through learning from spiritual models. Spiritual and religious traditions have long recognized that "spirituality is caught, not taught." But decades of SCT-guided research have extensively documented four major psychological processes that underlie all types of learning from human models of behavior: *attention* to the model, *retention* of information about the model's behavior and attitudes, *reproduction* of what is learned in behavior, and *motivation* to persist.[29] By extension, these same four processes can be theorized to underlie the effective transmission of spiritual behaviors and attitudes. Not surprisingly, therefore, evidence suggests that religious traditions have sought to foster these four processes throughout history (e.g., fostering *retention* through frequent repetition at worship services of key verses from scripture).[16]

These four modeling processes are also clearly evident in the EPP, which appears to foster them systematically. For example, memorizing and meditating on an inspirational passage gives focused *attention* to the modeling information contained in the passage. Repeatedly meditating on the words builds *retention*. This, in turn, enhances the *reproduction* of the ideals in the passages during the day. Many passages also recount positive experiences that come to those who persist in spiritual practice, thereby supporting *motivation* to practice ("It is in giving that we receive").[16] Other points in the EPP support observational spiritual learning as well. For example, inspirational reading fosters *attention* to the ideals and actions of exalted models and creates *motivation* to emulate their attitudes and actions. Slowing Down and One Pointed Attention help create the mental equanimity that facilitates *retention* and *reproduction* in behavior (in daily living) of an exemplar's values. Last but not least, Spiritual Association fosters learning from individuals within one's family or community who may also at important times function as spiritual models. For this reason, we have argued that the EPP holds interest not merely as a health intervention, but as a model of a more general educational approach. That is, the EPP demonstrates a nonsectarian approach, feasible in appropriate settings in a pluralistic society, for reintegrating spiritual modeling into education.[31]

Conclusions

We have described an empirically studied, comprehensive, nonsectarian, and wisdom-based program that has been used by lay practitioners for several decades in its present form. The EPP systematically reconciles a householder's need for daily coping supports with a deep contemplative engagement with wisdom traditions, traditionally a prerogative of monastics and religious orders. Emerging research shows promising and sometimes dramatic benefits of the EPP for health, spirituality, and personal effectiveness. Because of its nonsectarian character, its comprehensive set of tools, its support for direct engagement with spiritual wisdom traditions, and its crosscutting appeal to diverse populations, the EPP warrants careful consideration among healthcare organizations including campus health services, professionals, and laypersons.

Acknowledgment

The first three images in Figure 6.1 are copyright © 2001–2007 by http://www.arttoday.com.

References

1. Fetzer Institute. (1999). *Multidimensional measurement of religiousness/spirituality for use in health research*. Fetzer Institute, full text: http://www.fetzer.org), Kalamazoo, MI, p. 92).
2. Easwaran, E. (1991/1978). *Meditation: A simple eight-point program for translating spiritual ideals into daily life*. Tomales, CA: Nilgiri Press, full text also online: http://www.easwaran.org, p. 29.
3. Smith, H. (1991). *The world's religions: Our great wisdom traditions*. San Francisco CA: Harper San Francisco, p. 5.

4. Two of the authors (Tim Flinders & Carol Lee Flinders) have presented the EPP at workshops over several decades to thousands of individuals, and are personally acquainted with regular EPP practitioners who are observant in each of these faiths.
5. Easwaran, E. (2003/1982). *God makes the rivers to flow: Sacred literature of the world*. Tomales, CA: Nilgiri Press, large parts also online, http://www.easwaran. org.
6. Oman, D., Hedberg, J., Downs, D., & Parsons, D. (2003). A transcultural spiritually based program to enhance caregiving self-efficacy: A pilot study. *Complementary Health Practice Review, 8*, 201–224.
7. McEwen, B. S. (1998). Protective and damaging effects of stress mediators. *New England Journal of Medicine, 338*, 171–179.
8. Hedberg, J., Bowden, J., & Oman, D. (2002). A comprehensive non-sectarian program for integrating spirituality into health practice. (*Materials prepared for workshop at Conference on Spirituality, Culture and End-of-Life in Medical Education, sponsored by the Association of American Medical Colleges, Kansas City, MO, September 14, available online: http://apha.confex.com/apha/viewHandout.epl?uploadid=487*).
9. Walsh, R. & Shapiro, S. L. (2006). The meeting of meditative disciplines and western psychology: A mutually enriching dialogue. *American Psychologist, 61*, 227–239.
10. Seeman, T. E., Dubin, L. F., & Seeman, M. (2003). Religiosity/spirituality and health: A critical review of the evidence for biological pathways. *American Psychologist, 58*, 53–63.
11. Goleman, D. (1988). *The meditative mind: The varieties of meditative experience*. New York: Tarcher, p. 168)
12. Baumeister, R. F. & Exline, J. J. (1999). Virtue, personality, and social relations: Self-control as the moral muscle. *Journal of Personality, 67*, 1165–1194, pp. 1172, 1177.
13. Peterson, C. & Seligman, M. E. P. (2004). *Character strengths and virtues: A handbook and classification*. Washington, DC and New York: American Psychological Association and Oxford University Press.
14. Pargament, K. I. (1997). *The psychology of religion and coping: Theory, research, practice*. New York: Guilford.
15. Emmons, R. A. (1999). *The psychology of ultimate concerns: Motivation and spirituality in personality*. New York: Guilford.
16. Oman, D. & Thoresen, C. E. (2003). Spiritual modeling: A key to spiritual and religious growth? *The International Journal for the Psychology of Religion, 13*, 149–165, p. 159.
17. Oman, D., Hedberg, J., & Thoresen, C. E. (2006). Passage meditation reduces perceived stress in health professionals: A randomized, controlled trial. *Journal of Consulting and Clinical Psychology, 74*, 714–719.
18. Oman, D., Richards, T. A., Hedberg, J., & Thoresen, C. E. (in press). Passage meditation improves caregiving self-efficacy among health

professionals: A randomized trial and qualitative assessment. *Journal of Health Psychology*.

19. Oman, D., Shapiro, S., Thoresen, C. E., Flinders, T., Driskill, J. D., & Plante, T. G. (2007). Learning from spiritual models and meditation: A randomized evaluation of a college course. *Pastoral Psychology*, *55*, 473–493.

20. Oman, D., Shapiro, S., Thoresen, C. E., Plante, T. G., & Flinders, T. (in press). Meditation lowers stress and supports forgiveness among college students: A randomized controlled trial. *Journal of American College Health*.

21. Epel, E. S., Blackburn, E. H., Lin, J., Dhabhar, F. S., Adler, N. E., Morrow, J. D., et al. (2004). Accelerated telomere shortening in response to life stress. *Proceedings of the National Academy of Sciences of the United States of America*, *101*, 17312–17315.

22. Richards, T. A., Oman, D., Hedberg, J., Thoresen, C. E., & Bowden, J. (2006). A qualitative examination of a spiritually based intervention and self-management in the workplace. *Nursing Science Quarterly*, *19*, 231–239, p. 238.

23. Flinders, R., Cohn, D., Ruppenthal, B., Martindale, C. J., Freeman, E. M., Cole, V. J., et al. (1991). Reduction of risky sexual behavior in gay and bisexual men (abstract presented at the seventh international AIDS conference, June 17, 1991, Florence, Italy). In T. Flinders, M. Gershwin, & R. Flinders (Eds.), *The RISE response: Illness, wellness, and spirituality* (pp. 213–214, 218). New York: Crossroad (1994).

24. Earl, W., Flinders, R., Flahive, M., Bartholow, B., Kobayashi, J., & Cohn, D. (1990). Psychosocial adjustment to HIV infection: Efficacy of different group interventions in gay and bisexual men (abstract presented at the sixth international AIDS conference, June 21, 1990, San Francisco). In T. Flinders, M. Gershwin, & R. Flinders, (Eds.), *The RISE response: Illness, wellness, and spirituality* (pp. 211–212, 218). New York: Crossroad (1994).

25. Winzelberg, A. J. & Luskin, F. M. (1999). The effect of a meditation program on the level of stress in secondary school student teachers. *Stress Medicine*, *15*, 69–77.

26. Oman, D. & Beddoe, A. E. (2005). Health interventions combining meditation with learning from spiritual exemplars: Conceptualization and review. *Annals of Behavioral Medicine*, *29*, S126.

27. Wachholtz, A. B. & Pargament, K. I. (2005). Is spirituality a critical ingredient of meditation? Comparing the effects of spiritual meditation, secular meditation, and relaxation on spiritual, psychological, cardiac, and pain outcomes. *Journal of Behavioral Medicine*, *28*, 369–384.

28. Powell, L. H., Shahabi, L., & Thoresen, C. E. (2003). Religion and spirituality: Linkages to physical health. *American Psychologist*, *58*, 36–52.

29. Bandura, A. (1986). *Social foundations of thought and action*. Englewood Cliffs, NJ: Prentice Hall.

30. Oman, D. & Thoresen, C. E. (2006). Applying social cognitive theory to spirituality: Achievements, challenges and prospects. *Paper presented at symposium on*

Spiritual Transformation: New Frontiers in Scientific Research, Berkeley, CA, April 7, 2006.

31. Oman, D., Flinders, T., & Thoresen, C. E. (in press). Integrating spiritual modeling into education: A college course for stress management and spiritual growth. *The International Journal for the Psychology of Religion*.

CHAPTER 7

Mantram or Holy Name Repetition: Health Benefits from a Portable Spiritual Practice

JILL E. BORMANN AND DOUG OMAN

Much interest in the relation of spirituality to health has emerged in the past decade, in both popular culture and scientific research[1] (see also Chapter 1, this volume). This renewed interest has occurred at a time when people feel pressured and harried from the unrelenting demands of modern life. As a result, there is an ever-increasing interest to identify stress-relieving and health-promoting therapies that are low-cost and easily conveyed to others.[2]

This chapter focuses on a spiritual practice that meets many of these demands. Variants of this practice have been called *holy name repetition*[3] (in the West) and *mantram repetition* (in the East), and are found in nearly every major religious and spiritual tradition. To avoid confusion of various names, we primarily refer to "mantram repetition," following vocabulary used by Eknath Easwaran (1910–1999),[4, 5] whose writings have been useful as instructional materials in our studies. We emphasize that no one needs to change his or her religion in order to benefit from this practice. Furthermore, mantram repetition is personal, private, invisible, inexpensive, nonpharmacological, and nontoxic. There is good reason to believe it fosters spiritual benefits, regardless of one's religious faith or lack thereof. Both spiritual and health benefits are documented in empirical research that we will describe.

This chapter contains six sections. In the next section we describe the nature of mantrams and how they work. The third section describes scientific principles (mechanisms) through which mantram repetition may foster benefit. The fourth section reviews empirical intervention studies of the effects of teaching mantram repetition to a variety of populations. The final section describes implications for practice.

Mantrams: What Are They and How Do They Work?

A mantram is a short, fixed word or phrase that can be defined as a "powerful spiritual formula for the highest power we can conceive of—whether we call it God, or the ultimate reality, or the Self within"[4] (p. 8). Mantrams are ancient and found in both the West and the East. In the West, John Cassian (360–433 CE) recommended frequent repetition of a biblical verse (Psalm 70:l) that he viewed as "necessary and useful to each one of us and in all circumstances"[6] (p. 133). In the East, many Buddhists emphasize Nembutsu, repeating a Buddhist mantram;[7] in Islam, repeated prayers of "Allah" have long been used "in any place and at any time ... [unrestricted] to the exact hours of ritual prayer"[8] (p. 167); in Hinduism, Mahatma Gandhi reported that the name of God was "in my heart, if not actually on my lips, all the twenty four hours"[9] (p. 7), and that it "becomes one's staff of life and carries one through every ordeal"[9] (pp. 11–12). Table 7.1 supplies examples of mantrams from major traditions.

Mantram repetition, as we define it, involves frequent repetition (as often as possible) throughout the day and night. To experience maximal benefit, mantrams should be repeated silently every day: while walking, waiting in line, when sitting in a dentist's chair, or falling asleep. Constant repetition may help maintain awareness and connection with spiritual ideals through-out the day. Such repetition is likely to provide spiritual benefit in the form of comfort and inspiration, but may also offer health benefits, as we argue in the next section. It is recommended that a person should select a mantram carefully.[4, 5] Once chosen, it is best not changed, to avoid losing the benefit of earlier repetitions.

To introduce the mantram to diverse audiences, emphasis is placed on dif-ferentiating spirituality from religious doctrine. This is done by describing three philosophical assumptions: (1) All humans inherently possess access to a reservoir of spiritual resources experienced as peace, loving kindness, compassion, goodness, altruism, joy, health, and wholeness. (2) These re-sources often go untapped because our minds are agitated and unaware of them. (3) Mantram repetition is a tool to focus, calm, and quiet the mind, enabling us to tap these spiritual resources. For participants who are less spiritually inclined or interested, we use a variety of terms for mantram such as rapid focus tool, cue word, self-centering strategy, or a self-soothing word. Mantram repetition in this context is described as a tool for training attention.

Mantram repetition as a beneficial practice *by itself* is the focus of this chapter. Elsewhere, mantram repetition has been presented as one compo-nent of a comprehensive and integrated Eight-Point Program (EPP; for details see Flinders, Oman and Flinders, this volume). To clarify how a mantram is integrated into daily living, we have found it useful to teach mantram

Table 7.1

Selected Mantrams from Various Traditional Sources

Mantram	Explanation and/or Comment
Buddhist	
Om mani padmé hum	An invocation of the jewel (the Self) in the lotus of the heart
Namu Amidabutsu	An invocation of the Buddha of Infinite Light
Christian	
Jesus	Son of God
Hail Mary or *Ave Maria*	Divine Mother of Jesus or Virgin Mary
My God and my All	(Used by St. Francis of Assisi in his prayers)
Lord Jesus Christ, Son of God, have mercy on me	The Jesus Prayer
Kyrie Eleison	Lord have mercy
Om Yesu Christu	Jesus Christ
Hindu	
Rama	Eternal joy within (Mahatma Gandhi's mantram)
Om Sri Ram, jai Ram, jai jai Ram	May joy prevail
Om namah Shivāya	An invocation of beauty and fearlessness
Om Bhavani	An invocation of the Divine Mother
Islamic	
Alláh	One true God
Bismillāh ir-rahmān ir-rahīm	In the name of God, the merciful, the compassionate
Jewish	
Barukh attah Adonai	Blessed art thou, O Lord
Ribono shel olam	Lord of the universe

Note: See other instructional resources at http://www.easwaran.org.

along with two other EPP practices: slowing down and one-pointed attention. All three points work together synergistically. That is, repeating a mantram is helped by one-pointed attention and slows thinking. This allows "pause time" to make wiser choices, set priorities, and decrease stress from hurried behavior. Together, these practices are likely to elicit mindfulness, and the accompanying ability to experience one's thinking as separate from one's self.[10] When dealing with unwanted ruminative thoughts, for example, mantram repetition is readily available as an alternate focus for attention that can provide immediate relief.

Importantly, as we present it, mantram repetition is *distinct* from sitting meditation, and has distinct benefits. Many well-known forms of sitting meditation involve focusing attention on a single chosen or assigned word or phrase (for example, Transcendental Meditation and Benson's Meditation).[11] In contrast, mantram repetition uses a spiritual phrase *throughout the day*. Table 7.2 describes differences between mantram repetition and other spiritual practices with which it is sometimes confused.

How Mantram Repetition Provides Health Benefit

How might mantram repetition foster physical health? One central function of the mantram is to disrupt negative thoughts and behaviors by rechanneling the focus of attention and behavior. For example, study participants have reported that mantram repetition was useful for controlling anxiety and shifting attention away from unwanted thoughts and maladaptive, stressful emotions.[12] Shifting attention away from troublesome stimuli may be viewed as a "first line of defense" in efforts of self regulation, and can greatly assist efforts to refrain from smoking, substance abuse, or other unhealthy behaviors. In this regard, mantram repetition is similar to "thought stopping," a well-known technique from behavioral therapy.[3] Furthermore, by interrupting rumination or other maladaptive ("fight or flight") responses to stress, a mantram may help elicit the opposite of a physiological stress response, the *relaxation response*.[11]

More generally, mantram repetition may strengthen a person's ability to think and enact a wide variety of *positive* and *healthy* thoughts and behaviors. Just as an advertiser's jingle facilitates purchasing an advertised product, constant repetition of a mantram fosters remembrance of spiritual ideals. It may also foster remembrance of other ideals and states of mind that over time have become associated with a mantram. In psychological theory, this is called the "associative network" theory of memory and emotions.[3] Psychologists have long known that a person's ability to recognize a word (e.g., "teacher") is easier if a related word (e.g., "student") has been presented earlier. Similarly, words that evoke positive or

Table 7.2

Characteristics of Mantram Repetition Compared to Other Spiritual Practices

Other Spiritual Practice	Comparison to Mantram Repetition
Sitting Meditation	*Attention, Posture, and Location* Like Mantram Repetition, all practices of "sitting meditation" involve an effort to focus and train attention. But unlike Mantram, sitting meditation requires sitting for a longer period of time, in a reasonably quiet place, with eyes closed, and in a specific posture.
Centering Prayer, Transcendental Meditation, and Benson's Meditation	*When the Spiritual Word is Repeated* Like Mantram Repetition, these methods involve focus on a single meaningful prechosen word or phrase (which in some cases is spiritually meaningful). Unlike Mantram's focus on the chosen words at opportune times throughout the day, these methods involve using the chosen words during sitting meditation.
Passage Meditation	*Setting and Content of the Focus* Like Mantram Repetition, Passage Meditation involves focus on memorized spiritual language and is included in Easwaran's Eight-Point Program (see also Flinders, Oman, and Flinders, this volume). Unlike Mantram, Passage Meditation is a sitting meditation with focus on a longer memorized text. Mantram is portable and uses a much *shorter* word or phrase.
Informal Mindfulness Practices	*Focus of Attention in a "Portable" Practice* Like Mantram Repetition, "informal" practices of Mindfulness Based Stress Reduction are "portable" and may be used throughout the day. In Mantram, attention is repeatedly directed to spiritual words. But in informal mindfulness practices, attention is commonly redirected to the breath.

Note: As capitalized in this table, Mantram Repetition indicates repetition of a mantram, a holy name, or a spiritual word or phrase as described in instructional materials used in our research studies (see references 4 and 5).

negative feelings (e.g., "bunny" versus "cockroach") are easier to recognize after seeing other words with a similar positive or negative valence. Through associations, the mantram appears to engender what psychologists call a "spreading activation," making related memories and emotions more mentally available to consciousness.[3] Importantly, an associative network need not be conscious.

Often, the most important association that a mantram elicits may be a feeling of well-being or an attitude of self-confidence. Recall that mantram practitioners are encouraged to use a mantram repetition during nonstressful times, such as before sleep, or while waiting in line. In this way, as well as through any spiritual meaning that it possesses for the practitioner, the mantram can acquire a set of positive associations that gradually evolves and deepens over time. Behavioral psychologists long ago noted that words can acquire the power to elicit specific behaviors, a process called classical conditioning (evoked calmness could be viewed as the "conditioned response"). Through eliciting mental states, the mantram also elicits their physiological correlates, which may include a relaxation response. As Benson notes, remembrance may evoke "the calm and confidence associated with health and happiness, but not just in an emotional or psychologically soothing way. This memory is also physical"[11] (p. 20). One study has demonstrated cardiovascular improvements from mantram repetition.[13] Stress reductions may also foster physical health through "mind/body" processes related to improved functioning of the immune system, and reduced cellular aging.[14]

Compared to secular words, spiritually derived words have greater potential to activate spiritual attitudes. That is, a mantram derived from tradition may possess few associations at the outset (e.g., "Om mani padme hum" for an agnostic Westerner). But over months or years, a mantram's network of associations will slowly but inevitably evolve in ways that are shaped by both culture and individual experience. In this manner, over long periods, spiritually derived words appear to permit (but not require) substantially greater long-run access to the ideals of major spiritual and religious traditions. Importantly, all major traditions endorse similar character strengths and virtues, such as compassion and forgiveness.[15, 16] Spiritually derived mantrams may activate spiritual attitudes and behaviors not only directly, but also by bringing to mind traditional *spiritual models* who exemplify these qualities[17] (see also Oman and Thoresen, this volume).

Health consequences may flow from the spiritual attitudes elicited by mantram repetition. Spiritual and religious involvement, as noted earlier, has been associated with a broad array of positive health factors and outcomes[1] (see also Chapter 1, this volume). A portion of these benefits appears to be less attributable to spiritual attitudes than to membership in a faith or spiritual community. But substantial benefits also appear to emerge more directly from spiritual attitudes themselves. For example, for many people, spiritual thoughts and ideals may elicit feelings of comfort related to experiences of a loving God or Higher Power. Such comfort may alleviate distress, fostering physical health. Similarly, over time, a mantram may foster better health behaviors by reinforcing attitudes of stewardship toward the body, as encouraged by wisdom traditions.[16] Health consequences may also flow from spiritually encouraged character strengths and virtues such as compassion, forgiveness, optimism, and conscientiousness[15] (see also Wachholtz and Pearce, this volume).

Other potentially important functions of a mantram, most discussed in more detail elsewhere,[3] may include:

- Facilitating spiritual and religious methods of coping with stress.[18]
- Fostering mindfulness, a construct of increasing interest in health research. Mindfulness helps foster clear perceptions of one's thinking as separate from one's self, leading to reduced rumination and other maladaptive self-focused thought.[10]
- Supporting personal strivings for spiritual goals that facilitate personality integration and help reduce internal conflicts and distress.[3]
- Encouraging greater concern for other persons, leading to stronger interpersonal connections and greater social support, a well-established health factor.
- Fostering more supportive relations with a perceived divine being or higher power. Sociologists have presented evidence that such "divine relations" may foster health through processes analogous to social support.[19]

Over time, of course, as changes in thought and behavior are assimilated, it is plausible (if not inevitable) that mantram repetition may foster changes in the brain's neurological patterning. Other spiritual practices, such as meditation, have been demonstrated to foster such changes.[20]

Empirical Research

A program of empirical research on mantram repetition has been led since 2001 by Bormann (the first author of this Chapter). She and her colleagues have examined the acceptability and utilization of a mantram-based intervention in various groups. We have also examined the mantram's effects on health and spiritual outcomes, and how these effects arise ("mechanisms").

Table 7.3
Mantram Repetition Standardized Intervention: Main Topics of Weekly Meetings

Week	Main Topics
1	Introduction to Mantram Repetition and Relaxation Response
2	Choosing, Using, and Tracking Mantram Practice
3	The Stress Response and Mantram Repetition
4	Slowing Down versus Automatic Pilot
5	One-Pointed Attention versus Multitasking
6	Slowing Down and One-Pointed Attention for Making Healthy Choices
7	Making Mantram Repetition a Part of Your Life
8	Putting It All Together

A Standardized Program

The focus of the research program has been a structured health education intervention, initially developed for our first study. Over time, the intervention evolved from a 5-week (90 minutes/week) course to a standardized, 8-week course (see Table 7.3) based on a manual, instructor guidelines, textbook, and list of recommended mantrams (similar to Table 7.1). These materials are available on request for research purposes (readers can contact Bormann).

From the beginning, every intervention participant has been given a list of mantrams and a course text by Easwaran, who offers what we regard as the best available in-depth, nonsectarian description of mantram repetition.[3] Our earlier studies used his *Mantram Handbook*,[4] which includes practical examples and highlights the origins and spiritual characteristics of a mantram. Later studies have used *Strength in the Storm: Creating Calm in Difficult Times*,[5] which focuses primarily on applications and examples.

Most research participants have chosen a mantram that appeared on the recommended list. But in most groups, a small number have asked to make up their own mantrams. In response to such requests, instructors explain that the recommended mantrams have been used by people for centuries and have "weathered the test of time." They come with "extra value" because they remind us of our highest ideals associated with a higher power or a holy name. By repeating them, we save ourselves from using phrases that are less effective. In addition, emerging research provides evidence that spiritual words *do* offer greater benefit than secular words.[21, 22] Instructors therefore encourage participants to experiment for themselves. Class time has focused less on theories, and more on how to do mantram repetition in practice.

Vivid imagery and metaphors have been useful for motivating practice and conveying how mantrams can be used. For example, with U.S. older adults who have traditional religious backgrounds, we refer to mantram as a "prayer word" that serves as a "collect call to God"; for HIV-infected adults, often rejected by religious groups, we refer to a "rapid focus tool" or "self-soothing word"; for professionals, healthcare providers or other workers, we discuss a stress-reduction coping strategy that offers a 5-second "jacuzzi for the mind" or a "speed bump" during the day; for those afflicted with insomnia or chronic pain, we speak of a metaphorical "sleeping or pain pill"; and for veterans afflicted with posttraumatic stress disorder, we speak of "training the mind" to redirect attention away from disturbing flashbacks and as a "pause button" for managing anger, hypervigilance, or obsessive thoughts.

When presenting to groups, instructors avoid unnecessary and potentially divisive discussions of sectarian perspectives, including general differences between "Western" and "Eastern" religious perspectives. Such discussions easily disrupt a class by needlessly shifting attention to contentious issues. Theological understandings merit respect, and inevitably differ across traditions. But except for the precise spiritual words, the *practice* of mantram repetition is often very similar.

Effects on Health, Well-Being, and Spirituality

Using this mantram-based intervention, Bormann and colleagues have conducted studies among veterans, healthcare employees, and HIV-infected adults. Table 7.4 summarizes four of these published studies, which we now describe.

1. *Veterans.* The initial research examined U.S. military veterans, primarily male, who received healthcare through a Veterans Affairs facility in southern California. Sixty-two veterans interested in stress management were enrolled for the study in 2001 and 2002. Before and after attending mantram classes, they completed scientifically validated psychological questionnaires to assess perceived stress, anxiety, anger, quality of life, and symptoms of posttraumatic stress disorder (PTSD). Spiritual well-being was also assessed using a widely used, validated questionnaire. At the end of the intervention, these veterans demonstrated significant improvements in all outcomes (see Study #1, Table 7.4).[23]

These group changes were promising, but to what extent did improvement result from actual mantram practice, and to what extent might improvement have resulted from other benefits of group participation, such as social support? Anticipating this issue, we measured mantram practice by giving participants wrist-worn counters (golf scorers) and tracking sheets to record the number of mantram sessions done each day.[24] Since it was impractical to count each single repetition of a mantram, participants were instructed to count the number of mantram series or *sessions*, regardless of the number of repetitions per session. During the intervention, this measure of mantram "dose" was collected on a subset of fifty-two participants who

Table 7.4

Selected Published Studies of Mantram Repetition Intervention

Study No.	Population and Design	Main Findings	Reference
#1	Sixty-two veterans assessed at pre- and postintervention (without comparison group)	⇨ Significant improvements in stress, anxiety, anger, spiritual well-being, quality of life, and PTSD ⇨ Mantram practice fully mediated changes in anxiety and spiritual well-being and partially mediated improvements in all other outcomes ⌘	23
#2	Forty-two healthcare employees assessed at pre- and postintervention (without comparison group)	⇨ Significant improvements in stress, anxiety, anger, spiritual well-being, and quality of life ⇨ Mantram practice mediated favorable changes in anxiety and spiritual well-being ⌘	25
#3	Thirty veterans and 36 healthcare employees from studies #1 to #2 were interviewed about mantram use using critical incident research method	⇨ Most participants (83%) reported occasions when mantram was useful for managing stress, other emotions, sleep/insomnia, and unwanted thoughts. ⌘	12

(Continued)

Table 7.4
(Continued)

Study No.	Population and Design	Main Findings	Reference[a]
#4	Ninety-three HIV-infected adults randomized to: Mantram ($n = 46$) Controls ($n = 47$) who received similar levels of attention and followed for 22 weeks	⇨ Mantram group (compared to controls) had favorable changes in anger, faith/assurance, and spiritual connectedness ⇨ Mantram practice was associated with increased quality of life, faith/assurance, spiritual meaning/peace, and decreased non-HIV intrusive thoughts	26

Note: PTSD=Posttraumatic Stress Disorder.
[a]Number in reference list of article containing study results.

practiced an average of nine daily mantram sessions apiece. Some averaged as few as one or as many as forty-five sessions per day. This measure was used to statistically control for effects of mantram practice. The results suggested that mantram practice most likely explained (mediated) the observed changes in outcomes.[23]

2. *Healthcare employees.* Would such benefits only be found among veterans? To probe the generalizability of our findings, a similar study among healthcare employees was conducted. Forty-two employees with an interest in stress management volunteered at the same VA hospital. Analyses once again demonstrated significant pre- to postintervention reductions in several outcomes. Significant reductions were found in participants' perceived stress, as well as tendencies to feel anxiety and anger. Significant increases were found in spiritual well-being. Changes in anxiety and spiritual well-being appeared to be mediated by higher mantram use, as measured by wrist counters.[25]

These two quantitative studies of veterans and employees supply promising evidence that the intervention can produce beneficial changes, and that many changes are substantially mediated by greater adherence to mantram practice. But these studies did not tell us anything about the subjective experience of our study participants. Did *participants* experience mantram repetition as useful?

3. *Qualitative interviews.* A third study involved qualitative interviews with sixty-six randomly selected participants from these two earlier

studies: thirty veterans (3 percent female) and thirty-six employees (86 percent female).[12] Participants were contacted by phone and asked to describe examples (if any) of how they had applied the mantram to manage life situations. Interviews were tape-recorded and transcribed. Reported occasions or "incidents" were sorted into categories using an analysis technique called "critical incident methodology." Of the sixty-six participants contacted, fifty-five (83 percent) reported a total of 139 helpful incidents using mantram. Analyses revealed that participants had used mantram repetition for managing stress (thirty-five incidents), sleep/insomnia (nineteen incidents), and unwanted thoughts (ten incidents). They also commonly reported managing emotions other than stress (seventy-five incidents), including impatience, anger, frustration, and feeling upset, disgruntled, or out of control.

Here are examples of what veterans reported about their experiences of mantram repetition:

> Repeating the mantram seemed to stop post-traumatic stress disorder-type dreams that had recurred for 10 to 11 years.[12] (p. 508)

> The mantram has really calmed down my outbursts at persons who frustrated me![12] (p. 507)

> I use it [mantram] occasionally. It's helped me deal with things better that I have no control over, if you know what I mean.[12] (p. 507)

A healthcare employee described how mantram was useful for managing work stress:

> Well, lots of times when I am working, you know, I'm working and there's something happening around the area and I get stressed about it and I want to do something about it. So I just do some of my mantrams, just to take my mind out of it. It works.[12] (p. 507)

As a concerned parent, another healthcare employee found the mantram useful for managing family stressors:

> My son wanted to watch wrestling and had not, of course, followed through with some child requirements and was being a bit difficult, [{so}] I used some mantrams.[12] (p. 507)

These initial studies of veterans and healthcare employees gave promising preliminary evidence that mantram repetition could reduce stress and foster spiritual well-being. Both statistical analyses and subjective reports suggested that mantram practice itself was useful for two dissimilar populations. But from a scientific point of view, these results were inconclusive. One could not rule out, for example, the possibility that changes were due to the therapeutic effects of group participation, or to tendencies of distressed people (who self-elected to take a stress management intervention) to naturally recover over time.

4. *HIV patients* (randomized trial). The next study provided a more rigorous test of benefits. With funding from the National Center of Complementary and Alternative Medicine (NCCAM), we conducted a randomized controlled trial of a mantram intervention on health outcomes in HIV-infected adults.[26] Ninety-three participants interested in stress management were recruited using flyers distributed in the community. Participants were randomly assigned to either the mantram-based intervention ($n = 46$) or a control group ($n = 47$) that experienced equal contact time (controls viewed HIV educational videos, followed by group discussion). Questionnaires were administered to both groups before, during, and after the intervention and at 3 months follow-up. Compared to controls, the mantram group improved significantly on anger, faith/assurance, and spiritual connectedness. Group differences were not significant, however, in perceived stress, anxiety, and depression.

As in earlier studies, mantram dose was measured using wrist counters and logs. More frequent mantram practice was significantly associated with reduced non-HIV intrusive thoughts, increased quality of life enjoyment and satisfaction, faith/assurance, and sense of spiritual meaning/peace. Although these relationships could not be explained by demographics, baseline spiritual well-being, involvement in a religious group, or frequency of other religious practices, mantram practice might contribute to these improvements but more research is needed.

Other Studies

More understanding has come from several other studies:

Subjective effects on HIV and PTSD patients. We conducted qualitative interviews with the HIV patients in Study #4, as well as with a group of PTSD patients trained in mantram ($n = 14$). Interviews reveal the wide range of applications that these seriously ill patient populations found for the mantram, perhaps most importantly to manage common symptoms. For example, an HIV patient used the mantram for pain:

> I used it sometimes when I was in pain. And I would just say the mantram and focus on the pain . . . it somehow made it easier for me to process it . . . [in about] half the times, it would help the pain go away a little more quickly.

A veteran with PTSD described mantram benefits for managing irritation, a characteristic symptom of PTSD:

Somebody will say something to me when I am pissed off and I'll read it
wrong. They're not trying to piss me off... by doing the mantram, that cuts
down on the irritation and allows me to look at things just a little bit more
realistically.

Others have described how the mantram was useful for issues that include
managing grief of bereavement (common in communities of HIV patients),
and fostering increased concentration (a major need for PTSD patients).

Family caregivers. We are currently piloting studies of teaching mantram
repetition to family caregivers of veterans afflicted with dementia or other
debilitating diseases. Ten caregivers with an average of 3 years caregiving
experience have reported significant decreases in perceived stress and trends
toward increased mindfulness. They rated the intervention as beneficial (average of 3.87 on a 1 to 4 point scale).

Pregnant mothers and their partners. A pilot study is also underway to
explore how mantram repetition can assist pregnant mothers and their partners in managing anxiety and fear during and after childbirth. Initial reports
show that the mantram has provided calmness, peace, and a buffer against
the stress of a Caesarian section.

Mantram cardiovascular effects. Bernardi and colleagues found that repetition of a Buddhist mantram ("Om mani padmé hum") or a Roman
Catholic mantram ("Ave Maria") reduced arousal, slowed respirations, and
enhanced cardiovascular rhythms and in healthy adults. They recommend
that mantram repetition be viewed as a health practice.[13]

Maha-mantram repetition. Wolf and colleagues have examined the ancient Hindu "maha mantra" ("Hare Krishna...Hare Rama..."). They
studied community-dwelling U.S. adults who responded to newspaper ad-
vertisements ($n = 61$). Compared to a control group that repeated a mean-
ingless group of syllables as if it were a mantram, maha mantra repetition
was associated after 4 weeks with significantly less stress and depression.[21]

Mantram within a comprehensive program. As noted earlier, mantram
repetition is one practice within the EPP, an eight-point program of spiritual
practices. This comprehensive program has shown a number of benefits
among health professionals and college students (see Flinders, Oman, and
Flinders, this volume). The specific functions of mantram repetition, passage
meditation, and other EPP points are difficult to disentangle in quantitative
analyses. But qualitative findings have confirmed that nurses trained in the
EPP mention the mantram as one point most commonly used during the
day.[27] For example, one nurse stated:

I use the mantram at work too because, understandably in case management
you get into a lot of situations where families are frustrated and often times
you are the closest thing and they just sometimes take things out on you.
There's nothing you can do about the thing, but if you say your mantram and

just deal with them in a calm way, it's amazing that when you're calm, they usually calm down.[27]

Summary and Future Directions

We have reviewed several empirical studies of mantram repetition. These studies suggest that mantram repetition holds considerable promise for fostering spiritual and health benefits. Study participants from diverse populations have offered subjective reports of mantram repetition as useful for managing a variety of stressors. Improvements in health and spiritual measures have been documented, sometimes using randomized designs. Consistent with hypothesized mechanisms, more frequent mantram use has often been accompanied by larger benefits. From a cautious scientific point of view, these findings are far from conclusive, but quite encouraging.

Several questions require more research. Firm, scientifically rigorous recommendations will require additional replications using randomized designs. Also needed is careful exploration of which findings will generalize most broadly to diverse patient groups or other populations. Documentation should also be provided regarding physiological outcomes and underlying psychological mechanisms. Fuller research agendas have been suggested elsewhere.[3, 26]

Self-confidence, or *self-efficacy* for mantram repetition, is a future research topic that may merit special attention. How do people develop self-confidence that they can integrate mantram repetition into diverse spheres of daily activity? How does such self-confidence (self-efficacy) shape outcomes from mantram repetition? Can self-efficacy theory guide efforts to tailor mantram interventions to diverse populations? Self-efficacy theory is perhaps the most highly cited psychological theory of the past three decades. It has been highly practical and productive in many branches of psychology and health science, but is only now being systematically applied to spirituality.[17, 28] A fruitful synergy of self-efficacy theory with mantram repetition seems quite plausible.

Implications and Resources for Practice

Compared to most other health educational programs or spiritual practices, mantram repetition is remarkably simple and free from difficult, expensive, or time-consuming prerequisites. These features suggest a wide range of clinical, public health, and pastoral applications.[3] The available evidence, while not conclusive, supports potential health benefits in diverse populations. The simplicity of the practice makes it accessible to everyone, including those severely ill, or highly stressed by economic or personal circumstances. Potential applications include formal health promotion efforts (e.g., offering organized classes) as well as integration into individual practice by physicians, nurses, psychologists, social workers, and clergy.

Self-care is also an important application. Many persons have integrated mantram repetition into their daily life after becoming acquainted with it through word of mouth or popular books.[4, 5] In some faith traditions, parents have taught mantram repetition to young children.[3] In such cultures, pregnant mothers may sing a mantram to *prenatally* instill a spiritual inclination into the unborn child (the viability of prenatal conditioning is supported by empirical research in both animals and humans).[29] More generally, Oman and Driskill note that because mantram repetition

> *can potentially benefit both the ill (by making them well) and the well (by making them stronger and more efficacious), its benefits to a community are likely to be greatest when it is shared not only with the most needy, but with entire...populations.*[3] (p. 14)

Efforts to integrate mantram repetition into health education and clinical practice may be most effective when several issues are considered:

- To avoid confusion, mantram repetition should be clearly and explicitly distinguished from related practices (see Table 7.2).
- Choosing a mantram from a tradition can be facilitated by supplying a list of examples (e.g., a photocopy of Table 7.1). Some people are more comfortable with words or phrases that avoid theistic imagery, such as "Om mani padme hum," a Buddhist mantram. Although traditional mantrams are encouraged, the ultimate choice is an individual's own responsibility.
- People differ in their motives for practicing mantram repetition. Presentations should therefore be tailored to individual backgrounds and concerns. For example, traditional religious perspectives strongly motivate some people but are irrelevant to others. Many people, like the groups we have studied, are motivated by specific work- or health-related stressors.
- Mantrams contain extra psychological power (there is good reason to believe) if they have been hallowed by long use in a spiritual or religious tradition.
- Adopting mantram repetition, like any other habit or skill, may be fostered by social modeling (Oman and Thoresen, this volume). Presentations of mantram repetition are more persuasive if backed by authentic accounts of how one has benefited from using the practice personally, or from diverse third parties (e.g., from Gandhi, or the research participants quoted here).

- Mantram repetition can serve as a *gateway* to using additional practices. After practicing mantram repetition for a few months or years and experiencing its benefits, some people adopt additional practices, such as sitting meditation or contemplative prayer. Indeed, theory suggests mantram repetition is most potent when combined with additional practices[3] (see also Flinders, Oman, and Flinders, this volume).

Conclusions

We have highlighted several strong and compelling features of mantram repetition, sometimes also called repetition of a holy name or spiritual word. This practice possesses a strong historical basis in both Western and Eastern religious traditions. The effectiveness of this practice is supported by scientific theory as well as increasing empirical evidence from veterans, healthcare employees, HIV-infected adults, and other groups. Perhaps ironically, the mantram may in part be viewed as a much healthier application of a principle that today is most systematically exploited by commercial advertisers: mental repetition.

The simplicity, portability, long history, and cross-cultural, and multifaith theological grounding of this practice suggest the possibility of widespread popular interest. Indeed, findings from one recent scientific research study of mantram repetition were disseminated by media as diverse as *Web MD*, *Fox News*, the *Hindustan Times*, *Woman's Day*, and Andrew Weil's *Self-Healing Newsletter*.[12]

From a scientific point of view that demands rigor, many questions still remain before firm recommendations can be offered to professionals. But so far, the research findings are quite promising. In view of the many strengths of mantram repetition, we encourage everyone—including religious and health professionals as well as laypersons—to consider how this practice might merit a place in one's daily work or daily life.

References

1. Miller, W. R. & Thoresen, C. E. (2003). Spirituality, religion, and health: An emerging research field. *American Psychologist, 58*, 24–35.
2. Worthington, E. L., Jr., Kurusu, T. A., McCullough, M. E., & Sandage, S. J. (1996). Empirical research on religion and psychotherapeutic processes and outcomes: A 10-year review and research prospectus. *Psychological Bulletin, 119*, 448–487.
3. Oman, D. & Driskill, J. D. (2003). Holy name repetition as a spiritual exercise and therapeutic technique. *Journal of Psychology and Christianity, 22*, 5–19.

4. Easwaran, E. (1998/1977). *Mantram handbook*. Tomales, CA: Nilgiri Press.
5. Easwaran, E. (2005). *Strength in the storm: Creating calm in difficult times.* Tomales, CA: Nilgiri Press.
6. Cassian, J. & Luibhéid, C. (1985). *Conferences*. New York: Paulist Press.
7. Smith, H. & Novak, P. (2003). *Buddhism: A concise introduction.* San Francisco, CA: HarperSanFrancisco.
8. Schimmel, A. (1975). *Mystical dimensions of Islam.* Chapel Hill, NC: University of North Carolina Press.
9. Gandhi, M. K. (1949). *Ramanama*. Ahmedabad, India: Navajivan.
10. Teasdale, J. D., Moore, R. G., Hayhurst, H., Pope, M., Williams, S., & Segal, Z. V. (2002). Metacognitive awareness and prevention of relapse in depression: Empirical evidence. *Journal of Consulting and Clinical Psychology, 70,* 275–287.
11. Benson, H. & Stark, M. (1997). *Timeless healing: The power and biology of belief.* New York: Fireside.
12. Bormann, J. E., Oman, D., Kemppainen, J. K., Becker, S., Gershwin, M., & Kelly, A. (2006). Mantram repetition for stress management in veterans and employees: A critical incident study. *Journal of Advanced Nursing, 53,* 502–512.
13. Bernardi, L., Sleight, P., Bandinelli, G., Cencetti, S., Fattorini, L., Wdowczyc-Szulc, J., et al. (2001). Effect of rosary prayer and yoga mantras on autonomic cardiovascular rhythms: Comparative study. *British Medical Journal, 323,* 1446–1449.
14. Epel, E. S., Blackburn, E. H., Lin, J., Dhabhar, F. S., Adler, N. E., Morrow, J. D., et al. (2004). Accelerated telomere shortening in response to life stress. *Proceedings of the National Academy of Sciences of the United States of America, 101,* 17312–17315.
15. Peterson, C. & Seligman, M. E. P. (2004). *Character strengths and virtues: A handbook and classification.* Washington, DC and New York: American Psychological Association and Oxford University Press.
16. Smith, H. (1991). *The world's religions: Our great wisdom traditions.* San Francisco, CA: Harper San Francisco.
17. Bandura, A. (2003). On the psychosocial impact and mechanisms of spiritual modeling. *The International Journal for the Psychology of Religion, 13,* 167–174.
18. Pargament, K. I. (1997). *The psychology of religion and coping: Theory, research, practice.* New York: Guilford.
19. Pollner, M. (1989). Divine relations, social relations, and well-being. *Journal of Health and Social Behavior, 30,* 92–104.
20. Cahn, B. R. & Polich, J. (2006). Meditation states and traits: EEG, ERP, and neuroimaging studies. *Psychological Bulletin, 132,* 180–211.
21. Wolf, D. B. & Abell, N. (2003). Examining the effects of meditation techniques on psychosocial functioning. *Research on Social Work Practice, 13,* 27–42.

22. Wachholtz, A. B. & Pargament, K. I. (2005). Is spirituality a critical ingredient of meditation? Comparing the effects of spiritual meditation, secular meditation, and relaxation on spiritual, psychological, cardiac, and pain outcomes. *Journal of Behavioral Medicine, 28,* 369–384.

23. Bormann, J. E., Smith, T. L., Becker, S., Gershwin, M., Pada, L., Grudzinski, A. H., et al. (2005). Efficacy of frequent, mantram repetition on stress, spiritual well-being, and quality of life in veterans: A pilot study. *Journal of Holistic Nursing, 23,* 395–414.

24. Bormann, J. E., Smith, T. L., Shively, M., Dellefield, M. E., & Gifford, A. L. (2007). Self-monitoring using wrist counters for stress reduction: Mantram repetition. *Journal of Health Quality, 1,* 47–55.

25. Bormann, J. E., Becker, S., Gershwin, M., Kelly, A., Pada, L., Smith, T. L., et al. (2006). Relationship of frequent mantram repetition to emotional and spiritual well-being in healthcare workers. *Journal of Continuing Education in Nursing, 37,* 218–224.

26. Bormann, J. E., Gifford, A. L., Shively, M., Smith, T. L., Redwine, L., Kelly, A., et al. (2006). Effects of spiritual mantram repetition on HIV outcomes: A randomized controlled trial. *Journal of Behavioral Medicine, 29,* 359–376.

27. Richards, T. A., Oman, D., Hedberg, J., Thoresen, C. E., & Bowden, J. (2006). A qualitative examination of a spiritually based intervention and self-management in the workplace. *Nursing Science Quarterly, 19,* 231–239.

28. Oman, D. & Thoresen, C. E. (2006). Applying social cognitive theory to spirituality: Achievements, challenges, and prospects. *Paper presented at symposium on Spiritual Transformation: New Frontiers in Scientific Research, Berkeley, CA, April 7, 2006.*

29. Oman, D. & Thoresen, C. E. (2005). Religion, spirituality, and children's physical health. In E. C. Roehlkepartain, P. E. King, L. Wagener, & P. L. Benson (Eds.), *The handbook of spiritual development in childhood and adolescence* (pp. 399–415). Thousand Oaks, CA: Sage.

PART 3

SPIRIT AND ACTION

CHAPTER 8

Compassion and Health

AMY B. WACHHOLTZ AND MICHELLE PEARCE

It is six o'clock in the evening and you are sitting in your car impatiently waiting for the light to change. Even though the air conditioning is on full blast you feel sticky and irritable as you contemplate the never-ending projects piling up at work and the myriad of responsibilities you need to attend to this evening, including your children and the long-neglected baskets of laundry. While tapping your fingers on the steering wheel, you notice a man standing on the concrete medium between the lanes of traffic. He is in his mid-fifties, with long, shaggy gray hair, a torn, sweat-stained shirt, and a cardboard sign that reads, "I'm hungry! Please help! God bless you." Like a choose-your-own-adventure novel, you have at least two choices at this point, and both depend on your perspective. If you believe this man is begging you for money because he squandered his own on alcohol, and simply needs to clean up his act and get a job, you are likely to feel angry and keep your eyes firmly fixed on the traffic light.

However, you might have a very different response if you begin to wonder what it is like to be this man, and consider possibilities for his suffering, such as an accident that left him disabled and unable to work with no choice but to beg for enough money to survive. If you identify with his suffering as if it could be your own, and if you are moved with a desire to somehow alleviate his suffering, you are likely to reach into your wallet and hand him a few dollars. This latter empathetic view of the homeless man's suffering, your desire to relieve it, and subsequent action is an example of compassion. We are willing to bet that if you chose to demonstrate compassion you are probably feeling less anxious and stressed about your own problems, and perhaps even a little foolish for feeling that way in the first place. Notably, not only has your compassion improved this homeless man's situation, but research has demonstrated that it may also have tangible benefits for your own physical health, emotional well-being, and relationship satisfaction.

The purpose of this chapter is to explore and synthesize a number of areas of research, each of which suggests that compassion and related concepts have a beneficial effect on one's health and well-being; whereas a lack of compassion (e.g., anger, unforgiveness, etc.) has a detrimental effect. We will also discuss the role of religion and spirituality in the cultivation and demonstration of compassion. Finally, we will identify several interventions that have been designed to encourage compassion toward oneself and others that may prove useful for clinicians and their patients.

Definition of Compassion

A number of definitions of compassion have been proposed, most of which include the following four components: (1) an awareness of another's pain, perception of reality, and psychological state; (2) a feeling of kindness; (3) a desire to alleviate the suffering; and (4) doing what is within one's power and ability to alleviate the suffering.

Compassion is often confused with other similar emotion terms. Sympathy is defined as sorrow for another's suffering and a wish to see them better. Pity also sees the other as suffering as well, but views this suffering as an indication of weakness, and therefore implies an inequality in status. Neither sympathy nor pity involves an action to alleviate the suffering. Empathy is most closely related to compassion, as it is defined as the ability to recognize and understand the emotion of another. Yet, empathy is felt for both positive and negative emotions, not just for suffering, and is not necessarily action-oriented, which is a defining component of compassion. Despite these differences, the terms empathy and compassion are often used interchangeably in the literature.

There are stable personality differences in the tendency to feel compassion associated with organic, cultural, and socialization factors. Women, and girls as young as 2 years of age, tend to display higher levels of empathy, a concept similar to compassion, than do men and boys, although in both Eastern and Western cultures, women tend to show less compassion and more self-criticism toward themselves than toward others.[1] The tendency to feel compassionate may have an organic basis. Using fMRIs, Farrow and colleagues[2] found that empathetic judgments activated very specific areas of the brain. It appears that there may also be a neural mechanism for mapping others' feelings onto one's own nervous system. The authors suggest that this neural activation may help us to understand the intention of another. The environmental context, as well as the perceived responsibility of the individual for his or her suffering, also influences how much compassion we feel. We tend to feel more compassion for those we perceive as not responsible for their suffering.

Compassion in World Religions

Although a spiritual belief system is not necessary to feel compassion, because compassion often involves decreasing self-focus to consider the plight of others, there is usually a spiritual or ethical belief system that underlies and encourages the development and expression of this characteristic. Indeed, compassion is considered a virtue in most of the major world religions and philosophies. For example, in Buddhism, the first of the Four Noble Truths is the belief that the "unenlightened life is suffering." As such, to be enlightened, the ultimate goal of the Buddhist faith, one must demonstrate compassion. His Holiness the Dalai Lama has been quoted as saying, "The whole purpose of religion is to facilitate love and *compassion*, patience, tolerance, humility, forgiveness" (emphasis added). Compassion is also central in Christianity, evidenced in Christ's admonishment to his followers to pay particular care to the widow, the fatherless, and the poor, not to mention the Golden Rule, rooted in Judaic teachings, of doing unto others as you would have done unto you. In Islam, giving alms to the poor is a compassionate act and is identified as one of the five pillars of the faith. Interestingly, a working group, consisting of a panel of multifaith participants (Buddhists, Christian, Muslims, Jews, Atheists, Agnostics, and others), was gathered by the World Health Organization to develop an instrument to measure the role of spirituality in quality of life. They collaboratively and unanimously chose the phrase "self-less love and compassion" as the key component of spirituality.[3] This suggests a common central theme of compassion among diverse faiths and worldviews, and an agreement that compassion is an important concept when considering health and well-being.

Compassion and Health

Compassion, a subject of numerous spiritual, philosophical, and new age texts, has not been extensively examined in psychological research. However, there is a cluster of concepts that are similar to the defining components of compassion, involving prosocial attitudes and behaviors directed toward others and one's self, which have been the subject of scientific health research. We have identified five such areas of research that we believe provide collaborative evidence to suggest that there is a relationship between compassion and physical and mental health. Namely, we will examine the relationship between health and correlates of compassion in the domain of stress and negative emotions, positive emotions, religion and spirituality, forgiveness, and altruism/volunteering.

Stress, Negative Emotions, and Health

One means of ascertaining the relationship between compassion and health is to examine health outcomes when a lack of compassion is demonstrated. Our society spins faster and faster as the pressure to do more and produce more increases. Extensive social psychology research shows that when people are tired, harassed, and rushed, they are more likely to be self-centered, make snap judgments about others, display impulsive behaviors, and be less thoughtful of others. Over time, stress and the resulting behaviors are likely to have a significant negative impact on multiple dimensions of health (physical, mental, and spiritual). Chronic stress and the subsequent sympathetic nervous system arousal can have a large impact on the functioning of the immune system and an individual's resistance to illness.[4] Indeed, chronic stress is linked to high baseline levels of glucocorticoids, hormones that have been implicated in a number of mental and physical health disorders. The relationship between stress and health problems is more likely to appear in older adults, as the effects accumulate over time.

In many ways, anger and hostility are opposing emotions to compassion, and are also more likely to be experienced under perceived stressful conditions, and to create and maintain physiological arousal. When anger arises, we often are focused on our own position on a subject, and usually do not give much thought to the other person's side or suffering. A plethora of research shows the negative effects that anger has on the human body and the human psyche, including increased pain, depression, and disability. Anger can also have significant cardiac implications. In a study of almost 3,000 men, the researchers found that whether anger was suppressed or expressed, the presence of anger made it 1.7 times more likely that an individual will have an ischemic heart disease-related event, even after controlling for physiological, psychological, and behavioral risk factors.[5]

It should be noted that anger is not always a bad thing. Researchers have discovered that anger and motivation activate the same part of the brain. This makes sense, as often it is the feeling of anger that motivates us to change something in our environment. However, when anger is chronic, unexpressed, or accompanied by feelings of powerlessness, it is likely to be turned inward, causing a prolonged release of stress hormones, which will eventually take their toll on the physiology and health of the individual.

Hostility is another opposing emotion to compassion. Hostility comprises a number of negative attitudes or beliefs toward another person and may include other factors such as cynicism and denigration. It may also be accompanied by some form of verbal or physical aggression. Much research has established a relationship between hostility and negative health outcomes such as cardiac disease and stroke. Hostility has been identified as one of the most potent (or damaging) components of "Type A" behavior, and is an independent predictor of coronary heart disease.

Feelings of stress, anger, and hostility are incompatible with feelings of compassion, and are associated with physiological arousal, decreased immune functioning, increased pain levels, cardiac disease, and depression. However, the research reviewed thus far is not sufficient to conclude that there is a relationship between compassion and health, only that there seems to be a relationship between health and emotional states associated with a lack of compassion. To understand more about health and the presence of compassion we turn now to research on positive emotions and health.

Positive Emotions and Health

A growing body of research, including the relatively new area of "positive psychology," has demonstrated a relationship between health and positive emotions, such as love and empathy, which are closely related to several of the defining components of compassion.[3] Among others, positive emotions have been linked to spontaneous remissions of cancer, faster wound healing, protection from cardiovascular disease, and reduced chronic pain.

There are at least five reasons posited for the association between health and positive emotions. First, there appears to be a neurochemical pathway through which positive emotions influence physical health. For example, neurobiology research has demonstrated that when an individual is in love, positive neurochemical changes occur in the body, such as the release of oxytocin, a neurochemical related to bonding in relationships.[6] Second, research has also demonstrated a relationship between positive emotions and an increase in the immune system's ability to fight disease.[7] It may be that an individual who cultivates and experiences positive emotions is likely to have fewer health problems over the course of his/her life.

Third, emotions such as love and compassion, may also counter negative emotions and act as a buffer against stress by facilitating an overall positive mood, relaxation, decreased anger, and feelings of connectedness with others. Indeed, individuals who have participated in interventions designed to help them develop loving feelings and reduce anger and distress have reported reduced chronic pain and improved mental health.[8]

Fourth, positive emotions, such as compassion, may influence health through their influence on social support and relationship satisfaction. Relationship satisfaction between couples is correlated with compassionate activities such as empathic concern and perspective taking[9] because such behaviors often lead to good communication, warmth, and a positive outlook. The better one's relationships are the more social support one can expect. Moreover, social support was shown to be reliably associated to aspects of the cardiovascular, endocrine, and immune systems in a review of eighty-one studies.[10]

Finally, feelings of love and compassion for one's self may enhance a feeling of self-efficacy and trust in one's body's ability to maintain health. Trusting one's self to effectively deal with health-related situations can be a strong protective factor against illness and pain.[11] Therefore, compassion, like other positive emotions, may both rejuvenate and protect one's health through a myriad of direct and indirect pathways.

Religion/Spirituality and Health

A third way to elucidate the relationship between compassion and health is to examine the association between religion/spirituality, compassion, and health. Research indicates that religion can have a positive impact on a variety of areas, including physical and psychological health, interpersonal relations, and levels of distress during difficult times. From cancer, to HIV/AIDS, to heart attacks, to hypertension, correlational research has suggested that those individuals who have strong religious and/or spiritual lives are physically and psychologically healthier.[12] Not only is religion/spirituality often associated with compassion, but compassion may also help, in part, to illuminate why there is a relationship between religiosity and health. For example, Steffan and Masters[13] found that individuals with a high level of intrinsic religiousness and a high level of compassionate attitudes reported more positive psychosocial health outcomes than did those with lower reported levels of religiousness and compassion. Moreover, upon closer statistical examination, it was determined that the individuals' high level of compassion explained the relationship between religiousness and psychosocial health outcomes in that those who were religious were more likely to be compassionate and in turn were more likely to experience better psychosocial outcomes. Research is still needed to identify whether compassion plays a similar role in the relationship between religiousness and physical health.

The religion and health literature has identified multiple areas where research has indicated that religion and spirituality may have a positive influence on the individual. However, it is also important to note that at times religion/spirituality can spur a lack of compassion for oneself or others that may be detrimental to health. For example, research by Pargament[14] revealed that when patients identified God as a compassionate being they had significantly better physical and mental health outcomes compared to patients who identified God as a judgmental and noncompassionate being. In a study comparing long-term AIDS survivors (at least 4 years past the initial appearance of an AIDS defining symptom), and a HIV+ comparison group with similar CD4 counts, researchers found that feeling harshly judged by a higher power, or pronouncing religiously based judgment on one's self was inversely related to long-term survival.[15]

It appears that religion and spirituality can be a double-edged sword. For some, religion/spirituality encourages compassionate attitudes and behaviors. For others, specific religious/spiritual beliefs can promote judgementalness toward one's self and others who do not fit within a strict rubric of belief or behavior. It may be that those whose faith encourages them to think and act compassionately experience more positive mental and physical health outcomes than those whose religious/spiritual beliefs facilitate a more negative self and worldview.

Forgiveness

It has been said, "Before you criticize someone, you should walk a mile in their shoes. That way, when you criticize them, you're a mile away and you have their shoes." Of course, this is a humorous take on a familiar saying that is often used to encourage a compassionate and forgiving response. The research on forgiveness and health is relevant in understanding the association between compassion and health, as true forgiveness necessitates feelings of compassion toward others and/or one's self. Forgiveness has been defined as "the replacement of negative emotions of unforgiveness by positive, love-based emotions such as empathy, *compassion*, sympathy, and affection for the offender"[16] (emphasis added).

Forgiveness may be related to number of health issues including cancer and heart disease. A study that asked participants to recall experiences of betrayal found that those who were more likely to forgive not only had lower baseline blood pressure, but they also displayed less cardiovascular reactivity to the acute stress of discussing an event in which they were hurt by someone close to them. They were also much quicker in returning to their baseline cardiac activity after finishing the task.[17] The authors coined that forgiveness really does result in a "change of heart."

Old grudges and new ones show the same physiological pattern of arousal. This may be because we tend to rehearse the grudge over and over again, which causes physiological reactions to eventually become ingrained. Hormone (glucocorticoids) releases during periods of unforgiveness and when recalling unforgiven betrayals are consistent with those released during stress, which can impact the functioning of the immune system and the individual's resistance to illness.[4] In contrast, when a victim begins to develop feelings of empathy for a perpetrator the victim begins to show reduced allostatic load and his or her cardiovascular and sympathetic nervous system arousal begins to diminish. Moreover, those with generally higher trait forgiveness have lower resting blood pressure, improved immune system functioning, better physical health, and better poststress recovery, suggesting that there are long-term health effects of forgiveness.

If we judge someone responsible for a negative outcome, we are more likely to respond in anger and feel little compassion. This attitude is detrimental in negotiation situations because individuals have less desire to work with one another or to identify a solution that works for all involved. In contrast, empathetic concern and perspective taking, markers of compassion, are positively related to long-term relationship satisfaction,[9] perhaps because of the association between compassion and forgiveness.[18]

Overall, compassion through forgiveness can break the bonds of powerful negative emotions that tie the individual to the perpetrator and the offenses committed against them. By extending compassionate love through forgiveness there can be significant and positive health consequences for the individual. Therefore, in many ways, while forgiveness may not have any consequences for the offender, it can have very real consequences for the person who was wounded.

Altruism/Volunteering

It has been asserted that "compassion is never passive."[19] Indeed, research has shown that feelings of empathetic concern are positively related to helping and prosocial behavior.[20] Moreover, most studies show that giving instrumental or emotional support to others is related to decreased morbidity and improved health. Although concerns have been raised that giving too much of one's self can create problems, generally, those who have greater involvement with volunteer organizations tend to have better health outcomes, even after controlling for potentially confounding variables (e.g., demographic, personality, physical, and mental health variables).[21] Altruism has also been linked with brain release of endorphins.[22]

Helping others also appears to be related to long-term survival, even when the individual is coping with his/her own serious health issues. In the study discussed earlier on long-term AIDS survivors, the researchers also found that those who helped others who were struggling with HIV were more likely to have longer survival status than those in the HIV+ comparison group.[15] Helping others was significantly correlated with the Compassionate View of Others subscale on the Ironson-Woods Spirituality/Religiousness Index. Having a compassionate view of others was also correlated with healthier psychosocial status, increased social support, helping others, disclosing HIV status to partners, and longer survival status.

The familiar adage that it is better to give than to receive appears to have some merit. In a series of research studies, psychologists have found that those giving social and instrumental support actually have better long-term physical and mental health outcomes than do those who receive the support. Even after controlling the variables that may have an obvious impact on these findings (i.e., social economic status, physical and mental health status of giver and receiver, education, age, and gender), those individuals who gave social support had lower morbidity than those receiving the social support.[23] In a similar study, Brown and her colleagues[24] also found that giving both instrumental (e.g., rides to doctors appointments) and emotional (e.g., listening to another's concerns) reduced mortality over a 5-year period, a finding that is consistent across cultures, including African Americans, Caribbeans, Eastern Europeans, and U.S.-born European Americans.[23]

And the more you do, the greater the decrease in mortality. Oman, Thoresen, & McMahon[21] found a 44 percent reduction in mortality in community dwelling elderly among those who volunteered at two or more organizations, after controlling for physical functioning and social support. Given that being a nonsmoker was related to a 49 percent reduction in mortality, high levels of volunteering provided almost the same level of protective benefit as being a nonsmoker! These researchers also found that religious involvement seemed to go hand-in-hand with volunteering. Religious involvement provides an additional complementary benefit to volunteering, such that those who attended religious services at least once a week and volunteered had a 60 percent reduction in mortality rate.

Previous research has identified that people have multiple reasons for volunteering, such as: gaining social support, career advancement, personal enhancement, and altruistic values. As such, there may not be a direct link between compassion and volunteering. However, at some level, the benefits of altruism or compassionate love, may explain some of the beneficial effects observed among those who volunteer or provide support to others.

It is interesting to note that having a compassionate attitude while performing a compassionate helping behavior may be important for experiencing the positive effects of helping others. In a study assessing compassionate attitudes and behaviors, the researchers assessed both college students and a larger community sample. They found that compassionate attitudes had a greater protective effect on mental health than did compassionate behaviors alone.[13] The authors hypothesized that while compassionate behavior may lead to compassionate attitudes, the benefits of compassionate behavior alone may be more limited, since behavior may flow from external pressures rather than internal values.

Too Much Compassion: Compassion Fatigue and Caregiver Burden

For some people, demonstrating a high level of compassion for others can lead to feeling overwhelmed by their suffering, and can result in emotional and physical costs rather than benefits. "Compassion fatigue" or "caregiver burnout," as it is referred to in the literature, is a type of "deep physical, emotional and spiritual exhaustion accompanied by acute emotional pain."[25] The once compassionate individual becomes increasingly withdrawn, irritable, fatigued, and less empathetic as a means of coping and rebalancing. It has been theorized that some individuals may be more sensitive to the emotional state of others and less able to protect themselves from identifying with and/or taking on the burdens of others. Compassion fatigue can be detrimental to both the caregiver and the patient, decrease productivity, increase sick days, lead to higher job turnover, affect personal relationships, and can result in an overall decline in physical health.[25]

Clearly, not everyone who demonstrates a high level of compassion experiences negative outcomes, but it has been suggested that healthcare workers, caregivers, clergy, volunteers, and emergency care workers may be more vulnerable to compassion fatigue than are those in other professions. For example, one survey found that 54 percent of physicians reported a time when they felt that they no longer had any compassion left, even after a restful weekend.[26] Compassion fatigue is likely to be experienced more often by individuals in the "caring" professions because on top of the typical job stressors, they must also contend with caring for the emotional suffering and traumas of others. It is important that those who are vulnerable to compassion fatigue engage in good self care on a daily basis, such as doing the things that rejuvenate one's self, exercising, spending time with friends and family, developing hobbies, and engaging in prayer and meditation.

Putting Compassion into Practice

A few intervention studies have explored ways in which individuals can increase compassion and similar types of emotions toward themselves and others, primarily in the forgiveness and meditation research literature. Interventions in both of these areas have shown promising health-related benefits, though admittedly the research is somewhat limited.

Forgiveness interventions, both spiritual and secular-based methods, primarily center on increasing empathy/mercy for the transgressor, and letting go of the negative emotions related to the transgression resulting in the two-fold benefit of improved mental and physical health. A meta-analysis of forgiveness interventions showed that patients who took the time and energy to process the transgression and move toward forgiveness produced fewer stress hormones, and reported reduced psychological distress than individuals that continued to maintain negative feelings toward the transgressor.[27]

Many of the interventions designed to increase empathy have employed meditation. Meditation has been shown to improve one's ability to empathize with others' emotions after only 4 weeks of practice. It can enhance and rejuvenate romantic relationships by increasing feelings of connection and acceptance of the other partner,[28] as well as reducing anger toward oneself and others.[8] One study focusing on loving-kindness meditation, a form of meditation that targets increasing empathy for others, showed that meditation can effectively reduce chronic pain patients' anger toward themselves and others, while simultaneously increasing their ability to empathize with others. The critical aspect of this study was that the meditation did not create better mechanisms to help the patients suppress their anger (which as discussed previously can have negative health consequences); instead, the meditation focused on decreasing the frequency and intensity of anger toward the trangressor by increasing the patient's ability to empathize with others and to be compassionate toward themselves. Not only did this effectively increase compassion toward themselves and others, but the patients also reported health benefits such as a decrease in low back pain.[8]

Other meditation studies have found similar compassion and health connections, even in studies that were not explicitly designed to explore compassion. For example, one study exploring the effects of mindfulness based stressed reduction (MBSR) on immune response to a flu vaccine challenge, found that after the 8-week MBSR training program, not only did meditators create more antibodies in response to the flu vaccine, but they also demonstrated an increased capacity for empathy.[29] The study also showed that MBSR meditation may be related to altered brain activity that correlates with positive affect and immune functioning. Those who practiced MBSR meditation showed a significant increase in their left-side anterior activation, a site that has previously been shown to be related to positive affect. Interestingly, improved immune reactivity increased relative to the proportion of brain activity found in the left anterior section of the brain.[29]

The benefits of meditation may result by decreasing the feeling of time pressure and providing the mental space for the individual to feel more in control of his or her emotional reactions and lives. Both increased time pressure and decreased feelings of control are related to increased anger, which conflicts with feelings of compassion. However, as Feldman[26] astutely notes, "compassion . . . does not mean that pain will always disappear or that we will discover a solution to every dispute and conflict. We cannot always fix every event of distress, but we can always be present, awake, and receive each moment with compassion and simplicity."

We conclude this section by offering a relatively simple practice suggested by His Holiness the fourteenth Dalai Lama as a means of increasing love and compassion in the world:

1. Spend 5 minutes at the beginning of each day remembering we all want the same things (to be happy and to be loved) and we are all connected to one another.
2. Spend 5 minutes—breathing in—cherishing yourself; and breathing out—cherishing others. If you think about people you have difficulty cherishing, extend your cherishing to them anyway.
3. During the day, extend that attitude to everyone you meet. Practice cherishing the simplest person (clerks, attendants, etc., as well as the

"important" people in your life; cherish the people you love and the people you dislike).

4. Continue this practice no matter what happens or what anyone does to you.

Conclusion

Over the course of this chapter, we have discussed a number of ways in which people can show compassion and how compassion can influence one's health and relationships. To further our understanding about the role of compassion in health, a relatively unexplored relationship in the psychological research literature, we examined concepts highly correlated with compassion including empathy, love, spirituality, forgiveness, altruism, and feelings of interconnectedness. We also examined concepts incongruent and opposed to compassion, such as chronic stress, anger, hostility, holding grudges, and directing negative emotions toward one's self and others. By relating compassion to these other concepts that have more frequently been the subject of research, we do not mean to imply that compassion is only a conglomeration of other emotions and behaviors. Instead, we view compassion as a multifaceted concept involving the direction of kind awareness to another, a perception of the other's suffering, a desire to relieve the suffering, and subsequent action to do so. The concepts we examined in this paper—positive emotions, emotions that oppose compassion, and behaviors that often necessitate compassion, such as forgiveness and altruism—help to elucidate each of the different components of the definition of compassion.

Research on the concepts stated above points toward a relationship between compassion and health outcomes, including mitigated physiological stress arousal, improved immune functioning, decreased cardiovascular reactivity, morbidity and mortality, lower blood pressure and pain levels, and greater levels of relaxation, feelings of connectedness, and relationship satisfaction. From the way we choose to perceive and respond to the homeless man on the street corner to the driver who cut us off on the way to work, to our coworker who is late to yet another meeting, we experience countless opportunities every day to choose to be compassionate. And, how we decide to respond in each of these moments may have both short- and long-term consequences for our bodies, emotions, and relationships. As Thomas Merton has said, "Compassion is the keen awareness of the interdependence of all things." Understanding the vital interdependence between both ourselves and others and between our body and psyche, as well as the consequences thereof, may make the admonishment to do unto others as we would have others do unto us is more important than we have ever realized.

References

1. Kitayama, S. & Markus, H.R. (2000). The pursuit of happiness and the realization of sympathy: Cultural patterns of self, social relations, and well-being. In E. Diener & E. Suh (Eds.), *Subjective well-being across cultures* (pp. 43–86). Cambridge, MA: MIT Press.
2. Farrow, T.F.D., Zheng, Y., Wilkinson, I.D., Spence, S.A., Deakin, J.F., William, J., et al. (2001). Investigating the functional anatomy of empathy and forgiveness. *Neuroreport, 12,* 2433–2438.
3. Underwood, L.G. (2005). Interviews with Trappist monks as a contribution to research methodology in the investigation of compassionate love. *Journal for the Theory of Social Behavior, 35,* 285–302
4. Cacioppo, J.T., Berntson, G.G., Malarkey, W.B., Kiecolt-Glaser, J.K., Sheridan, J.F., Poehlmann, K.M., et al. (1998). Autonomic, neuroendocrine, and immune responses to psychological stress: The reactivity hypothesis. *Annals of the New York Academy of Sciences, 840,* 664–673
5. Gallacher, J.E.J., Yarnell, J.W.G., Sweetnam, P.M., Elwood, P.C., & Stansfeld, S.A. (1999) Anger and incident heart disease in the Caerphilly study. *Psychsomatic Medicine, 61,* 446–453
6. Esch, T. & Stefano, G.B. (2005) The neurobiology of love. *Neuroendocrinology Letters, 26,* 175–192.
7. Davidson, R.J., Kabat-Zinn, J., Schumacher, J., Rosenkranz, M., Mueller, D., Santorelli, S.F., et al. (2003). Alterations in brain and immune function produced by mindfulness meditation. *Psychosomatic Medicine, 65,* 564–570.
8. Carson, J.W., Keefe, F.J., Lynch, T.R., Carson, K.M., Goli, V., Fras, A. et al. (2005). Loving-kindness meditation for chronic low back pain: Results from a pilot trial. *Journal of Holistic Nursing, 23,* 287–304.
9. Davis, M.H. & Oathout, H.A. (1987). Maintenance of satisfaction in romantic relationships; Empathy and relational competence. *Journal of Personality & Social Psychology, 53,* 397–410.
10. Uchino, B.N., Kiecolt-Glaser, J.K., & Cacioppo, J.T. (1996). The relationship between social support and physiological processes: A review with emphasis on underlying mechanisms and implications for health. *Psychological Bulletin, 119,* 488–531.
11. Wachholtz, A.B. (2006). *Does spirituality matter? Effects of meditative content and orientation on migraineurs.* PhD dissertation, Bowling Green State University, KY.
12. George, L.K., Larson, D.B., Koenig, H.G., & McCullough, M.E. (2000). Spirituality and health: What we know, what we need to know. *Journal of Social and Clinical Psychology, 19,* 102–116.
13. Steffen, P.R., Masters, K.S. (2005). Does compassion mediate the intrinsic religion-health relationship? *Annals of Behavioral Medicine, 30,* 217–224.

14. Pargament, K.I. (1997). *The Psychology of Religion and Coping.* New York: Guilford Press.

15. Ironson, G., Solomon, G.F., Balbin, E.G., O'Cleirigh, C., George, A., Kumar, M., et al. (2002). The Ironson-Woods Spirituality/Religiousness Index is associated with long survival, health behaviors, less distress, and low cortisol in people with HIV/AIDS. *Annals of Behavioral Medicine, 24,* 34–48.

16. Berry, J.W. & Worthington, E.L. (2001). Forgivingness, relationship quality, stress while imagining relationship events, and physical and mental health. *Journal of Counseling Psychology, 48,* 447–455.

17. Lawler, K.A., Younger, J.W., Piferi, R.L., Billington, E., Jobe, R., Edmondson, K., et al. (2003). A change of heart: Cardiovascular correlates of forgiveness in response to interpersonal conflict. *Journal of Behavioral Medicine, 26,* 373–393.

18. McCullough, M.E., Worthington, E.L.J., & Rachal, K.C. (1997) Interpersonal forgiving in close relationships. *Journal of Personality & Social Psychology, 73,* 321–336.

19. Feldman, C. (2004). *The Buddhist path to simplicity: Spiritual practices in everyday life.* New York: Element Books, p 99.

20. Batson, C.D. (1987). Prosocial motivation: Is it ever truly altruistic? In L. Berkowitz (Ed.), *Advances in experimental social psychology* (Vol. 20, pp. 65–122). New York: Academic Press.

21. Oman, D., Thoresen, C.E., & McMahon, K. (1999). Volunteerism and mortality among the community-dwelling elderly. *Journal of Health Psychology, 4,* 301–316.

22. Hafen, B.Q., Karren, K. J., Frandsen, K. J., & Smith, N.L. (1996). *Mind/body health: The effects of attitudes, emotions, and relationships.* Boston, MA: Allyn & Bacon.

23. Brown, W.M., Consedine, N.S., & Magai, C. (2005). Altruism relates to health in an ethnically diverse sample of older adults. *The Journal of Gerontology (Series B): Psychological Sciences and Social Sciences, 60,* 143–152.

24. Brown, S.L., Nesse, R.M., Vinokur, A.D., & Smith, D.M. (2003). Providing social support may be more beneficial than receiving it: Results from a prospective study of mortality. *Psychological Science, 14,* 320–327.

25. Pfifferling J.H. & Gilley, K. (2000). Overcoming compassion fatigue. *Family Practice Management, 7,* 39–46.

26. Pfifferling, J.H. (1994, April). Can you care too much? *Hippocrates, 1,* 32–33

27. Baskin, T.W. & Enright, R.D. (2004). Intervention studies on forgiveness: A meta-analysis. *Journal of Counseling & Development, 82,* 79–90.

28. Carson, J.W., Carson, K.M., Gil, K.M., & Baucom, D.H. (2004). Mindfulness-based relationship enhancement. *Behavior Therapy, 35,* 471–494.

29. Shapiro, S.L., Schwartz, G.E., & Bonner, G. (1998). Effects of mindfulness-based stress reduction on medical and premedical students. *Journal of Behavioral Medicine, 21,* 581–599.

CHAPTER 9

The Calling Protocol: Promoting Greater Health, Joy, and Purpose in Life

DIANE E. DREHER AND THOMAS G. PLANTE

Whenever we face new challenges or complain of anxiety, depression, or a host of other problems, we have another opportunity to discover our callings, to ask, "What should I do with my life?" A calling or vocation (from the Latin, *vocare*) originally meant to be called by God to celibate religious life. This concept expanded during the Renaissance in Western Europe, when people believed that God gave everyone, from kings to commoners, a personal set of "gifts" or talents to be used in loving service to their neighbors, a loving tribute to their creator. In our own time, research in positive psychology has found that people who see their work as a calling, a source of joy and meaning, are healthier, happier, and more satisfied with life than those with jobs or careers.[1] Responding to personal challenges, job layoffs, retirement, or longing for something more in life, an increasing number of people today are seeking their callings, stepping back from the rush of external demands to ask how they can live with greater meaning and purpose.

Helping people find their callings has become a valuable aspect of psychotherapy. In many therapy sessions, questions of calling, meaning, and purpose naturally come up. One example is Rebecca, a 60-year-old women recently laid off from her high-power Silicon Valley job in human resources when her company was bought out by another company. During the course of merger transitions, her position was eliminated. Rebecca came to therapy feeling lonely and depressed, unsure of her next step in life. She was also keenly aware that her adolescent son would be graduating from high school and would most likely go off to college in another state, leaving her without any children at home. Her husband is a busy professional himself with no plans to retire any time soon. With her therapist, she reflected on her strengths, weaknesses, and questions about possible next steps in life. Through this process of reflection and discovery, she decided to attend law school (a dream she had many decades ago but abandoned along the way) and work for social justice in nonprofit agencies, focusing on health concerns of the aging population.

Principles of the Calling Protocol

An effective tool in psychotherapy, spiritual direction, and personal develop-ment, the calling protocol used by Rebecca and other people in this chapter is based on studies of Renaissance lives and current research in positive psychology.[2] Designed to help people look within, identify their strengths and values, and chart a more authentic direction for their lives, the protocol involves four steps: Discovery, Detachment, Discernment, and Direction.

1. *Discovery:* We all have personal strengths, vital keys to greater joy and fulfillment in life. In the Renaissance these were known as "gifts." In positive psychology, they are known as "signature strengths," the five major character strengths possessed by every individual.[3] The first step in the protocol encourages people to discover their strengths and find ways to use them on a daily basis.

2. *Detachment*: Detaching from inauthentic and debilitating behaviors (such as consumerism, workaholism, or excessive TV) helps us achieve greater clarity. The protocol uses a variety of detachment practices from traditional psychotherapy to meditation and exercise.

3. *Discernment*: Recognizing our values helps us live more congruently. The protocol helps people become more aware of their values through psychotherapy, by reflecting on the qualities of people they admire, or by practicing Ignatian discernment, developed in the Renaissance by St. Ignatius Loyola and used by many spiritual directors today.

4. *Direction*: For the fourth and final step, the protocol incorporates insights from Hope Theory, helping people turn their strengths and values into action by showing them how to set meaningful, manageable goals.

Step 1: Discovery

Recognizing our strengths.   Research in positive psychology has validated the Renaissance concept of "gifts," the belief that everyone has a unique set of talents and strengths. After an extensive international study, psychologists Martin Seligman and Christopher Peterson identified twenty-four character strengths and virtues, concluding that each of us has five major strengths, or "signature strengths." To experience greater joy and meaning in life, they recommend that people find ways to use these strengths regularly.[3]

Focusing on our strengths—on what we love to do and do well—seems like it would be easy. As children, we are naturally drawn to explore our world, to reach out to do what we love. Research has shown that people are healthier, happier, and more successful when they concentrate on what they do well. But somewhere along the road from childhood to adulthood, many of us forget this simple truth. A Gallup survey has revealed that most men and women in the United States, Britain, Canada, France, Japan, and China concentrate more on their weaknesses than they do on their strengths.[4] This focus on weakness not only makes people unhappy but also less effective. Too many people become demoralized, haunted by feelings of inadequacy. Even when they work to build up their weak areas, they can become, at best, more competent. For research has shown that we can only achieve excellence by building on our strengths.[4]

The first step in the calling protocol helps people identify their strengths and find ways to use them regularly. Three ways to do this are by drawing upon memories, using the VIA-IS signature strengths survey, and consulting with people they know.

1. *Drawing upon Memories.* In this practice, people take time to relax and reflect, remembering a time when they felt joyously, vitally alive, filled with a deep sense of being themselves. They capture this memory by jotting down a few notes, then share it with a therapist or other empathic listener who points out whatever strengths the process reveals. (Did the person demonstrate courage? Curiosity? Compassion? Strong interpersonal skills? Perseverance? Something else?). Learning about their strengths, people feel empowered and encouraged. In group sessions and workshops, the result is always a buzz of excitement, a heightened sense of energy in the room. Therapists and counselors can use this process with their clients, helping them identify their strengths, then brainstorm together about new ways to use them.

   One client, Zach, came to therapy struggling with severe ulcerative colitis. He has never been successfully employed following college, lives with his parents, and takes classes at a local community college to keep him busy. When he turned 30, he became increasingly depressed and anxious that his life has "stalled" with little hope of improvement. He even considered suicide. After reflecting on his strengths and times when he felt more alive and competent, he talked about his love of swimming and his success as a young competitive swimmer in high school. He glows when he describes his swimming competitions and his feelings of success. Connecting with these strengths convinced him to obtain his lifeguard certification and seek employment at a local country club with a large and successful swimming program. He is also enthusiastically looking into coaching swimming at the club as well.

2. Using the VIA-IS signature strengths survey on http://www.authentichappiness.org (survey is also available in Martin Seligman's book, *Authentic Happiness*).[5] The Web site asks people to sign in, answer a few demographic questions (age, occupation, etc.), and respond to an extensive on-line survey that gives them their top five "signature strengths." People can take the survey on-line at home or at their local public library, then print out the results and reflect on them. They can bring the printout to their therapist or counselor, working together to develop ways to use their strengths and connect them to new possibilities in life.

    Zach in the above example used the signature strength survey, learning a great deal about himself that he had never realized before. He reported that he now saw strengths that he never really thought he had. He and his therapist followed this experience up with more in depth psychological testing that helped better illustrate his personality strengths and weaknesses as well as careers consistent with his strengths.

3. *Consulting other people about their strengths.* People can also learn about their strengths by asking three people who know them well to tell them their top five strengths, and then comparing the results. Combining this exercise with the signature strengths survey provides another source of insight as well as additional personal reinforcement for their strengths. Some people respond better to the survey, while others are much more affected hearing people they know tell them about their strengths.

    Emily, a 20-year-old college student, had always had low self-esteem. Having family and friends reinforce her for her strengths meant a great deal to her. Feeling much better about herself, she has become more proactive, speaking up in her classes, and signing up for a retreat to reflect on her values and future goals.

    Zach's therapist asked him to talk with several people about his strengths. He spoke with a faculty member at the local community college with whom he had several classes and whose opinion he respected. He also talked with his mother, with whom he maintains a close relationship, and an old friend from the high school swim team. Zach found the conversations fascinating since he had no idea that people saw certain strengths he had. His conversation with his teacher ultimately led him to enter into a new program at the college that involves creative writing as well as an internship with a television station.

When people are struggling with low self-esteem, depression, burnout, or confusion we've found that discovering their strengths brings them greater agency, shifting their focus from problems to possibilities. Research in positive psychology has confirmed our observations. In 2005, Martin Seligman, Tracey Steen, Nansook Park, and Christopher Peterson conducted an on-line study asking over 500 people to discover their signature strengths with the VIA-IS survey, and then use one strength in a new way each day for a week. A large number of participants said they kept on using their strengths, and a follow-up survey revealed a significant improvement in happiness and decreased depressive symptoms 6 months later. Proposing a new emphasis for clinical practice, the researchers concluded, "Psychotherapy has long been where you go to talk about your troubles, a strangely untested assumption. We suggest that psychotherapy of the future may also be where you go to talk about your strengths."[6]

Step 2: Detachment

Discarding unproductive activities. The next step in the calling protocol is detachment, looking beneath all the noise and confusion around us to ask, "Who am I, really?"

People often need help detaching from unhealthy messages within and around them. Finding a calling means listening to ourselves, which we cannot do when our minds are burdened with problems, information overload, unhealthy self-concepts, and other peoples' demands and expectations. To find their callings people must detach from the false to embrace the true, releasing unproductive habits and unhealthy inner dialogues.

Three effective detachment practices are working with a psychotherapist or counselor, exercise, and meditation.

1. *Psychotherapy and Counseling.* Working with empathic professionals can help us begin listening to ourselves at a deeper level. Supportive teachers and counselors can help young people listen to their hearts when consumer culture distracts them with artificial values or when their parents pressure them to pursue lucrative careers while their strengths draw them to other fields. Therapists can help their clients detach from addictive behavior (from drugs, tobacco, and alcohol, to compulsive shopping, overeating, and overwork), and stop ruminating on their problems.

   Lucy came to therapy complaining about several family members who have been trying to take advantage of a wealthy relative. Disgusted by what she feels is their greedy, selfish, and entitled behavior, Lucy became so upset that she had trouble sleeping at night, lying awake thinking hateful thoughts about these individuals. She also read over their e-mails and other communications regularly, sharing them with her friends and supportive relatives. Obsessing about these family members was negatively impacting the quality of her life. Working with Lucy to detach from these unproductive activities through a variety of techniques gave her a greater sense of peace and calm.

2. *Exercise.* Studies have shown that regular exercise can reduce symptoms related to stress, anxiety, depression, and thought disturbance, improving mood and psychological well-being.[7]

    Lucy has a history of anxiety and depressive symptoms that have been debilitating for her in the past. In fact, she has never worked, driven a car, been on an airplane, or even left her home state of California. She was encouraged to exercise on a regular basis to better deal with her anxious and depressive symptoms. Her exercise had the happy consequence of helping her lose weight and spend more quality time with her husband. She now walks 5 miles each day with her husband after having their morning coffee. This has become a daily ritual that helps her manage her moods, control her weight, and have time to connect with her husband.

3. *Meditation.* Studies have shown that meditation not only relieves stress but also helps people overcome a number of problems—including insomnia, eating panic, and phobic disorders—so they can focus more effectively on their personal goals.[8]

    Monica, an 18-year-old college freshman, was feeling overwhelmed and stressed. With her mind racing about all the things she had to do, she often became so anxious and tense that she couldn't concentrate on her studies and had trouble falling asleep at night. When she was given a short passage meditation [9] to practice each day, she wondered when she'd find the time. But now she looks forward to her daily meditation practice, saying that it helps her relax. She also uses a short form of the meditation to help her deal with anxiety before an exam and often before falling asleep at night. She now says she feels noticeably less tense and more in charge of her life.

Step 3: Discernment

Discovering our values, examining our lives. The third step in the calling protocol is discernment, discovering and living by our own deepest values, achieved through the Ignatian discernment process, psychotherapy, or spiritual modeling.

1. *Ignatian Discernment.* The Renaissance saint, Ignatius Loyola, developed a discernment practice as part of his *Spiritual Exercises*. He taught people to reflect on their daily lives, asking which events bring

them *consolation* (joy, clarity, meaning, vitality, peace, community, closeness to God) and which ones bring *desolation* (isolation, anxiety, confusion, bitterness, boredom, and a host of other alienating emotions). As a young soldier and courtier, St. Ignatius developed this practice while recovering from serious leg injuries suffered at the Battle of Pamplona. As he lay in bed at his family castle for many long, painful months, enduring repeated settings of his shattered leg, he wanted to read some of his favorite tales of adventure and chivalry, but the only books in the house were a life of Christ and a collection of saints' lives. Ignatius read them, then thought about his former life at the courts of princes, his duels, deeds of chivalry, and a fair princess admired from afar. These reminiscences brought a pleasant nostalgia, but left him feeling empty and discontent. But when he read the saints' lives and thought of living like St. Francis or St. Dominic, he felt a deep and lasting joy. Discernment, he realized, means reflecting on our feelings, recognizing which choices bring only momentary pleasures, which ones offer deeper joy.[10, 11] Ignatian discernment—focusing on the deep feelings associated with our choices—is still used today by many people in retreats, spiritual direction, therapy, and personal reflection.

2. *Psychotherapy.* Psychologist John Neafsey has noted the "striking parallels" between Ignatian discernment and practices in psychotherapy that help people "listen carefully to their inner experience, with the aim of learning to recognize and follow the calling of their own inner voice."[12] By using such practices, therapists help their clients learn to honor their feelings to discern their values and live more authentically.

3. *Spiritual Modeling* is another way people can discern their values. Spirituality and health researchers Doug Oman and Carl Thoresen have found that our values are profoundly influenced by spiritual role models in our religious traditions, families, and communities. As St. Ignatius recognized his values by reflecting on the lives of St. Francis and St. Dominic, so people today can develop greater wisdom and discernment by reflecting on the lives of men and women they admire. These exemplary individuals can become powerful role models, inspiring people to live their values with courage and conviction, discovering their callings and finding a greater sense of the sacred in their lives. [13]

Michelle, an English professor in her mid-40s, has always admired Eleanor Roosevelt. Over the years, she has read her autobiography and several books about her. When Michelle took on new responsibilities as the head of her department, she focused on Roosevelt's qualities of courage and compassion to guide her in her work, hanging a photograph of her spiritual model in her office as a daily reminder and reinforcement. She found new inspiration in her work, handling her responsibilities, even the daily challenges, guided by a deeper sense of purpose and meaning.

Discerning our values not only helps us live with greater courage and authenticity, but it is also good for our health. A recent UCLA study found that when people reflect on their personal values before facing a stressful situation, they experience significant reductions in their neuroendocrine and psychological responses to stress.[14] By regularly reflecting on our values, we can build better health on many levels.

Step 4: Direction

Setting meaningful, achievable goals.   In the fourth and final part of the calling protocol, people combine their strengths and values to chart new directions in life. Drawing upon research in Hope Theory, developed by psychologist C. R. Snyder from the University of Kansas,[15] this process helps people set meaningful, achievable goals.

People can find out their current "hope" skills by answering the questions on Snyder's "Hope Scale"[15] or by reflecting on a time when they pursued an important goal, recalling what they did and how successful they were. For all of us, there are patterns. Some of us are great initiators, beginning projects with enthusiasm but then losing momentum, afraid to continue and face the risk of failure, while others persevere to the end. Some people have difficulty getting started, while others rush into new projects. Some don't succeed because their goals aren't clear enough. Others have strong motivation but became bogged down and frustrated because they don't know the right pathways to get them where they want to go.

By remembering how we approached an important goal in the past and looking for personal patterns, we can discover our own areas of strength and weakness, then learn how to build our strengths, for hope is a skill that improves with practice.

For years, Snyder studied people with high levels of hope—leaders in religion, business, academic, and civic life. Interviewing them to find out what they had in common, he discovered that they all had similar thought patterns: superior strengths in what Snyder called Goals, Pathways, and Agency. [16]

1. *Developing Effective Goals.* Snyder found that hopeful people have *meaningful* goals, goals they can believe in. The first three steps in the calling protocol help people set meaningful goals. By discovering their strengths and values, they can create goals that are truly their own, not something they've been told they "should" do.

Successful goals are also *specific* and *measurable*. Vague goals produce only vague results. Instead of "I'd like to feel better," hopeful people ask what they would do if they felt better, how feeling better would look and feel like. "I'd like to be able to climb the stairs at work without getting out of breath" is a more specific goal. Goals should also be *positive*. Instead of "I'd like to stop being out of shape," hopeful people frame their goal positively: as being more fit. They ask what fitness looks like and how they would measure it, such as "I'd like to walk 2 miles a day four times a week."

Oscar came to therapy because he needed to lose weight. At age 62, he said his physician told him that he had to lose weight, alter his diet, and exercise to combat the impact of both diabetes and cardiovascular disease. Oscar has tried many diets and weight loss programs over the years but has always regained his weight and felt like a failure in his attempts. One intervention he and his therapist used successfully was to work toward the goal of walking 10,000 steps per day using a small pedometer on his belt. Oscar wrote down his daily step count and charted it on a computer spreadsheet, enjoying working with graphs, tables, and statistical procedures to review his progress. After 3 years with his pedometer, he has maintained a 35-pound weight loss. While he is still overweight, his physician is very pleased with his progress and no longer very worried about his diabetes and heart troubles.

2. *Developing Effective Pathways*. After setting a goal, the next step is pathways: finding out how to get there. Some people set themselves up for failure by going after a big goal all at once. If you set a goal to walk 2 miles a day and you were really out of shape, you'd first need to break your goal into a series of smaller subgoals: walking a block or two around the neighborhood, then gradually adding more distance as you build your strength and stamina.

In the previous example, Oscar set himself a goal of walking 10,000 steps a day, then met with his therapist to come up with a set of pathways that worked for him. Since he liked working with charts and computers, he used a pedometer and computer spreadsheet to track his progress.

Another key hope practice is visualization: seeing yourself doing what it takes to achieve a goal.[16] Visualizing pathways helps you see the steps to success laid out before you, bringing vital revelations. As you visualize, when you come to a step and find that you don't know how to do it, you'll know you need to develop new skills or ask for help.

Heidi dreamed of becoming a magazine writer. She took college courses in nonfiction writing and magazine journalism, then interviewed local writers to find out how they managed to write and publish. She used these details to visualize herself working at her favorite magazine: doing on-line research, interviewing people, going after a story, generating new story ideas. As she practiced her visualization, Heidi realized she needed further training to reach this level, so she applied to a graduate program in journalism. Now, with a master's degree in magazine journalism, she has become a staff writer for a national health magazine.

Therapists, teachers, and counselors can support people in developing their pathways, encouraging them to develop strategies, like Oscar's, which work for them, or like Heidi, to find out more about their long-range goal by doing an information interview, taking a class, or asking someone they know for advice. Helping people develop better pathways also means supporting them in developing backup plans, asking what they would do if their initial plan doesn't work. Just as they'd take an alternate route if they came to a roadblock, they need to come up with alternate pathways. Hopeful people do this in advance, so they're well prepared.

3. *Developing a Sense of Agency.* The final part of Hope Theory is agency—or motivation. Successful people stay motivated by realizing that hope is an ongoing, dynamic process. If things don't work out, they don't beat up on themselves. They think of alternatives, ask for help, modify their pathways or change their goals when necessary, moving forward in their lives with energy and optimism.

People can renew their sense of agency by thinking of a past success in reaching a goal, asking, "What did I do then? How can I do something similar today?" They can also build agency through:

- Positive self-talk ("You can do it!"),
- Remembering past successes,
- Seeing problems as challenges,
- Staying balanced: getting enough sleep, as well as a healthy diet, and regular exercise,
- Remembering to laugh and not take themselves too seriously.

Dave is an engineer working in a Silicon Valley computer company. He fully admits that he can be too serious, obsessive, and take himself and others too seriously. Dave enjoys doing magic tricks, juggling, and telling jokes as a hobby. In fact, he periodically performs at children's birthday parties and even at several work parties and events. He especially enjoys juggling. He also sees juggling as a metaphor for life trying to keep many things going at once hoping that none fall down. He and his therapist use his hobby as a way to engage in positive self-talk, stay balanced, and see the humor in things. When stressed, he starts to juggle and does a card trick. These skills have helped him better manage both his work life and home life with several active teenagers and his spouse.

Helping people develop their own vital balance, the calling protocol draws upon their natural resources—their personal strengths and values—to help them find greater joy and purpose in life. The protocol is not pathology-focused so it is widely applicable and benefits a wide range of ages and populations. Used in therapy, spiritual direction, counseling, classes, or individual reflection, the protocol creates a powerful ripple effect, for discovering a sense of calling brings new possibilities, as well as greater meaning and vitality to people's lives. Finally, the calling protocol turns research in positive psychology into positive action, for as psychologists Martin Seligman and Christopher Peterson have affirmed, "The best therapists do not merely heal damage: they help people identify and build their strengths and their virtues."[17]

References

1. Wrzesniewski, A., McCauley, C., Rozin, P., & Schwartz, B. (1997). Jobs, careers, and calling: People's relations to their work. *Journal of Research in Personality*, *31*, 21–33.
2. Dreher, D.E. (in press). *Your Personal Renaissance*. New York: Marlowe. This book provides an extensive discussion of the Renaissance concept of calling, validation by research in positive psychology, personal exercises, and examples from Renaissance and contemporary lives.
3. Peterson, C. & Seligman, M.E.P. (2004). *Character Strengths and Virtues*. Washington, DC: American Psychological Association.
4. Hodges, T.D. & Clifton, D.O. (2004). Strengths-based development in practice. In P.A. Linley & S. Joseph (Eds.), *Positive Psychology in Practice*, pp. 256–268. Hoboken, NJ: Wiley.
5. Seligman, M.E.P. (2002). *Authentic Happiness*. New York: Simon & Schuster.
6. Seligman, M.E.P., Steen, T.A., Park, N., & Peterson, C. (2005). Positive psychology progress: Empirical validation of interventions. *American Psychologist*, *60*, 410–421; quote on p. 421.
7. Plante, T.G. (1996). Getting physical: Does exercise help in the treatment of psychiatric disorders? *Journal of Psychosocial Nursing*, *34*, 38–43.
8. Walsh, R. & Shapiro, S.L. (2006). The meeting of meditative disciplines and western psychology: A mutually enriching dialogue. *American Psychologist*, *61*, 227–239.
9. Easwaren, E. (1991). *Meditation*. Tomales, CA: Nilgiri Press.
10. Puhl, L.J. (Ed.) (1951). *The Spiritual Exercises of St. Ignatius*. Chicago, IL: Loyola Press.

11. Olin, J.C. (Ed.), (1992). *The Autobiography of St. Ignatius Loyola*. New York: Fordham University Press (translated by J.F. O'Callahan).
12. Neafsey, J.P. (2004). Psychological dimensions of the discernment of vocation. In J.C. Haughey (Ed.), *Revisiting the Ideal of Vocation*, pp. 163–195. Washington, DC: Catholic University of America Press. Quotes on pp. 168, 165.
13. Oman D. & Thoresen C.E. (2003). Spiritual modeling: A key to spiritual and religious growth? *International Journal for the Psychology of Religion, 13*, 149–165.
14. Cresswell, J.D., Welch, W.T., Taylor, S.E., Sherman, D.K., Gruenewald, T.L., & Mann, T. (2005). Affirmation of personal values buffers neuroendocrine and psychological stress responses. *Psychological Science, 16*, 846–851.
15. Snyder, C.R. (1994). *The Psychology of Hope*. New York: Simon & Schuster. All references to Hope Theory are from this book: an excellent source for building hope.
16. Feldman, D.B. Personal communication. October 2006.
17. Seligman, M.E.P. & Peterson, C. (2003). Positive clinical psychology. In L. G. Aspinwall & U. M. Staudinger (Eds.), *A Psychology of Human Strengths*, pp. 305–317. Washington, DC: American Psychological Association. Quote on 306.

PART 4

SPECIAL POPULATIONS

CHAPTER 10

Religion/Spirituality and Health in Adolescents

SIAN COTTON, DANIEL H. GROSSOEHME, AND JOEL TSEVAT

- *All eyes were fixed on NB, a 16-year-old African American girl, as she relayed her life story of eight foster placements, a series of abusive relationships, cutting her arms repeatedly, and being within inches of taking her own life in utter desperation. When the doctor asked, "How had she made it through these terrible times? How was she still getting up every day to face herself and her painful life once again?" She replied, steadfastly, "If I didn't have God . . . I wouldn't be here today."*

- *TJ was a 14-year-old boy who had been frequently hospitalized for treatment of a lymphoma. During his hospitalizations, his room lights were off throughout the day and he stared at the TV. He was a member of Jehovah's Witnesses, as was his mother, who was able to visit only on weekends. His father had not been a part of his life since the divorce 8 years ago. Having heard that TJ was being treated for his disease without much success, his father showed up at the hospital one day, and among other things, talked about his side of the family's Native American roots. The following Monday, TJ ordered burritos for lunch, asked a nurse to make him microwaved popcorn, and hung up an extra blanket between the counter and his bed. He invited several staff with whom he was close to sit with him on the floor and share in his "Native American" meal. TJ turned on the lights in his room and began to read during the day, especially about Native peoples. He learned about "smudging," a Native ritual in which one is surrounded in the smoke of burning sage incense and prayers are chanted for purification and cleansing from evil. TJ said he felt better after smudging, as if he was ready to "do battle" with the "bad blood cells" or face whatever tests he might have to go through.*

- *AP was a 17-year-old male "honor" student who had been very active in his Protestant congregation—a choir member and an usher. He was confirmed when he was 16 and now said, "Only one more year and I won't have to come anymore. That confirmation class where all we did was watch videos that told us what to believe … no discussion, and some of the other kids' behaviors—I didn't feel safe asking a serious question there. I believe in God, but I don't want anything to do with the Church anymore."*

There is growing evidence and acceptance of the link between religion/spirituality and health outcomes in adults,[1] yet comparatively less attention has been paid to those issues in adolescents. In this chapter, we address the relevance and importance of religion/spirituality in the lives of adolescents. We briefly review the scientific evidence linking religion/spirituality with adolescent health outcomes (health risk behaviors, mental heath, and physical health) and discuss possible explanatory pathways for those links. We review measurement issues and tools to assess spirituality in adolescents. Placing adolescents within the larger context of their families, their communities, and their developmental tasks, we describe the basics of spiritual development in adolescents. We close with a brief discussion of evidence-based real world applications that incorporate these findings into adolescent health promotion efforts. Future directions for this growing area of interest are highlighted. Given the limited data available on international and cross-cultural perspectives on adolescent religion/spirituality,[2] this chapter will focus primarily on findings relevant to American youth, ages 12–20.

Is Religion/Spirituality Relevant for Adolescents?

The stories above are but a few examples of the importance of religious and spiritual issues to today's adolescents. Recent studies show that an estimated 84–95 percent of American adolescents believe in God, 85–90 percent state that religion is important in their life, 93 percent believe God loves them, 67 percent believe in life after death, more than 50 percent attend religious services at least monthly, and close to half frequently pray alone and participate in religious youth groups.[3, 4] In addition, the majority report that their faith has helped them make major life decisions and that their relationship with God contributes to their sense of well-being, and many use their faith (sometimes referred to as "spiritual coping") to manage adverse events or trauma.[3, 5] On the other hand, 50 percent of teenagers do not attend religious services and are not involved with a religious youth group;[3] moreover, those who are involved are often unsure what role faith actually plays in their lives. In a national study of more than 3,000 teenagers, Smith and colleagues state that "religion seems very much a part of the lives of many U.S. teenagers, but for most of them it is in ways that seem quite unfocused, implicit, in the background, just part of the furniture" (p. 262).[3] Nevertheless, religion/spirituality is important to many teens, appears to be linked to positive health outcomes (see subsection below), and is the subject of much scholarly work.[2, 3, 5-7]

Some might pause here and say, well religion/spirituality may be important to adolescents, but in what way does that influence their health? And what do we mean when we say adolescent "spirituality" anyway?

Definition of Terms

Similar to the adult literature on religion and health, disagreements exist within the scientific community over how to define "spirituality."[1, 8] Experts do agree that religion/spirituality is a complex and multidimensional construct—incorporating attitudes, behaviors, and beliefs related to faith and how it operates in one's life. The terms most often used in the scientific literature on religion/spirituality are "religiosity" and "spirituality." Religiosity is the formal, institutional, and outward expression of the sacred as often measured by importance of religion, belief in God, frequency of religious service attendance, frequency of prayer, and/or frequency of meditation. Spirituality (from the Latin word "*spirare*," meaning "to breathe") is the internal, personal, and emotional expression of the sacred and is measured by spiritual well-being, peace and comfort derived from faith, spiritual connectedness, or the use of spiritual coping.[1] Some suggest that spirituality is the broader construct; it may incorporate formal religion, but it may also incorporate other broader avenues through which adolescents might seek "transcendence" (going beyond the limits of oneself), such as through nature or the arts. Others argue against the "bifurcation" of the terms "religious" versus "spiritual."

Whether adolescents consider themselves to be "spiritual" as opposed to "religious" is less an issue for adolescents—but rather seems to be more of an academic issue. This is true at least for American adolescents; international data appear to support the dichotomy (i.e., the "yes, spiritual but not religious").[2, 3] Contrary to popular views, it seems that most American teenagers identify with formal religious traditions rather than seeking spirituality via other modalities.[3] So, while we mostly use the term "spirituality" in this chapter, we describe research on religiosity and spirituality, an academic bifurcation that does not appear to resonate with most American teenagers.

What Is the Scientific Evidence Linking Religiosity/Spirituality with Adolescent Health Outcomes?

The evidence over the last two decades or so of research in this regard is fairly conclusive: in general, adolescents who have higher levels of religiosity and/or spirituality fare better than their less religious or spiritual peers: those with higher levels of religiosity and/or spirituality have lower rates of risky health behaviors and fewer mental health problems—even when taking into account other factors that may affect health outcomes such as age, sex, or family income. While the association between religion/spirituality and health in adolescents is fairly small-moderate, it is nevertheless consistent across many studies, as summarized in several reviews.[5-7] The overwhelming majority of research has focused on religion/spirituality in relation to risky health behaviors, with less research on relationships with mental health (e.g., trauma), physical health (e.g., chronic illness such as asthma), or health-promoting behaviors (e.g., exercise or healthy diet).

Health Risk Behaviors

Engaging in risky behaviors, including risky sexual behaviors, violent behaviors, and substance use, is the leading cause of adolescent morbidity and mortality nationwide.[9] Religion/spirituality is but one of a wide variety of factors (including family factors and quality of peer relationships) that have been associated with lower rates of risky behaviors in adolescents. Overall, levels of religiosity and/or spirituality are inversely related to rates of substance use (hard drug use and alcohol), risky sexual activity (early sexual initiation, multiple sexual partners), and delinquency in adolescents.[5-7] These findings are consistent across ethnic/racial groups (though data in non-Caucasian population are scant) and age spans (e.g., 7th–12th graders), and are usually more consistent among adolescent girls than boys.[7] Regarding healthy behaviors, higher rates of church attendance among adolescents are related to health-promoting behaviors such as healthier diet, exercise, sleep, and seatbelt use.[10]

Mental Health

Rates of mental health problems, especially depression, continue to be alarmingly high among adolescents: suicide is the third leading cause of death in adolescents ages 15 to 19.[9] Mental health problems such as depression or anxiety are associated with poorer performance in school, poorer quality of life, less social interaction, and higher suicide rates in adolescents.[9] Most previous studies have focused on depression and anxiety vis-à-vis church attendance and importance of religion, finding that religiosity and/or spirituality are inversely related to levels of depression, anxiety, hopelessness, and self-esteem.[5-7, 11] Preliminary evidence suggests that the meaning/purpose facets of spirituality and the institutional aspects of religion/spirituality (involvement in a religious community) have perhaps the most robust relationships with mental health.[11] Conversely, some studies have indicated possible negative effects of religion/spirituality on adolescent mental health. For example, although certain aspects of religion/spirituality (e.g., personal commitment to core spiritual beliefs) are related to lower rates of suicidal ideation, other aspects, such as negative interpersonal religious experience, have been linked to depressive symptoms, possibly from negative personal experiences with religious congregations.[12]

Physical Health

A third area of lesser focus has been the role of religion/spirituality in relation to physical health outcomes, specifically for adolescents with potentially life-threatening illness (e.g., cancer) or with chronic conditions requiring strict adherence to medical regimens (e.g., asthma). The very limited number of studies in this area (as compared with the many studies of adults with cancer or HIV/AIDS) are primarily descriptive (or have very small sample sizes) and suggest that adolescents with physical illnesses may have heightened spiritual concerns.[7] Preliminary evidence suggests that adolescents may utilize spiritual coping in ways similar to those used by adults, for example, by creating meaning and social support through the crisis of the illness. However, much work remains to be done in this area. For example, do adolescents use more or fewer spiritual coping strategies (e.g., prayer) to manage their illness in comparison with say, use of cognitive strategies? Oman and Thoresen (2006)[2] call for additional research on how religion/spirituality impacts major morbidity and mortality in adolescents with diseases such as obesity, asthma, or diabetes.

How Might Spirituality Be Related to Health in Adolescents?

Hypotheses abound regarding how spirituality may influence health in adolescents, and some hypotheses are beginning to be formally tested in adolescents. For example, perhaps teenagers who attend religious services have greater levels of social support than those who do not attend services—and thus it could be the social support per se that contributes to better health outcomes (an indirect effect of religion/spirituality). Alternatively, perhaps teenagers who are more religious and/or more spiritual have a greater sense of meaning and purpose in their lives through their faith, which in turn (again maybe indirectly) leads to better mental health outcomes and fewer risky behaviors. Scholars have hypothesized other direct and indirect possi-ble mechanisms, including: (1) health beliefs/practices associated with many religions; (2) psychosocial resources/psychological factors (e.g., self-esteem); or (3) religious/spiritual coping (e.g., prayer).[2, 13] Those mechanisms could also be synergistic, such that adolescents might have positive role models through their local or national religious organizations, plus utilize spiritual coping (e.g., prayer) to cope with stressors.

Religious/Spiritual Coping

Religious/spiritual coping, that is, using religion/spirituality to deal with life stressors, has been associated with physical and psychological out-comes in adults.[14] Relatively little is known about the effectiveness of religious/spiritual coping in adolescents. Mahoney and colleagues (2006) reviewed the available empirical research and concluded that "given the well-established power of religious coping for adults, far more attention should be devoted to this topic in the lives of youth" (p. 352).[2] The authors recommend that future research address both positive and negative effects of religious coping, focus on refining and evaluating psychometrically sound measurement tools, incorporate family based religious coping, assess the uniqueness of religious versus secular coping processes on outcomes, and develop theoretical models of the use of religious coping by adolescents.[2]

Unfortunately, very few hypothesized mechanisms, including religious/spiritual coping, have been formally tested. As studies begin to tease out more of the actual effects of spirituality on health,[15] the resultant information can be used to inform adolescent health promotion interventions. For example, if gaining meaning/purpose directly improves certain health outcomes (e.g., lowers rates of depressive symptoms or risky behaviors), one could develop health promotion programs that, in addition to targeting negative behaviors, could also foster spiritual well-being (e.g., through meaning-making).

What About the Possible Negative Influences of Religion/Spirituality on Health in Adolescents?

Though the majority of research findings support a salutary, constructive role of faith in adolescents' lives, religion/spirituality may also play a neg-ative role for adolescents. Some studies have shown that highly religious but sexually active teenagers are actually less likely to use contraception, placing them at greater risk for unintended pregnancy or perhaps sexually transmitted diseases.[16] Other teenagers who feel judged or criticized by their religious communities have higher rates of depression.[12] Given the negative health outcomes associated with "spiritual struggles" (e.g., anger at God or perceived punishment from God) among adults,[14] attention to those issues in adolescents is vital. For example, a gay/lesbian/bisexual/transgender adolescent may be at risk for feeling ostracized by her/his religious community, or a teenager might feel caught between what her/his religion teaches regarding appropriate sexual behavior versus what her/his peer group advocates (e.g., premarital sexual intercourse).

Do Good Research and Clinical Tools to Assess Adolescent Spirituality Exist?

In short, the answer is no. Currently, no gold standard research measure of adolescent spirituality exists. Measures used in the past were typically: (1) not responsive to developmental changes in adolescents; (2) adult-focused in language and content; (3) unidimensional; and/or (4) developed for one particular study (and not generalizable). Large national adolescent health surveys utilize standard religiosity items such as importance of religion or church attendance, but such items are, as we have mentioned, limited in scope because they only assess a single dimension. Furthermore, all too often, religion/spirituality is studied as a demographic variable (similar to age or sex) rather than as the primary variable of interest. Time and money would be well spent developing and validating assessment tools to examine a variety of religious/spiritual factors in adolescents (e.g., a developmentally appropriate spiritual coping measure or a measure of adolescent spiritual well-being).

Spiritual Screening versus Spiritual Assessment

Although "spiritual screening" or "spiritual assessment" may conjure images of research, in a professional or healing relationship, the purpose of spiritual screening of the adolescent is to develop an appropriate plan of care. Spiritual screening comprises a relatively short list of questions. One such screening tool is the FICA:[17]

- F (faith): What is your faith tradition?
- I (important): How important is your faith to you?
- C (church): What is your church or community of faith?
- A (address): How would you like me to address these issues in your healthcare?

Once the treating clinician adjusts the questions to be age-appropriate for the adolescent (e.g., one might not say "apply to your health" for a 12-year-old, but rather use more specific and concrete language), a simple tool like this can be used in a wide variety of professional settings (e.g., youth group settings, hospitals, and juvenile detention facilities). Another screening tool, the Child/Adolescent Spiritual Screening Tool (CASST), developed by Grossoehme (in press), screens for a balance between an adolescent's spiritual resources and needs; those whose needs exceed their resources are presumed to be at risk for adverse health outcomes and therefore in need of an appropriate health intervention.[18] Performing spiritual screening in any therapeutic, medical, or religious setting is important so as not to "miss" those who have substantial needs, which, if unresolved, might be associated with poorer health outcomes. Spiritual assessments, on the other hand, are generally more formal, written means used for gaining very specific information about a person's religious/spiritual experiences, particular beliefs, or practices. They are generally used to develop a plan of care (by a chaplain or some mental health professional) during a hospitalization, or a long-term outpatient program (such as a substance abuse recovery program).

What Is Unique Developmentally and Contextually About Adolescent Spirituality?

Adolescents live within the context of their families, communities, schools, and peers—all of which exert great influence on the developing adolescent whose many tasks include establishing an identity across multiple domains (e.g., social, vocational, sexual, or spiritual). Regarding parental influence on adolescent's religiosity, consider these findings from the National Study on Youth and Religion:[3] (1) the majority of adolescents are similar to their parents when it comes to identifying with a specific religious tradition; (2) six in ten adolescents say they would still attend religious services regularly if it was entirely up to them; and (3) the importance of faith for adolescents is fairly closely related to the importance of faith for their parents. Smith concludes that "the single most important social influence on the religious and spiritual lives of adolescents is (still) their parents" (p. 261).[3]

Although adolescent researchers often examine developmental issues in part by examining differences among adolescents in their younger, middle, or later years, very few studies on religion/spirituality have looked at differences by age (or other developmental dimensions). For example, no studies to date have examined developmental patterns in the use of religious coping, differences one might expect to find because of differences in cognitive development (e.g., development of abstract thinking).

Spiritual Development

Fowler describes the faith development of adolescents along sequential age/developmental trajectories—with faith being "the dynamic pattern which makes life meaningful to us" (p. 3).[19] In the "mythic-literal,"[19] phase of development, younger adolescents are generally quite concrete, using stories told in their religious communities or stories told about nature or meaning as their primary source of spiritual identity. Their spirituality assures them that the world is just and fair; for those who are religious, God is scrupulously fair—perhaps like their parents, only perfectly good. It is possible to have a relationship with something greater than themselves at this developmental stage. Faith takes on a unified quality as one's personal story begins to merge with their awareness of a larger environment. The adolescent's understanding of this "something greater" frequently develops from a more general, global "force" to an actual person, or a being, endowed with a personality that can feel and express love, anger, or sadness—typically projections based on experiences in actual relationships. Religious adolescents may refer to this person as God, Allah, the goddess, or other names. As they mature, adolescents realize that there is more to life than "fairness," and that sometimes in life, things that are not fair, just, or moral happen. This realization signifies the transition into the next stage of faith development: "synthetic-conventional." Abstract thinking develops, and with it, the ability to reflect on stories they have heard. Sometimes taking the form of "adolescent rebellion," adolescents often deconstruct what they have been taught about the meaning of life or religious/spiritual issues, and search for answers to their questions.

Developing a sense of identity is paramount in all aspects of teenagers' lives, including their spiritual lives. Lacking a fully formed identity, they look for, and depend on, feedback cues from others to tell them who they are. The "group think" mentality helps create a spiritual identity built around relationships with others who believe in the same way. Exploratory questions such as, "How are you and God doing?" or "So how's your relationship with God these days?" make sense with this age group and can serve as a "spring-board" into deeper discussion of their spiritual lives. Encouraging adolescents to engage in activities such as writing letters to God, or keeping a journal about their questions and ideas about the Divine, can also be useful ways to engage the adolescent in a substantive discussion of their beliefs and their meaning about their faith.

How Do We Practically Apply These Findings to Improve Adolescent Health Outcomes?

As scientific evidence mounts that spirituality is related to better adolescent health outcomes along a variety of dimensions, the question becomes: How can these findings translate into real world interventions to improve the health of today's youth? The ultimate question really is: How do we bridge the divide between (1) clinicians/practitioners (educators, youth group leaders, teachers, social workers, therapists, and medical professionals) working in the trenches with today's youth; and (2) academics writing about developmental theory and spiritual factors related to health, in order to improve the well-being of adolescents?[2]

A few spiritual interventions have been tried in adults. For example, adult studies have examined meditation retreats to reduce stress, church-based yoga classes to enhance well-being, and mantram repetition to aid with focus and attention in the bustle of daily living (see other chapters in this book). Other than some anecdotes and a few sporadic studies, however, we know very little about the effectiveness of those (or other) types of spiritually based programs with regard to adolescent health issues such as mental health, risk behaviors, or coping with chronic physical illness. A few studies of spiritually based interventions for adolescents have been reported. For example, a retrospective study of 583 adolescents in a residential program for juvenile delinquents found an association between partaking in chaplain-led spiritual/religious activities and being in a less restrictive environment 1 year after discharge, a finding that was independent of age and length of stay in treatment.[20]

Some examples of spiritual interventions one might test in adolescents include (1) a mindfulness meditation group to reduce stress or to treat attention deficit hyperactivity disorder (offered, in say, a school, a community health setting, or a psychiatric inpatient facility); (2) a 4-session (or probably longer) chaplain-based intervention at a juvenile delinquency facility to decrease recidivism; (3) meaning-based psychotherapy (group or individual treatment) for illness/traumatic experiences; (4) spiritually oriented psychotherapy that emphasizes the role of spiritual development and reframes "obstacles" as opportunities for spiritual growth; (5) religious or spiritual imagery in anger management programs for at-risk teens; and (6) depression educational or screening programs based in churches/temples.

The gap between science and practice is not unusual and will require multiple proactive perspective shifts and systems-approach thinking to overcome. At our own institution, we formed a multidisciplinary Spirituality-Health Special Interest Group, which meets quarterly in an effort to foster academic-community partnerships for health promotion efforts. Typically, we have about fifteen participants representing medicine, nursing, clinical psychology, sociology, lay ministry, pastoral care, and even data management. At our meetings, we present ideas for clinical programs and research related to spirituality and health. These sorts of partnerships are but one example of ways to bridge the academic-community gap in an effort to advance the field and to translate research findings into actual practice.

Where Do We Go From Here?

The future of developing, evaluating, and implementing spiritually-based adolescent health promotion programs depends in large part on addressing key methodological issues. Listed below are ten promising areas to consider:

1. *Test mediating pathways of effect.* A critical next step is to understand the potential mediating pathways through which religion/spirituality influences adolescent health. By using more advanced statistical techniques (e.g., structural equation modeling), one can test how, and in which particular subpopulations, religion/spirituality influences health. Possible pathways might include: (1) communicated values regarding appropriateness of health behaviors as taught in one's religious congregation; (2) meaning/purpose in life; and (3) social support. A clearer understanding of how such pathways operate will provide critical information for developing effective interventions.

2. *Use longitudinal designs.* Most studies to date have assessed relationships at one point in time (cross-sectional), making it difficult to assess causation in observed relationships, or to take into account potential developmental influences—particularly vital in understanding adolescent health. For example, does (and how does) the use of religion/spirituality shape decisions regarding health risk behaviors more strongly or more weakly as an adolescent ages? Developmental and temporal information gained from using longitudinal designs could be incorporated into age-specific interventions to thwart negative behaviors and promote health.

3. *Include diverse samples.* The majority of past research with adolescents, in relation to both religiosity and spirituality has involved Caucasian—primarily Judeo-Christian—samples. With the growing diversity of the U.S. population, studies should include adolescents of various faiths and ethnic groups. For example, although African American teenagers have been shown to be more religious than their Caucasian counterparts and religion is particularly important to African Americans during times of stress, few studies have focused on how religion/spirituality relates to health outcomes for African American adolescents.

4. *Develop and use psychometrically sound measures of adolescent religion/spirituality.* Measures used in the past are typically (1) not responsive to developmental change in adolescents, and (2) adult-focused in language and content. Given the complex multidimensional nature of religiosity and spirituality, measures should attempt to assess various dimensions to examine attitudes, beliefs, behaviors, and function.

5. *Examine potential negative influences of religion/spirituality.* Although most research supports a salutary relationship between religion/spirituality and health, religion/spirituality could have a negative influence. Such negative religious influences may be particularly salient

for teenagers who may already be vulnerable due to social ostracism (e.g., gay or bisexual teens), peer pressure, or a feeling of being singled out or punished.

6. *Develop and test spiritually based interventions.* The field will only make progress by testing hypotheses. Federally funded research to examine meaning-based psychotherapy for terminally ill patients and mantram repetition for reducing stress and improving well-being has been carried out in adults. Given the dearth of the scientific evidence in adolescents, the field would benefit from pilot studies and feasibility studies of spiritually based interventions in adolescents.

7. *Incorporate qualitative methods* (interviews or focus groups as opposed to surveys with structured questions). Using qualitative study designs to complement and inform quantitative measures designed specifically for teenagers would be invaluable for furthering the field. Previous studies using quantitative methods exclusively have neglected key information about adolescent spirituality (e.g., by assuming that all teenagers are "religious," when some might actually consider themselves as "spiritual" but not "religious").

8. *Determine adolescents' preferences for incorporating spirituality in their healthcare.* Adult studies have shown that many patients want their care providers to ask about faith during a health encounter, but we lack such information on adolescents. Studies asking adolescents questions such as, "Do you want your healthcare provider to ask you about your religious/spiritual beliefs and how they impact your health?" or "Would you be interested in joining a spiritually based support group (e.g., meditation group) to help cope with your illness?" would be helpful.

9. *Create multidisciplinary networks.* Addressing spirituality and health effectively will require collaborative efforts from a variety of persons/disciplines. Imagine a team comprised of an adolescent psychologist, a chaplain, a physician, a nurse, a community youth group leader, an adolescent patient, and a parent—all providing input on a proposed health promotion program incorporating spiritual principles.

10. *Learn from the adult religion-health literature.* Those methodological advances that have been reported in the adult literature could take a long time to trickle into research on adolescent health—if they ever make it. Valuable lessons from adults about measuring religiosity/spirituality, implementing spiritually based interventions, and incorporating religion/spirituality into the medical setting with adults— if reinterpreted and reframed within a developmental context—could hold much promise for adolescents.

Final Thoughts

Religion/spirituality plays a role in adolescent health. Many interesting questions remain though, such as what role do adolescents themselves see religion/spirituality playing in their health; how to incorporate findings from adolescents into evidence-based programs; and how to incorporate findings from adult studies to inform programmatic efforts with teenagers. With the development of more sophisticated measures and study designs, researchers should be able to better understand how religion/spirituality actually operates to affect adolescent health and well-being and thus to design appropriate interventions. Interdisciplinary approaches that actively work to break down the academic-community gap can help translate advances in spirituality-health science to improve adolescent health outcomes.

References

1. Koenig, H.G., McCullough, M.E., & Larson, D.B. (Eds.), (2001). *Handbook of religion and health*. New York: Oxford University Press.
2. Roehlkepartain, E., King, P., Wagener, L., & Benson P. (Eds.), (2005). *The handbook of spiritual development in childhood and adolescence*. Thousand Oaks, CA: Sage Publications.
3. Smith, C. & Lundquist-Denton, M. (2005). *Soul searching: The religious and spiritual lives of American teenagers*. New York: Oxford University Press.
4. Gallup, G.J. & Bezilla. (1992). *The religious lives of young Americans*. Princeton, NJ: The George H. Gallup International Institute.
5. Bridges, L.J. & Moore, K.A. (2002). *Religion and spirituality in childhood and adolescence*. Washington, DC: Child Trends.
6. Benson, P.L., Donahue, M.J., & Erickson J A. (1989). Adolescence and religion: A review of the literature trom 1970 to 1986. *Research in the social scientific study of religion: A research annual*, Vol. 1., 153–181.
7. Cotton, S., Zebracki, K., Rosenthal, S.L., Tsevat, J., & Drotar, D. (2006). Religion/spirituality and adolescent health outcomes: a review. *Journal of Adolescent Health*, 38, 4, 472–480.
8. Hill, P.C. & Pargament, K.I. (2003). Advances in the conceptualization and measurement of religion and spirituality: Implications for physical and mental health research. *American Psychologist*, 581, 64–74.
9. Centers for Disease Control and Prevention (2006). *Department of Health and Human Services*. Accessed on November 27, 2006, http://www.cdc.gov.
10. Jessor, R., Turbin, M.S., & Costa, F.M. (1998). Protective factors in adolescent health behavior. *Journal of Personality and Social Psychology*, 75, 3, 788–800.
11. Wong, Y.J., Rew, L., & Slaikeu, K.D. (2006). A systematic review of recent research on adolescent religiosity/spirituality and mental health. *Issues of Mental Health Nursing*, 27, 2, 161–183.

12. Pearce, M.J., Little, T.D., & Perez, J.E. (2003). Religiousness and depressive symptoms among adolescents. *Journal of Clinical Child & Adolescent Psychology*, *32*, 2, 267–276.
13. George, L.K., Ellison, C.G., & Larson, D.B. (2002). Explaining the relationships between religious involvement and health. *Psychological Inquiry*, *13*, 3, 190–200.
14. Pargament, K.I., Koenig, H.G., Tarakeshwar, N., & Hahn J. (2004). Religious coping methods as predictors of psychological, physical and spiritual outcomes among medically ill elderly patients: A two-year longitudinal study. *Journal of Health Psychology*, *9*, 6, 713–730.
15. Regnerus, M.D. (2003). Linked lives, faith, and behavior: Intergenerational religious influence on adolescent delinquency. *Journal for the Scientific Study of Religion*, *42*, 2, 189–203.
16. Studer, M. & Thornton, A. (1987). Adolescent religiosity and contraceptive usage. *Journal of Marriage & the Family*, *49*, 1, 117–128.
17. Pulchalski, C. & Rommer, A.L. (2001). Taking a spiritual history allows clinicians to understand patients more fully. *Journal of Palliative Medicine*, *3*, 1, 129–137.
18. Grossoehme, D.H. (in press). Developing a spiritual screening tool for hospitalized children's and adolescents' spiritual needs and resources. Doctor of Ministry Project 2006; Louisville Presbyterian Theological Seminary.
19. Fowler, J.W. (1981). *Stages of faith: the psychology of human development and the quest for meaning* (1st ed). San Francisco, CA: Harper & Row.
20. Hausmann, E. (2004). Chaplain contacts improve treatment outcomes in residential treatment programs for delinquent adolescents. *Journal of Pastoral Care and Counseling*, *58*, 3, 215–224.

CHAPTER 11

Spirituality and Cancer

ALLEN C. SHERMAN AND STEPHANIE SIMONTON

Cancer can have a daunting impact on multiple spheres of functioning, disrupting an individual's physical status, emotional well-being, and personal relationships. Patients may grapple with depleting treatment toxicities and existential concerns. For many, religious and spiritual (R/S) practices are a central resource. In the last few years researchers have focused growing attention on R/S factors in the oncology setting, seeking to explore some of the ways in which patients draw on spiritual resources, and whether these beliefs and practices influence health outcomes. In this chapter, we examine both helpful and detrimental facets of religiousness and spirituality at different phases of illness, ranging from early detection through advanced disease. Is R/S involvement associated with cancer screening practices among healthy individuals? For those who have been diagnosed with a malignancy, does R/S engagement color treatment decisions, enhance adjustment, or bolster quality-of-life? Do these relationships differ for individuals with early versus advanced disease? If faith does play a role, through what pathways does it influence these outcomes? Can these elements be incorporated into clinical services?

Definitional issues have been addressed at length in earlier sections of this volume (see Chapter 1). Cancer researchers have examined a number of different aspects of religiousness and spirituality, which seem to fall roughly into three broad domains. The first focuses on religiousness and spirituality as a *general orienting system*, a framework that organizes one's experiences and provides direction for living.[1, 2] Commonly used measures such as strength of religious faith, spiritual salience, and private or public religious activities might be considered in part as reflections of an individual's R/S orienting system. Other investigators have focused more specifically on

R/S coping. That is, how do individuals turn toward their faith in response to medical crisis—what particular strategies are marshaled to manage these demands (e.g., praying for strength, drawing assistance from the congregation, seeking meaning in misfortune?).[3–5] Finally, other researchers have explored *R/S outcomes*—the quality of one's religious/spiritual life in the aftermath of major upheaval. Most attention in this area has focused on spiritual well-being (e.g., experiences of harmony or meaning), but other constructs such as alterations in spiritual strivings,[6, 7] doubts, or posttraumatic growth[8] may be relevant as well.

Cancer Prevention and Screening

Health Behaviors

Cancer prevention and early detection are critical national priorities. Thus, one area of keen interest concerns whether religiousness might influence vulnerability to cancer, particularly in view of the relevance of lifestyle factors in contributing to this disease. Religious involvement has been tied to a number of important health behaviors that lower risk for cancer. Early epidemiological studies focused on denominational differences, noting lower rates of smoking, alcohol use, and other risky practices among religious groups that strictly proscribe such behaviors (e.g., Mormons, Seventh Day Adventists). More recent studies have demonstrated that greater attendance at religious services is tied to lower rates of smoking and alcohol use, and greater improvement over time for those who initially report poor health practices.[8, 9] On the other hand, findings regarding some other relevant health behaviors, such as obesity[10] and physical exercise,[9] have been more mixed and complex. For example, in a national survey that followed participants for 8 years, women who spent more time with religious media (e.g., religious TV or radio) were more likely to become obese over the course of the study, while conversely women who attended services more often or men who sought spiritual comfort to cope with difficulties were less likely to become obese.[10]

Screening Practices

Religious involvement may also have an impact on cancer screening practices. This line of inquiry is given added impetus by findings that stronger religious orientation is associated with use of other beneficial healthcare services, such as routine medical visits, dental exams,[8] and flu shots.[11] Cancer screening is a particularly important target for health professionals because early detection is tied to reduced disease severity and more successful treatment. Thus, a number of investigations have begun to focus on this area. In several national studies, women who attended religious services more often reported increased mammography screening compared with their less observant peers, after controlling for other important factors (e.g., socioeconomic status, age, and health insurance).[12, 13] Attendance at services also was tied to greater use of pap smears among middle-aged women,[12] and among subgroups of lower-income African American women who were uninsured or more ill.[14] Similarly, religious salience (i.e., the personal importance of religion) and religious affiliation (i.e., belonging to a religious group) were related to improved prostate screening.[11] Interestingly, relationships between religiousness and screening were not linear in some studies (beyond a certain threshold, the very highest levels of religious involvement were not always tied to further improvements in screening),[12, 13] and not all investigations found beneficial associations for particular practices.[14] Overall, however, evidence suggests a salutary connection between religiousness and screening for some individuals. Additional longitudinal studies (in which sustained adherence is examined over time) are needed to strengthen conclusions, and to clarify which R/S dimensions are important for which screening practices in which populations.

In what ways might religiousness be helpful? Knowing that a woman attends services often does not help us much in understanding why she undergoes screening mammography. Thus, investigators have begun to explore the impact of more specific religious beliefs, such as the sanctity of the body or religious injunctions to maintain good health.[13] In a study of women in rural North Carolina, the conviction that God works through health professionals to cure cancer (as opposed to healing independently from them) was associated with higher rates of mammography.[15] Additional factors that merit further exploration include some of the social resources that religiousness might confer, such as help from the congregation regarding awareness of guidelines, motivation to undergo screening, or transportation to an appointment.

Treatment Decisions

Once individuals have developed this harrowing disease, do R/S factors shape the types of medical decisions that they make? Does faith influence their choices about treatment options, participation in research trials, or end-of-life care? As yet, few studies have touched on these questions,[16–18] but we can find indications of distancing from as well as embracing medical care.

One area of major concern involves avoidance or delay in seeking treatment, resulting in more advanced, intractable disease—a problem that may be especially pronounced (though by no means limited to) underserved minority groups. Among women with breast cancer for example, African

Americans are more likely to be diagnosed with advanced stage tumors and have higher mortality rates than white women, even though their incidence of the disease is lower. These findings are not entirely explained by ethnic disparities in economic resources or screening practices, and appear to be influenced in part by culturally and religiously embedded beliefs about medical treatment.[15] One series of investigations examined whether delay in seeking treatment was related to beliefs about God's role in healing, among rural Southern women. Community residents who believed that God would cure them without medical treatment were more likely to indicate that they would delay pursuing care if they detected a breast lump[15]; moreover, breast cancer patients who held this belief were more likely to have been diagnosed with advanced rather than early-stage disease.[19] These fundamentalist beliefs were endorsed by only a minority of participants but were more common among African American women. Thus, particular types of religious beliefs may be among the broader tapestry of sociocultural factors (e.g., folk beliefs about tumors, fatalism), economic impediments (e.g., access to mammography, health insurance) and medical variables (e.g., physician recommendations, biological characteristics of the tumor) that influence mortality risk among rural African American women.

Disinclination to pursue health services was illustrated in another study as well, which focused on genetic testing among predominantly well-educated Caucasian women.[20] Breast cancer patients were offered free genetic testing if they were identified as being at high risk for the hereditary form of the disease. More religious/spiritual women were less likely than their peers to undergo testing, particularly if they also perceived themselves to be at low risk for recurrence of the disease. (Women who believed they were at *high* risk for a return of the illness were likely to pursue testing regardless of their religiousness.)

Other investigators have begun to explore religious responses to care at the end of life rather than during earlier phases of diagnosis and treatment (see Chapter 12 for a more extensive discussion). End-of-life care has become a topic of considerable concern in both medical and public discourse, as reflected most poignantly in the recent Terri Schiavo case. When curative treatment strategies fail, patients and families face wrenching decisions about what kind of care to pursue. Several clinical and epidemiological studies suggest that religious individuals are more apt to desire ongoing life-preserving treatment compared with less religious participants. Although most research has not focused specifically on oncology patients, a recent study of individuals with advanced cancer inquired what kind of life-sustaining treatments participants would want if they were near death.[18] Several facets of religiousness/spirituality were tied to stronger preferences for life-extending care. Specifically, those who used spirituality to cope with their illness were more likely to desire hospitalization (rather than home care) if they entered a terminal phase, and those who believed in divine intervention or who turned to a higher power for support were more likely to want cardiopulmonary resuscitation (CPR), after controlling for ethnic differences. These results seem consistent with findings from studies conducted outside the oncology setting. For example, in a national survey of healthy adults, more frequent religious attendance was associated with greater opposition to "terminal palliative care" (i.e., pain relief at the end of life that might inadvertently shorten survival), as well as stronger opposition to physician-assisted suicide.[21] Of course, religious groups vary in their doctrinal positions regarding end-of-life care, and thus perhaps it is not surprising that surveys have sometimes uncovered denominational differences as well (e.g., Catholics or Conservative Protestants versus moderate Protestants), but these findings have not been consistent.[21]

As research continues to explore the interface between medical decision-making and religion, it will be helpful to assess an array of critical decisions at various phases of illness, such as pursuit of active therapy versus watchful waiting, participation in clinical trials,[16] preparation of advanced directives,[18] and enrollment in hospice. Important R/S beliefs might include, among others, those focusing on the immanence of a personal God in healing illness, the sanctity of the body, divine versus human control over the end of life, and the relative value ascribed to minimizing suffering/maximizing quality-of-life versus preserving the preciousness of life.

General R/S Orientation and Adjustment to Cancer

A more active area of research has explored the role of R/S factors in shaping adjustment to cancer or quality-of-life (QOL). Most individuals regard religion or spirituality as an important resource as they confront the myriad burdens of illness.[22–24] Does a patient's R/S orientation (e.g., depth of faith, intrinsic religiousness, or private spiritual practices) have any bearing on particular health outcomes (e.g., emotional well-being, physical symptoms)?

Some investigations have focused on patients with *early stage disease*. In a study of Croatian breast cancer patients with predominantly localized disease, for example, stronger religious faith was associated with lower rates of clinical depression.[25] Among Israeli patients with malignant melanoma (skin cancer), stronger religious beliefs/practices were tied to lower levels of distress and more active cognitive coping responses, after accounting for demographic and disease variables.[26] Religiousness was not related to QOL or stress symptoms.

Other investigations involved patients with *advanced or terminal disease*. Among women with predominantly advanced ovarian cancer, stronger R/S involvement was tied to improved emotional and functional well-being, fewer disease-specific concerns, and more favorable overall QOL, after accounting for demographic and disease variables.[27] In a study of terminally ill patients, belief in an afterlife was associated with less despairing reactions to the end of life (i.e., less hopelessness, desire for death, and suicidal ideation), though it was unrelated to broader aspects of distress.[28]

Other investigations included more *heterogeneous samples* of patients who varied widely in disease severity and time since diagnosis. Increased prayer was associated with better psychological well-being among patients with diverse stages of breast cancer[29] and lung cancer,[30] while greater meaning in life was tied to better physical as well as psychological well-being in these studies. Greater faith or intrinsic religiousness was tied to higher levels of hope[31–32] and life satisfaction,[23] and sometimes lower emotional distress[31] in studies that included patients with various malignancies.

While most patients in these studies were receiving or had recently completed active treatment, other investigations focused on *cancer survivors* who were several years removed from diagnosis. Among long-term survivors of breast cancer, spiritual salience was associated with better QOL and diminished distress, after controlling for a number of medical and demographic covariates,[33] while a stronger spiritual perspective was tied to increased hope and sense of coherence.[34] On the other hand, in a small study of prostate cancer survivors, Gall[4] noted poorer role functioning, social functioning, and emotional functioning among those who attributed their disease to God's anger.

In the aggregate, these research efforts suggest that general religious orientation may be tied to several dimensions of adjustment. Favorable outcomes have been noted at both early and advanced stages of disease. Notably, however, a number of studies have not found significant results.[5, 35–37] Moreover, among those investigations that have uncovered meaningful relationships with R/S orientation, the particular outcomes that have emerged vary across studies. Evidence seems strongest regarding personal resources (e.g., trait hope, optimism) and coping strategies (e.g., active engagement), while findings regarding other endpoints (e.g., emotional distress) are more mixed. More recent investigations are generally characterized by greater methodological rigor than older ones, as one would expect in a new field, but many studies in the existing database have notable limitations. Almost all studies have relied on cross-sectional research designs, in which participants are assessed at a single point in time; this approach offers little guidance about temporal or causal relationships. Additional problems, particularly in earlier investigations, include small samples; missing information about medical characteristics; reliance on heterogeneous samples that mix together patients with different malignancies and phases of treatment; and lack of controls for important demographic or medical factors.

To the extent that general R/S orientation has a salutatory effect on health outcomes for some patients, what pathways or mechanisms might help explain these relationships? As an orienting system that helps interpret and guide one's experiences, religiousness/spirituality may enhance a sense of meaning or control during a period of painful uncertainty, activate personal resources and coping responses, and provide comfort and reassurance. Additionally, it may offer access to support from the religious community and from inspirational role models (past or present). Some of these connections have been explored in interesting qualitative studies with cancer patients, but investigators are only beginning to test explanatory models more rigorously. Initial results suggest that coping strategies (e.g., active engagement with the challenges of illness),[27] as well as personal resources such as optimism,[38] hope,[34] and meaning,[39] may be among the pathways through which R/S factors influence health outcomes.

Religious/Spiritual Coping and Adjustment to Cancer

Another important line of investigation has explored R/S coping patterns. Rather than inquiring about participants' typical involvement in religious or spiritual pursuits, these studies focus more specifically on how patients draw on their faith to manage the burdens of illness.

The tools that researchers have used for this job have evolved over time. An initial wave of studies assessed religious coping in a rather limited way, by using a single subscale drawn from broader questionnaires designed to measure an array of secular coping strategies (e.g., COPE).[40] These initial studies were a good start, as they helped shift attention from an exclusive focus on general religiousness and highlighted the importance of coping. However, they provided little information about the many divergent forms that R/S coping may take. Reactions to life-threatening illness can be complex and multifaceted. Patients may experience unsettling doubt and uncertainty as well as comfort and conviction. Some may feel ambivalent, abandoned, or punished. Thus, subsequent studies have begun to make use of more recently developed measures that encompass, within the same instrument, a number of distinct R/S coping strategies (e.g., RCOPE;[3] Religious Problem-Solving Scales).[41] These measures were intended to provide a somewhat more nuanced and complex understanding of R/S responses to challenging circumstances, including alienated and well as more affirming reactions.

Initial Approaches to Studying Religious/Spiritual Coping

As one might anticipate, cultural and developmental factors powerfully shape the use of R/S coping in response to illness. For example, older patients with head and neck cancer relied more heavily on religious coping than did their younger counterparts,[42] and Hispanic and Black breast cancer patients made more use of religious coping than did non-Hispanic white women, controlling for other demographic and medical variables.[43] Other investigators found denominational differences, with Evangelical patients reporting higher levels of religious coping than Catholics in a group of Hispanic women with breast cancer.[44]

For the most part, studies relying on unidimensional measures of religious coping have not found significant associations with health outcomes among cancer patients. We evaluated 120 patients with advanced head and neck cancer at various phases of illness, using a cross-sectional design.[24] Participants were assessed: (1) prior to treatment; (2) during active treatment; (3) within 6 months of completing treatment; or (4) more than 6 months post-treatment. At each of these phases of treatment, religious coping was one of the most frequently endorsed coping strategies—particularly for women and older participants. However, religious coping was not related to measures of emotional distress or cancer-related stress symptoms. Other investigators have noted similar findings,[22, 42] in studies encompassing patients with varying types and stages of cancer.

Interestingly, however, in two studies involving newly diagnosed breast cancer patients, women who drew more heavily on religious coping reported *greater distress*.[45, 46] The cross-sectional analyses make these findings difficult to interpret; a plausible and commonly invoked explanation is that greater distress "mobilizes" more intensive reliance on religious coping in response.[47] That is, individuals are more apt to turn to religion when they are experiencing greater distress. There is some evidence to support this explanation among noncancer patients;[47] regrettably the data for these breast cancer patients offer only a snapshot in time, and more sophisticated research designs are needed to better understand these relationships.

More intriguing findings emerged from a longitudinal study by Stanton and colleagues.[48] Women with early stage breast cancer were followed prospectively from shortly after diagnosis to 1-year follow-up. The effects of religious coping depended on participants' level of hope (construed as a personality characteristic rather than a specific attitude toward illness). For women with *little hope*, use of religious coping shortly after diagnosis predicted better outcomes at 3- and 12-month follow-ups (i.e., lower emotional distress, higher vigor, and less fear of recurrence). For these women, faith may have provided a sense of comfort and control. For those *high in hope*, however, religious coping was tied to poorer outcomes over time. Religious coping appeared related to avoidant rather than adaptive coping strategies for these individuals.

Multidimensional Approaches to Studying Religious/Spiritual Coping

As noted, more recent studies have sought a somewhat richer portrait of coping, employing a newer generation of measures that examine R/S struggle as well as R/S comfort or support. Pargament's[49] work has suggested that specific religious coping strategies reflect two broad underlying dimensions, encompassing a movement toward religious resources in response to difficult circumstances ("positive religious coping") and a sense of questioning, conflict, or movement away from religious involvement ("negative religious coping"). A few investigations have explored these dimensions among cancer patients at varying stages of disease.

Religious struggle ("negative religious coping") is generally reported by only a minority of patients, but it has been tied consistently to poorer outcomes. Some of this work has targeted patients with *early stage disease*. After accounting for control variables, religious struggle was associated with poorer QOL and life satisfaction among breast cancer patients recruited from an Internet site,[50] increased depression (but not anxiety) among Australian women with gynecological cancer,[35] and more depressive coping/brooding among German women with breast cancer.[51] In contrast, patients who relied on positive religious coping reported significantly less depressive coping[51] and marginally less depression[35] in these studies.

Other investigations have focused on patients with *advanced disease*. Among patients receiving palliative care, religious struggle was related to poorer overall QOL, while positive religious coping was tied to better QOL, after controlling for demographics and self-efficacy.[52] Similarly, in a smaller group of palliative care patients, religious struggle was associated with greater emotional distress and poorer QOL; positive religious coping was not significant.[53]

In our own work, we have been exploring R/S coping among multiple myeloma patients for a number of years. Myeloma patients often experience an array of taxing symptoms including lytic bone lesions, spinal fractures, pain, anemia, and fatigue. In a recent project, we assessed a large group of myeloma patients at a similar point in treatment—while undergoing initial medical work-up for autologous stem cell transplantation.[5] Stem cell transplant protocols involve a demanding course of treatment. In view of these difficulties, we anticipated that R/S concerns might be especially poignant. As is true in the broader literature, we found that positive religious coping was much more characteristic of patients' responses than religious struggle. However, those who did experience conflict or ambivalence about their faith reported a range of poor health outcomes, including greater depression, increased emotional distress, poorer mental health, and increased pain and fatigue, after adjusting for relevant control variables. Positive religious coping was not related to these outcomes. We found similar results when we assessed a different group of myeloma patients at a later phase of treatment, during stem-cell harvest.[54] In that study, religious struggle was tied to greater distress and cancer-related stress, and lower life satisfaction, emotional well-being, and social well-being, after controlling for demographic and disease variables. We continue to follow these patients over the course of long-term treatment.

While assessment of positive and negative coping patterns represents an improvement over earlier unidimensional evaluations, it still offers only a limited picture. In a more fine-grained analysis, Gall[4] scrutinized more specific types of religious coping strategies in a small group of prostate cancer patients, most of whom were far removed from their initial diagnosis. Expressions of religious discontent were associated with poorer emotional and role functioning, while efforts to cope via performing good deeds were tied to better social functioning, after controlling for demographic characteristics and secular coping responses.

Nairn and Merluzzi[55] explored a different aspect of religious responses to cancer. Among patients with diverse malignancies, they examined how individuals perceived the role of God in their efforts at coping and problem-solving. A style of coping in which God was viewed as a partner is managing difficulties ("collaborative religious coping") or in which difficulties were turned over to God to manage ("deferring religious coping") was related to improved adjustment to cancer and greater self-efficacy. In contrast, those who perceived that God was not involved in their coping efforts ("self-directed religious coping") reported poorer adjustment. Beliefs about God's versus one's own role in handling life difficulties ("who is steering the ship?") represent an important area of inquiry and touch on fundamental questions regarding control, responsibility, and theodicy. Notably, however, the measure of self-directed coping used in this study appears to encompass not only efforts to solve problems autonomously (without God's intervention), as intended by the authors of the scale, but also a sense of abandonment by God, which was not intended to form part of the construct. Therefore, attempts have been made to revise this instrument to ensure greater interpretative clarity,[41] and we await results from further research regarding perceptions of divine control and God's immanence in earthly affairs.

In sum, the database on R/S coping among cancer patients rests on methodologically firmer footing than the more uneven (and older) literature on general religious orientation. Though some studies are characterized by a few of the limitations discussed earlier (e.g., small samples, lack of information about medical parameters, use of heterogeneous samples, and incomplete control for covariates), for the most part these difficulties are less pervasive.

As Pargament[2] has observed in other settings, when we focus on R/S coping among cancer patients we learn something more than we would know by considering only general R/S orientation[5] or secular forms of coping.[4] Findings have become more meaningful as investigators have turned from simple to somewhat more elaborated measures of R/S coping. Thus far, results are most consistent regarding correlates of *negative* R/S coping patterns: religious struggle or ambivalence seems to be a reliable marker for poor health outcomes across a number of domains. Findings for positive religious coping are more variable. Notably, all of these results stem from cross-sectional studies; thus, while painful or conflicted religious responses may be tied to difficulties in broader aspects of QOL, we have little under-standing about casual relationships. Nor do we know how these religious struggles unfold over time. Traumatic experiences that rupture an individ-ual's traditional worldview sometimes become a foundation for personal growth.[7] One would expect that religious struggle might follow a number of different trajectories, with some individuals continuing to express painful alienation, some becoming more resigned or indifferent to spiritual pursuits, some embracing their faith with new vitality and passion, and some turning to other R/S paths instead.[1, 38] Longitudinal studies and qualitative research would help enrich our understanding of these divergent responses.

Spiritual Outcomes

Aside from the varied R/S resources that patients carry with them as they confront the crisis of cancer (general R/S orientation), and the specific R/S strategies they employ to manage it (R/S coping), another important dimen-sion concerns the R/S outcomes that they experience. Spiritual well-being—a sense of peacefulness, reassurance, or existential meaning—has become the focus of considerable attention among investigators. Traditional measures of health-related QOL neglected to include a spiritual or existential domain, but as its importance became better appreciated in recent years several in-struments were developed to help rectify this omission (e.g., World Health Organization QOL scale).[56] This dimension of well-being is clearly valued by patients and provides information not assessed by other QOL domains.

Although research on spiritual well-being has helped illuminate a salient aspect of patients' experience, this work has also been marked by concep-tual confusion. Investigators often refer to measures of spiritual well-being as "spirituality;" we think using these terms interchangeably obscures distinc-tions between spiritual resources and spiritual outcomes. As we have noted elsewhere,[38, 57] measures of spiritual well-being generally include items that overlap with adjustment or mood, so the common practice of using spiritual well-being to predict other psychosocial outcomes may generate spurious results. Thus, though a large number of studies have highlighted associa-tions between spiritual well-being and psychosocial adjustment,[36, 50, 58] it is not always clear whether this is the most profitable approach. It may be more helpful to consider spiritual well-being as an important outcome in its own right, or to focus on its relationships with other variables with which it is less confounded, such as physical symptoms,[59] biological indices, or treatment decisions.[17]

Another interesting area that is closely tied to R/S outcomes involves posttraumatic growth[7] or benefit-finding.[60] Posttraumatic growth refers to positive life changes in the aftermath of crisis. Shifts in spiritual or exis-tential perspectives are often a prominent part of this process. Work on posttraumatic growth among oncology patients is advancing, though few investigations have focused specifically on the spiritual dimension. In a study of breast cancer patients, we found that stronger religious faith was associated with greater posttraumatic growth.[61] Longitudinal studies using both quantitative and qualitative approaches are needed to further our understanding of how and for whom spiritual changes unfold over the trajectory of illness. Additionally, there is a need to explore changes in other related constructs such as spiritual strivings,[6] spiritual doubts, and found meaning (i.e., order and purpose).

Religious/Spiritual Interventions

Efforts to Improve Cancer Screening

Aside from charting connections between R/S factors and health outcomes, investigators also have sought to *improve* health by incorporating these factors into creative interventions. Some of the earliest efforts focused on health education, particularly in underserved minority communities where the church plays a central role. African American churches have been an especially active venue for health promotion projects, consistent with their historical role in addressing a full range of community needs. Churches often provide influential role models, motivating messages, and vibrant networks of support and communication.[62] Over the years, partnerships have been crafted between community churches and health professionals to address smoking, diet, and other important health concerns. Recently, innovative studies have been directed toward cancer screening as well. Erwin and colleagues,[63] for example, enlisted African American cancer survivors to teach screening practices in local rural congregations, where they shared their experiences and served as models of survivorship. Spiritual expression was an important aspect of the program. The project was associated with significant gains in breast self-exam and mammography rates, relative to control communities, and has subsequently evolved into a national model. Other church-based programs have targeted screening for breast,[62] colorectal,[64] and prostate cancer;[65] thus far, outcome data from these types of programs have been limited but promising, and many projects are under development. Creative collaborations between religious leaders and health professionals may serve as a valuable resource in cancer control, particularly for vulnerable populations.

Efforts to Improve Adjustment to Cancer

Other spiritually informed interventions have been developed for patients who have been diagnosed with cancer.[66] A number of established programs are designed to provide support and enhance QOL. Some of these have incorporated within their models an explicit emphasis on existential concerns; regrettably, thus far very limited attention has been devoted to testing their effects specifically on existential/spiritual outcomes as opposed to other domains of functioning (e.g., supportive-expressive therapy;[67] mindfulness-based stress reduction).[68] More recently, there have been efforts to develop new interventions with a stronger emphasis on spiritual/existential content and outcomes. Miller and colleagues[69] evaluated a yearlong group program targeting patients with diverse types of life-threatening illness. The group focused on spiritual needs, end-of-life planning, and legacy, as well as other topics. At the end of the intervention, participants reported fewer difficulties with one aspect of death anxiety (meaninglessness) compared with those in the control condition. In less conservative analyses focusing on treatment completers, there were indications of additional improvements in depression and spiritual well-being.

Other studies have evaluated brief, "meaning-centered" interventions administered in individual rather than group formats. In one such program, patients with recently diagnosed cancer were helped to find a richer sense of meaning in life by focusing on previous challenges, current illness, and future mortality.[70] Relative to control patients, participants who completed the intervention reported significantly higher optimism, self-esteem, and self-efficacy. On the other hand, Coward[71] did not find improvements for newly diagnosed breast cancer patients who had participated in a group that focused on enhancing self-transcendence, relative to those in a non-randomized comparison condition. On balance, these preliminary projects offer hints that existentially or spiritually based programs may lead to favorable changes in relevant outcomes. Additional pilot projects have been completed and larger trials are underway,[66, 72] so our understanding about these types of services is apt to expand appreciably in the next few years.

Conclusions and Future Directions

Research on religiousness/spirituality and cancer has grown markedly in recent years. A number of trends seem heartening. The questions being asked are becoming more specific and refined, and investigators are beginning to approach them in more methodologically sophisticated ways. Our base of knowledge has been extended in several important areas (e.g., screening, adjustment/QOL), and initial forays have been made into important new domains (e.g., medical decision-making). Findings are variable but suggest salutary connections between certain facets of religiousness/spirituality and health (e.g., improved screening practices among healthy individuals, and more adaptive resources among those who are ill). On the other hand, other less commonly expressed dimensions of religiousness have been tied to poor health outcomes (e.g., exclusive reliance on God as healer may contribute to dangerous delay in seeking care). Thus, associations between R/S factors and health are multifaceted rather than uniform.

As the field moves forward a number of important questions require further scrutiny: (1) For whom are these effects most pronounced? Relationships between R/S factors and health may be strongly colored by differences in the cultural context in which individuals are embedded (e.g., ethnicity, geographical region), the personal characteristics they bring to the illness (e.g., gender, personality), and the specific medical challenges that they encounter (e.g., phase of treatment). It will be important to explore these factors more fully. (2) How do relationships between R/S factors and health change over time? Because most research has focused on concurrent associations, we know little about how R/S involvement may predict later changes in health outcomes, or how particular spiritual processes may shift and evolve over the course of treatment. (3) Which specific dimensions of health are most closely tied to R/S factors? Thus far most attention has focused on early detection among community residents and adjustment/ QOL among patients receiving treatment. Many other clinically and conceptually relevant areas await exploration, ranging from behavioral endpoints (e.g., treatment adherence, doctor-patient communication) to biological processes (e.g., proinflammatory cytokines, immune surveillance).

Cancer is a harrowing illness. The ways in which individuals protect themselves from this disease and adapt to its manifold challenges appear to be influenced by their R/S commitments. We look forward to learning more about these intriguing processes as the field develops.

References

1. Hill, P.C. & Pargament, K.I. (2003). Advances in the conceptualization and measurement of religion and spirituality: Implications for physical and mental health research. *American Psychologist, 58*, 64–74.
2. Pargament, K.I. (1997). *The psychology of religion and coping: Theory, research, and practice.* New York: Guilford.
3. Pargament, K.I., Koenig, H.G., & Perez, L.M. (2000). The many methods of religious coping: Development and initial validation of the RCOPE. *Journal of Clinical Psychology, 56*, 519–543.
4. Gall, T.L. (2004). The role of religious coping in adjustment to prostate cancer. *Cancer Nursing, 27*, 454–461.
5. Sherman, A.C., Simonton, S., Latif, U., Spohn, R., & Tricot, G. (2005). Religious struggle and religious comfort in response to illness: Health outcomes among stem cell transplant patients. *Journal of Behavioral Medicine, 28*, 359–367.
6. Emmons, R.A. (2005). Striving for the sacred: Personal goals, life meaning, and religion. *Journal of Social Issues, 61*, 747–759.

7. Shaw, A., Joseph, S., & Linley, P.A. (2005). Religion, spirituality, and post-traumatic growth: A systematic review. *Mental Health, Religion & Culture, 8,* 1–11.
8. Hill, T.D., Burdett, A.M., Ellison, C.G., & Musick, M.A. (2006). Religious attendance and the health behaviors of Texas adults. *Preventive Medicine, 42,* 309–312.
9. Strawbridge, W.J., Shema, S.J., Cohen, R.D., & Kaplan, G.A. (2001). Religious attendance increases survival by improving and maintaining good health behaviors, mental health, and social relationships. *Annals of Behavioral Medicine, 23,* 68–74.
10. Cline, K.M.C. & Ferraro, K.F. (2006). Does religion increase the prevalence and incidence of obesity in adulthood? *Journal for the Scientific Study of Religion, 45,* 269–281.
11. Benjamins, M.R. & Brown, C. (2004). Religion and preventative health care utilization among the elderly. *Social Science & Medicine, 58,* 109–118.
12. Benjamins, M.R. (2006). Religious influences on preventive health care use in a nationally representative sample of middle-age women. *Journal of Behavioral Medicine, 29,* 1–16.
13. Benjamins, M.R., Trinitapoli, J., & Elliison, C.G. (2006). Religious attendance, health maintenance beliefs, and mammography utilizations: Findings from a nationwide survey of Presbyterian women. *Journal for the Scientific Study of Religion, 45,* 597–607.
14. Aaron, K.F., Levine, D., & Burstin, H.R. (2003). African American church participation and health care practices. *Journal of General Internal Medicine, 18,* 908–913.
15. Mitchell, J., Lannin, D.R., Mathews, H.F., & Swanson, M.S. (2002). Religious beliefs and breast cancer screening. *Journal of Women's Health, 11,* 907–915.
16. Daugherty, C.K., Fitchett, G., Murphy, P.F., Peterman, A.H., Banik, D.M., Hlubocky, F., et al. (2005). Trusting God and medicine: Spirituality in advanced cancer patients volunteering for clinical trials of experimental agents. *Psycho-Oncology, 14,* 135–146.
17. Donovan, K.A., Greene, P.G., Shuster, J.L., Jr., Partridge, E.E., & Tucker, D.C. (2002). Treatment preferences in recurrent ovarian cancer. *Gynecologic Oncology, 86,* 200–211.
18. True, G., Phipps, E.J., Braitman, L.E., Harralson, T., Harris, D., & Tester, W. (2005). Treatment preferences and advance care planning at end of life: The role of ethnicity and spiritual coping in cancer patients. *Annals of Behavioral Medicine, 30,* 174–179.
19. Lannin, D.R., Mathews, H.F., Mitchell, J., Swanson, M.S., Swanson, F.H., & Edwards, M.S. (1998). Influence of socioeconomic and cultural factors on racial differences in late-stage presentation of breast cancer. *Journal of the American Medical Association, 279,* 1801–1807.
20. Schwartz, M.D., Hughes, C., Roth, J., Main, D., Peshkin, B.N., Issacs, C., et al. (2000). Spiritual faith and genetic testing decisions among high-risk

breast cancer probands. *Cancer Epidemiology, Biomarkers & Prevention, 9,* 381–385.

21. Burdette, A.M., Hill, T.D., & Moulton, B.E. (2005). Religion and attitudes toward physician-assisted suicide and terminal palliative care. *Journal for the Scientific Study of Religion, 44,* 79–93.

22. Carver, C.S., Pozo, C., Harris, S.D., Noriega, V., Scheier, M.F., Robinson, D.S., et al. (1993). How coping mediates the effect of optimism on distress: A study of women with early stage breast cancer. *Journal of Personality and Social Psychology, 65,* 375–390.

23. Ringdal, G.I. (1996). Religiosity, quality of life, and survival in cancer patients. *Social Indicators Research, 38,* 193–211.

24. Sherman, A.C., Simonton, S., Adams, D.C., Vural, E., & Hanna, E. (2000). Coping with head and neck cancer during different phases of treatment. *Head & Neck, 22,* 787–793.

25. Aukst-Margetic, B., Jakovljevic, M., Margetic, B., Biscan, M., & Samija, M. (2005). Religiosity, depression and pain in patients with breast cancer. *General Hospital Psychiatry, 27,* 250–255.

26. Baider, L., Russak, S.M., Perry, S., Kash, K., Gronert, M., Fox, B., et al. (1999). The role of religious and spiritual beliefs in coping with malignant melanoma: An Israeli sample. *Psycho-Oncology, 8,* 27–35.

27. Canada, A.L., Parker, P.A., de Moor, J.S., Basen-Engquist, K., Ramondetta, L.M., & Cohen, L. (2006). Active coping mediates the association between religion/spirituality and quality of life in ovarian cancer. *Gynecologic Oncology, 101,* 102–107.

28. McClain-Jacobson, C., Rosenfeld, B., Kosinski, A., Pessin, H., Cimino, J.E., & Breitbart, W. (2004). Belief in an afterlife, spiritual well-being and end-of-life despair in patients with advanced cancer. *General Hospital Psychiatry, 26,* 484–486.

29. Meraviglia, M. (2006). Effects of spirituality in breast cancer survivors. *Oncology Nursing Forum, 33,* E1–E7.

30. Meraviglia, M. (2006). The effects of spirituality on well-being of people with lung cancer. *Oncology Nursing Forum, 31,* 89–94.

31. Fehring, R.J., Miller, J.F., & Shaw, C. (1997). Spiritual well-being, religiosity, hope, depression, and other mood states in elderly people coping with cancer. *Oncology Nursing Forum, 24,* 663–671.

32. Herth, K.A. (1989). The relationship between level of hope and level of coping response and other variables in patients with cancer. *Oncology Nursing Forum, 16,* 67–72.

33. Romero, C., Kalidas, M., Elledge, R., Chang, J., Liscum, K.R., & Friedman, L.C. (2006). Self-forgiveness, spirituality, and psychological adjustment in women with breast cancer. *Journal of Behavioral Medicine, 29,* 29–36.

34. Gibson, L.M.R. & Parker, V. (2003). Inner resources as predictors of psychological well-being in middle-income African American breast cancer survivors. *Cancer Control, 10,* 52–59.

35. Boscaglia, N., Clarke, D.M., Jobling, T.W., & Quinn, M.A. (2005). The contribution of spirituality and spiritual coping to anxiety and depression in women with a recent diagnosis of gynecological cancer. *International Journal of Gynecological Cancer, 15*, 755–761.

36. Mickley, J.R., Soeken, K., & Belcher, A. (1992). Spiritual well-being, religiousness and hope among women with breast cancer. *Image: Journal of Nursing Scholarship, 24*, 267–272.

37. Nelson, C.J., Rosenfeld, B., Breitbart, W., & Galietta, M. (2002). Spirituality, religion, and depression in the terminally ill. *Psychosomatics, 43*, 213–220.

38. Sherman, A.C. & Simonton, S. (2001). Religious involvement among cancer patients: Associations with adjustment and quality of life. In T.G. Plante, A.C. Sherman AC (Eds.), *Faith and Health: Psychological Perspectives* (pp. 167–194). New York: Guilford.

39. Mullen, P.M., Smith, R.M., & Hill, E.W. (1993). Sense of coherence as a mediator of stress for cancer patients and spouses. *Journal of Psychosocial Oncology, 11*, 23–46.

40. Carver, C.S., Scheier, M.F., & Weintraub, J.K. (1989). Assessing coping strategies: A theoretically based approach. *Journal of Personality and Social Psychology, 56*, 267–283.

41. Phillips, R.E., III, Pargament, K.I., Lynn, Q.K., & Crossley, C.D. (2004). Self-directing religious coping: A deistic God, abandoning God, or no God at all? *Journal for the Scientific Study of Religion, 43*, 409–418.

42. Derks, W., de Leeuw, J.R.J., Hordijk, G.J., & Winnubst, J.A.M. (2005). Differences in coping style and locus of control between older and younger patients with head and neck cancer. *Clinical Otolaryngology, 30*, 186–192.

43. Culver, J.L., Alferi, S.M., Carver, C.S., Kilbourn, K.M., & Antoni, M.H. (1999). Coping and distress among women under treatment for early-stage breast cancer: Comparing African Americans, Hispanics and non-Hispanic whites. *Psycho-Oncology, 11*, 495–504.

44. Alferi, S.M., Culver, J.L., Carver, C.S., Arena, P.L., & Antoni, M.H. (1999). Religiosity, religious coping, and distress: A prospective study of Catholic and Evangelical women in treatment for early-stage breast cancer. *Journal of Health Psychology, 4*, 343—356.

45. Ben-Zur, H., Gilbar, O., & Lev, S. (2001). Coping with breast cancer: Patient, spouse, and dyad models. *Psychosomatic Medicine, 63*, 32–39.

46. Harcourt, D., Rumsey, N., & Ambler, N. (1999). Same day diagnosis of symptomatic breast problems: Psychological impact and coping strategies. *Psychology, Health & Medicine, 4*, 57–71.

47. Fitchett, G., Rybarczyk, B.D., DeMarco, G.A., & Nicholas, J.J. (1999). The role of religion in medical rehabilitation outcomes: A longitudinal study. *Rehabilitation Psychology, 44*, 333–353.

48. Stanton, A.L., Danoff-Burg, S., & Huggins, M.E. (2002). The first year after breast cancer diagnosis: Hope and coping strategies as predictors of adjustment. *Psycho-Oncology, 11*, 93–102.

49. Pargament, K.I., Smith, B.W., Koenig, H.G., & Perez, L. (1998). Patterns of positive and negative religious coping with major life stressors. *Journal of Scientific Study of Religion, 37*, 711–725.

50. Manning-Walsh, J. (2005). Spiritual struggle: Effect on quality of life and life satisfaction in women with breast cancer. *Journal of Holistic Nursing, 23*, 120–140.

51. Zwingmann, C., Wirtz, M., Muller, C., Korber, J., & Murken, S. (2006). Positive and negative religious coping in German breast cancer patients. *Journal of Behavioral Medicine, 29*, 533–547.

52. Tarakeshwar, N., Vanderwerker, L.C., Paulk, E., Pearce, M.J., Kasl, S.V., & Prigerson, H.G. (2006). Religious coping is associated with the quality of life of patients with advanced cancer. *Journal of Palliative Medicine, 9*, 646–657.

53. Hills, J., Paice, J.A., Cameron, J.R., & Shott, S. (2005). Spirituality and distress in palliative care consultation. *Journal of Palliative Medicine, 8*, 782–788.

54. Sherman, A.C., Simonton, S., Plante, T., Moody, V.R., & Wells, P. (2001). Patterns of religious coping among multiple myeloma patients: Associations with adjustment and quality of life (abstract). *Psychosomatic Medicine, 63*, 124.

55. Nairn, R.C. & Merluzzi, T.V. (2003). The role of religious coping in adjustment to cancer. *Psycho-Oncology, 12*, 428–441.

56. WHOQOL SRPB Group (2006). A cross-cultural study of spirituality, religion, and personal belief components of quality of life. *Social Science & Medicine, 62*, 1486–1497.

57. Sherman, A.C., Simonton, S., Adams, D.C., Latif, U., Plante, T.G., Burns, S.K., et al. (2001). Measuring religious faith in cancer patients: reliability and construct validity of the Santa Clara Strength of Religious Faith Questionnaire. *Psycho-Oncology, 10*, 436–443.

58. Laubmeier, K.K., Zakowski, S.G., & Bair, J.P. (2004). The role of spirituality in the psychological adjustment to cancer: A test of the transactional model of stress and coping. *International Journal of Behavioral Medicine, 11*, 488–55.

59. Brady, M.J., Peterman, A.H., Fitchett, G., Mo, M., & Cella, D. (1999). A case for including spirituality in quality of life measurement in oncology. *Psycho-Oncology, 8*, 417–428.

60. Schulz, U. & Mohamed, N.E. (2004). Turning the tide: Benefit finding after cancer surgery. *Social Science and Medicine, 59*, 653–662.

61. Sherman, A.C., Latif, U., Simonton, S., Fowler, J., & Suen, K. (2002). Religious faith and adjustment to breast cancer (abstract). *Annals of Behavioral Medicine, 24* (Suppl), S172.

62. Duan, N., Fox, S., Derose, K.P., & Carson, S. (2005). Maintaining mammography adherence through telephone counseling in a church-based trail. *American Journal of Public Health, 90*, 1468–1471.

63. Erwin, D.O., Spatz, T.S., Stotts, R.C., & Hollenberg, J.A. (1999). Increasing mammography practice by African American women. *Cancer Practice, 7*, 78–85.

64. Campbell, M.K., James, A., Hudson, M.A., Carr, C., Jackson, E., Oates, V., et al. (2004). Improving multiple health behaviors for colorectal cancer prevention among African American church members. *Health Psychology, 23,* 492–502.
65. Boehm, S., Coleman-Burns, P., Schlenk, E.A., Funnell, M.M., Parzuchowski, J., & Powell, I.J. (1995). Prostate cancer in African American men: Increasing knowledge and self-efficacy. *Journal of Community Health Nursing, 12,* 161–169.
66. Breitbart, W. (2006). Spirituality and meaning in supportive care: Spirituality- and meaning-centered group psychotherapy interventions in advanced cancer. *Supportive Care in Cancer, 14,* 888–901.
67. Spiegel, D., Bloom, J.R., Kraemer, H.C., & Gottheil, E. (1989). Effect of psychosocial treatment on survival of patients with metastatic breast cancer. *Lancet, 338,* 888–891.
68. Speca, M., Carlson, L.E., Goodey, E., & Angen, M. (2000). A randomized, wait-list controlled clinical trial: The effect of a mindfulness meditation-based stress reduction program on mood and symptoms of stress in cancer patients. *Psychosomatic Medicine, 62,* 613–622.
69. Miller, D.K., Chibnall, J.T., Videen, S.D., & Duckro, P.N. (2005). Supportive-affective group experience for persons with life-threatening illness: Reducing spiritual, psychological, and death-related distress in dying patients. *Journal of Palliative Medicine, 8,* 333–343.
70. Lee, V., Cohen, S.R., Edgar, L., Laizner, A.M., & Gagnon, A.J. (2006). Meaning-making intervention during breast or colorectal cancer treatment improves self-esteem, optimism, and self-efficacy. *Social Science and Medicine, 62,* 3133–3145.
71. Coward, D.D. (2003). Facilitation of self-transcendence in a breast cancer support group: II. *Oncology Nursing Forum, 30,* 291–300.
72. Dann, N.J. & Mertens, W.C. (2004). Taking a "leap of faith": Acceptance and value of a cancer program-sponsored spiritual event. *Cancer Nursing, 27,* 134–141.

CHAPTER 12

Spirituality and HIV/AIDS

HEIDEMARIE KREMER AND GAIL IRONSON

"If it wasn't for Him, I wouldn't be here today," explained an African American woman who was diagnosed with the Human Immunodeficiency Virus (HIV) more than 10 years ago. When she was diagnosed she felt that this was her death sentence, a curse from God, which drew her further into the world of drugs and unprotected sex, ending up as a prostitute in the streets. She subsequently described that she felt touched by the Holy Spirit during an intense prayer for her by people at church. This dramatic spiritual experience led her back to God, helped her to get off drugs, and to accept her disease as a plan of God. In a study done by our group,[1] people living with HIV describe how a profound spiritual experience can initiate a quantum change or spiritual transformation, which leads to an extensive change in behavior, attitude, beliefs, and one's view of the world and the self, and may contribute to the discovery of a new meaning in living with HIV.

Similarly, 10 years ago, the availability of highly active antiretroviral therapy (ART) changed the HIV diagnosis from almost being a death sentence to a life with a chronic disease. The introduction of ART in 1996 is a benchmark in the history of HIV, a quantum change in HIV treatment and research, changing the focus from preventing death to living and aging with HIV. Since then, the impact of spirituality and religiousness on HIV has shifted from an emphasis on end-of-life care to its recognition as an important factor contributing to quality of life and coping with a chronic disease. After a brief introduction to HIV/AIDS, this chapter will give an overview of the current research on the role of spirituality in relation to the biological and psychological aspects of HIV/AIDS. Next, research on spirituality in the face of HIV as a life-threatening disease, as well research on spirituality and coping with HIV as a chronic disease will be discussed.

Studies on spirituality in different populations of people living with HIV, such as African American women, gay men, and people with substance use problems will also be addressed. To conclude, this chapter will consider HIV as a potential trigger for spiritual growth and its implications for health.

HIV as a Challenge of the Millennium

According to the WHO report from 2006,[2] of the almost 40 million people living with HIV worldwide (of which one million live in the United States), about 7 million require ART. Due to international efforts in scaling up the availability of treatment, about one quarter of those in need of ART now have access to treatment. In the absence of antiretroviral therapy, it takes on average up to 10 to 12 years from the onset of the HIV infection until the Acquired Immune Deficiency Syndrome (AIDS) develops.

AIDS is defined as either a decline in the CD4-Lymphocyte cells below $200/mm^3$ or as the onset of characteristic opportunistic infections or some specific types of cancer. People with AIDS often suffer infections of the lungs, the intestinal tract, the brain, the eyes, and other organs, as well as debilitating weight loss, diarrhea, neurological conditions, and cancers such as Kaposi sarcoma or certain types of lymphomas.

However, rates of HIV disease progression vary largely. Rapid progressors (10 percent of people living with HIV) develop AIDS within 2 to 3 years following HIV infection, whereas long-term nonprogressors (5 percent) remain asymptomatic even after 12 or more years. The amount of HIV RNA, the viral load, can be measured in the blood. Those with higher viral loads have a higher likelihood of developing AIDS or of dying/death. ART is able to reduce the viral load and if treatment is effective, the virus is no longer detectable in the blood. Having an undetectable viral load in the blood does not indicate that the body is cleared of the virus. Since HIV replicates intracellularly, the virus remains in the body's cells, and in latent reservoirs, such as the brain cells and the lymphoid tissue, where it can replicate itself. Although effective antiretroviral therapy is no cure for HIV infection, it is able to control viral replication for decades and to reconstitute the immune system. For people living with HIV, who take antiretroviral therapy, the mean age at death is estimated to be above 60 years with 41 percent dying of illnesses not directly attributable to HIV.[3]

Spirituality in the Face of HIV as a Life-Threatening Disease

Before the introduction of highly active ART, 85 percent of the people living with HIV died within approximately 3 years after the onset of AIDS. Before the availability of antiretroviral therapy, spirituality in relation to

HIV/AIDS was mostly studied qualitatively, with the view that the person with HIV was confronting a terminal illness. Being diagnosed with an imminent life-threatening disease such as HIV/AIDS, in combination with the stigma associated with the disease, threatened people's sense of identity and assumptions about the future. In response to this existential experience people often develop the feeling that time is of essence and experience transformations in values, spirituality, and life priorities. Hall et al.[4] examined the role of spirituality in people who had spiritual or religious experiences that helped them cope with AIDS. They found a sequence of first finding new spiritual meaning and purpose in life emerging from the stigmatization associated with HIV/AIDS, then moving from stigmatization to the realization that HIV may have a positive purpose, and then developing a new spiritual understanding of life in the context of a terminal diagnosis. Pierson at al.[5] interviewed people in the end-stage of AIDS, mainly gay white men, to determine which components are necessary for optimizing the quality of dying. One quarter spontaneously mentioned spiritual aspects as essential, but some expressed indifference about spirituality or religion, or did not want to have the beliefs of others imposed on them as they were dying. In contrast, Fryback et al.[6] found that five men facing HIV/AIDS as a fatal diagnosis viewed spirituality as a bridge between hopelessness and meaningfulness in life, and often felt that they had a better quality of life now than they had before the diagnosis. Thus, before the availability of ART, the importance of spirituality in people living with HIV/AIDS was mainly studied in gay white men in an advanced stage of the disease living in industrial nations. For those who were turning to spirituality, spirituality enhanced their quality of dying and helped them to find deeper meaning in living with the disease. Few studies examined the role of spirituality in longevity with HIV. Barosso et al.[7, 8] discovered themes among long-term nonprogressors with HIV to which they attributed their health. The four themes were: finding meaning in HIV/AIDS, taking care of their health (physical and mental), perceiving human connectedness (supportive relationships and helping others), and spirituality (belief in a supportive, protective higher power, and surrender to a higher power). Tsevat et al.[9] developed a questionnaire to measure life satisfaction, health rating, and time-tradeoffs in fifty one patients in an HIV treatment center between 1996 and 1997, just when effective ART became available. Half of the patients felt that they had better life-satisfaction after they were diagnosed with HIV/AIDS, whereas only 29 percent experienced a decrease in life-satisfaction following their diagnosis. Those who felt at peace with God and the universe, those who stopped using drugs, and women, were significantly more likely to perceive that their life had improved after the diagnosis. Despite their compromised health (65 percent of the patients had AIDS), most patients strongly preferred to live longer, even if their health was not excellent. In particular, participants who felt at peace with God and the universe and those who had children had a stronger will to live.

Antiretroviral Treatment—The Quantum Change in the History of HIV

Today, 95 percent of the people who take antiretroviral therapy survive more than 3 years after being diagnosed with AIDS. Currently in the United States, the majority of the people with HIV can take treatment if needed, and the issues affecting treatment have shifted from the lack of access to treatment to the lack of adherence to treatment. Lack of adherence to therapy is one of the main causes of treatment failure in people living with HIV in the industrial world.

Nevertheless, only a few studies have examined the relationship between spirituality and adherence to ART. Holstad et al.[10] found a weak significant correlation between existential well-being (e.g., viewing life as positive and meaningful) and self-reported adherence in 120 HIV-positive people (measured with the Antiretroviral General Adherence Scale). However, religious well-being, spiritual beliefs, and the level of spiritual involvement were not significantly associated with the general tendency to adhere to ART. In contrast, Simoni et al.[11] found a significant strong association between self-reported adherence (using the AIDS Clinical Trials Group measure) and spirituality in 139 HIV-positive people. Spirituality was assessed with the Systems of Belief Inventory, which measures spiritual and religious beliefs and practices, as well as spiritual support and coping. Furthermore, a survey conducted by Parsons et al.[12] indicated that positive religious practices and beliefs were associated with better adherence to medication and keeping up with medical appointments. However, those who believed that HIV is a sin (15 percent) were more likely not to seek health care for HIV, and those who felt that HIV is a punishment of God (21 percent) were more likely to postpone the initiation of ART. Although all three studies were conducted in urban metropolitan cities in a low-income population of mainly African American origin these results are inconsistent. This may be due to each study's use of instruments that captured different aspects of spirituality and self-reported adherence.

Kremer et al.[13] interviewed seventy-nine people with HIV who had been offered ART by their physician in order to determine the factors they considered in their medical decisions to accept/initiate/adhere to treatment. For 58 percent of the participants, spirituality and worldview played an important role in the decision to accept or reject ART and was considered as often as treatment side effects and whether ART was easy to take for them. They often perceived that their spirituality helped them to adhere to treatment, to cope better with the side effects, and motivated them to take treatment.

Some felt that their spiritual beliefs and the belief in the mind-body connection helped them to remain healthy even without taking treatment (in one instant leading to death due to an opportunistic infection, which could have been prevented by taking ART).

Spirituality in the Face of HIV as a Chronic Disease

Even after effective ART transformed the HIV infection into a chronic disease, psychobiosocial factors continue to play an important role in the health and the survival of people with HIV. A longitudinal study of the psychobiological factors of long-survival with HIV, conducted by Ironson et al.[14, 15] observed 177 patients over 2 years. Findings were that depression, avoidant coping, hopelessness, low dispositional optimism, and lower education predicted faster disease progression, as indicated by a decline in CD4 cells and an increase in viral load. CD4 cells declined twice as fast in people with HIV with high cumulative depression and avoidant coping, even after accounting for the effects of ART and adherence.[14] Those low on optimism had less proactive behavior, more avoidant coping, and more depression, which may explain why they lost their CD4 cells 1.5 times faster than those high on optimism.[15] In the following discussion, we will examine the findings for the association between spirituality and psychosocial factors contributing to the health of people with HIV/AIDS.

Spirituality, Depressive Symptoms, and the Health of People with HIV/Aids

Depressive symptoms are very common in people living with HIV,[16] in particular in women.[17] Several investigators have observed that spirituality [11, 16, 18, 19] and spiritual well-being [16, 20] are associated with less depressive symptoms. The association between spirituality and depression was mediated by mastery (the belief that one's life chances are under one's own control), self-esteem,[11] and positive reappraisal coping and benefit finding.[18]

Spiritual Coping as a Path to Turning HIV into a Positive Life Change

Even after the onset of ART, people living with HIV/AIDS often relied on religiousness and spirituality to cope with their disease, as shown by a national survey[21] of 2,266 patients in 1998. Although people living with HIV often feel marginalized by religious institutions, most (85 percent) HIV-positive people in the United States have a religious affiliation, which is similar to the U.S. population in general according to the Gallup poll. Being a woman, nonwhite, older than 45 years, and being educated beyond high school were the characteristics associated with being both more spiritual and religious.[21] A majority indicated that spirituality (85 percent) and religiousness (65 percent) were important in their lives, and that they relied sometimes or often on their spirituality or religiousness in decision-making or problem solving.

Between 59 and 83 percent of people living with HIV/AIDS perceive positive changes since their HIV/AIDS diagnosis,[22] even more than the 49 percent reported by Tsevat et al.[9] at the onset of effective ART. Experiencing a significant positive life change, resulting from the confrontation with a major medical diagnosis such as HIV, has been labeled by researchers as benefit finding, positive reappraisal coping, posttraumatic growth, or self-transcendence. A positive life change may play an important role in improving both the quality and the quantity of life, even in the era of ART. Turning to spirituality/religiousness may be a catalyst for this process.

People who perceived their HIV diagnosis as a path to a radical positive turnaround, such as a spiritual transformation[1] initially described a sequalae of depression, anxiety, fear of death, guilt, worthlessness, and helplessness after being diagnosed with HIV. After hitting rock bottom, often struggling with both substance use and HIV, there was a search for help, the call for God or a Higher Power, and the surrender to the spiritual. Spiritual beliefs that were described as helpful were the belief in a loving and forgiving God, the belief in life after death, and the belief of being selected by God or a Higher Power to have HIV. A variety of spiritual experiences, such as near-death experiences, out-of body experiences, perceived visitations with diseased relatives, and perceived encounters with the Divine were also pathways to spiritual transformations. Turning to spirituality/religiousness can transform the challenge of living with HIV to a life with higher quality with a greater sense of peace, love, and connectedness to life and others.

The central role of spirituality/religiousness in coping and bringing a sense of meaning and purpose in living with HIV/AIDS as a chronic illness has been emphasized in several qualitative and quantitative studies[1, 19, 23–29]. Different sociodemographic backgrounds of the study populations, the lack of coherent measures of spirituality/religiousness, the lack of biological markers, and cross-sectional designs make it difficult to assess the contribution of spiritual coping to the health of people living with HIV.

Tarakeshwar et al.[23] interviewed ten women and ten men living with HIV on how spirituality influenced their coping with the illness. Themes suggested a relationship-based framework following the HIV diagnosis, including the relationship with God or a Higher Power, the relationship with family, and the relationship with life. Beyond the attempts to build a connection with a Higher Power via prayer, meditation, reading spiritual/religious literature, and church attendance, the relationship with God could be both a source of gratitude and a source of struggle. Consistent with the findings of other studies,[1, 7, 12, 19, 24, 28, 30, 31] spiritual/religious coping strategies can be positive or negative. Positive coping strategies build on a loving view of God or a Higher Power and a sense of connectedness with the religious community. Conversely, negative coping strategies reflect a feeling of being punished by God and are often concomitant with a sense of alienation from the religious community. Spirituality was important in sustaining family relationships, which contributed to finding a sense of purpose. The tie between spirituality and family relationships could be both the source of support as well as strain. Subthemes within spirituality and the relationship with life included taking care of health, transformation of life goals from a self-centered to an other-centered focus, and accepting mortality, which has also been documented by other researchers.[1, 4, 26, 30, 31]

Since spiritual coping and posttraumatic growth are more prevalent in women,[22] Siegel at al.[29] interviewed fifty-four women with HIV (34 percent African American, 34 percent white, 32 percent Latina, and 55 percent former iv drug users) on positive changes that they attributed to their HIV/AIDS diagnosis. Overall, 83 percent perceived at least one positive change since diagnosis, which included health behavior, spirituality, relationships, self-view, life values, and life goals. Some variation was found in the forms of growth, depending on the women's sociodemographic characteristics. Spiritual growth was more prevalent in African American and Latina women. Women with past drug use reported the most changes in health behavior, such as getting off drugs, eating healthier, and engaging in safer sex behaviors. Those with a history of drug use often experienced improved living conditions because of the entitlements they received due to their disability. Conversely, educated workingwomen reported more negative career changes. At least one positive change as a result of the diagnosis was reported in 93 percent of the women with AIDS.[29] Siegel et al.[29] suggested that the perception of benefits or positive changes, in particular when the health declines, plays a role in finding a "silver lining" in the temporal process of coming to terms with the illness.

Perceiving benefits in adversity is further examined in a multicenter study[24, 31] of 450 people with HIV/AIDS (86 percent male; 50 percent African American, and 45 percent white), which examines the mechanisms by which spirituality/religiousness improves the quality of life after being diagnosed with HIV. One-third of the participants felt that their life had improved after being diagnosed with HIV and 29 percent reported that their life had gotten worse. Higher education, being employed, and having a religion were associated with reporting positive changes after the HIV diagnosis. The majority (80 percent) indicated a religious preference, and one third reported praying or meditating at least daily. Three-quarters of the participants indicated that being faced with HIV/AIDS had strengthened their faith at least a little. Positive religious coping strategies were significantly more common than negative ones. For example, 35 percent endorsed seeking God's love and care and only 7 percent wondered whether God had abandoned them. Spirituality/religiousness was a composite score of the Duke Religion Index (organized and nonorganized religious activities, and intrinsic religiosity), the Functional Assessment of Chronic Illness Therapy-Spirituality-Expanded Scale (meaning/peace, faith, and overall spirituality), and the Brief Religious Coping Scale (positive and negative religious coping). Higher levels of optimism, self-esteem and life satisfaction, worse overall physical functioning, African American ethnicity, and less use of alcohol were associated with higher spirituality/religiousness scores. Spirituality/religiousness had the second strongest association with the perception of a positive change since the diagnosis, next to optimism. Almost half of the effect of spirituality/religiousness on perceiving a positive change was direct; the other half was indirect, mostly through higher levels of optimism, and partially via worse health and more health concerns. The latter is in line with the findings of Siegel et al.[29] who describe a tendency to find benefit in adversity as health declines.

Spirituality as a Source of Hope and Coping with HIV

Beyond optimism, hope was another predictor of slower HIV disease progression.[14] Two studies, one in women and one in men, assessed the link between spirituality and hope as a path to coping and improving the perceived health in people living with HIV/AIDS.[32, 33] Phillips et al.[32] found that African American women with HIV/AIDS had significantly lower levels of hope compared to women with breast cancer. Lower levels of hope were significantly associated with more avoidant coping. Conversely, maintaining a sense of hope for the future was significantly correlated with a higher coping score, managing the illness, and more spiritual activities in HIV-positive African American women. Heinrich et al.[33] examined 125 HIV-positive men (40 percent African American, 40 percent Latino, and 20 percent white) and found that scores on the Spiritual Well-Being Scale and the Herth Hope Scale were highly correlated ($r = 0.63$), which may indicate that both scales measure a similar construct. Heinrich et al.[33] found an indirect link between spiritual well-being and better perceived health (measured with the Perceived Heath Index and the HIV Specific Health Status Assignment) via hope. Hope was directly associated with better-perceived health, which includes physical, emotional, and social well-being.

Spiritual Growth and HIV Disease Progression

While the studies mentioned above focused on the association between spirituality and living a better life, other studies have investigated the link between spirituality and slower disease progression, which may lead to living a longer life. Cotton et al.[25] examined changes in spirituality and religiousness attributed to HIV/AIDS in 347 patients (52 percent non-Latin white, 58 percent African American). Whereas 41 percent of the sample reported an increase in spirituality after the diagnoses, only 25 percent reported an increase in religiousness, and 25 percent felt less welcomed in their religious community. Half of the participants believed that their spirituality/religiousness prolonged their life. However, Cotton et al. observed that African Americans, compared to whites, were significantly more likely to experience an increase in spirituality after their HIV/AIDS diagnosis (52 percent versus 37 percent), were more likely to feel alienated from their religious groups (21 percent versus 44 percent), and were more likely to believe that their spirituality/religiousness helped them to live longer (68 percent versus 41 percent). There were no gender differences in changes in spirituality/religiousness attributed to HIV/AIDS in this study. However, only 13 percent of the participants were female.

The findings of Ironson et al.[28] provide biological evidence for a predictive connection between spiritual growth and sustained health with HIV/AIDS. In a subsample of 100 participants of the longitudinal study of Ironson et al.[28] (64 percent male; 38 percent African American, 29 percent white, and 27 percent Latin), an increase in spirituality/religiousness after being diagnosed with HIV was reported by 45 percent of participants, and this increase predicted slower disease progression over 4 years. In fact, CD4 cells dropped 4.5 times faster in those with a decline in spirituality/religiousness after their diagnosis, compared to those who became more spiritual/religious. These results were independent of adherence, medication at every time point, and initial disease stage. Further, the slower disease progression among those with an increase in spirituality/religiousness could not be explained by depression, coping, hopelessness, optimism, social support, church attendance, substance use, age, gender, ethnicity, or education.

In contrast to Ironson et al., Milam[26] did not find a relationship between posttraumatic growth and HIV disease progression over 19 months in 412 people with HIV (87 percent male; 40 percent Latin, 39 percent white, 15 percent African American). However, all participants were taking ART and the observational period was too brief to expect meaningful disease progression. In addition, spiritual change is just one aspect of the Posttraumatic Growth Index, which also includes new possibilities, relating to others, personal strength, and appreciation of life. Nevertheless, Latin versus non-Latin, as well as female versus male individuals reported more posttraumatic growth. Among the Latin population, posttraumatic growth was associated with a preservation of CD4 cells. Although posttraumatic growth was related to less depressive symptoms and substance use, these factors did not explain the association between posttraumatic growth and slower CD4 decline in the Latin population. However, excluding the religious items from the scale reduced the significance results, suggesting that religious change may partially account for the relationship between posttraumatic growth and immune preservation in the Latin individuals. Milam[26] found a beneficial connection between posttraumatic growth and viral load among participants with low pessimism. Surprisingly, he[26] also reported an association between posttraumatic growth and a preservation of CD4 cells among those with low optimism, which is in contrast to the findings of other studies[15, 22] and requires further examination.

Posttraumatic growth might be a construct that is more prevalent among the Latin culture than self-transcendence, as a study of Ramer et al.[27] in 420 people with HIV/AIDS (87 percent male; 72 percent Latin, 14 percent white, and 12 percent African American) suggests. Self-transcendence refers to a developmental characteristic that expands one's boundaries of the self to take on broader life perspectives, activities, and purposes that help one discover or make meaning of one's life.[27] Latin individuals scored lower on the self-transcendence scale but higher on spirituality (measured with a quality of life subscale, with items related to life satisfaction, peace of mind, and personal faith in God). Conversely, African Americans reported higher self-transcendence and less spirituality than Latin or white individuals did. Higher self-transcendence was related to higher acculturation and experiencing higher energy levels. Higher spiritual well-being was associated with perceiving less depressive symptoms, higher energy levels, and less pain. Cross-sectionally, CD4 cells, viral load, HIV disease stage, and ART were not associated with self-transcendence and spirituality. However, this study did not examine the changes over time.

Very few studies on spiritual growth and health include biological measures. Ironson et al.[18, 19, 28] observed that the four factors of the Ironson-Woods Spirituality/Religiousness Index (sense of peace, faith in god, religious behavior, and compassionate view of others) were associated with lower urinary levels of cortisol and long-survival with HIV. Benefit finding may partially explain the association between spirituality and decreased cortisol levels in the urine.[18] In addition, lower urinary-cortisol levels have been associated with altruistic behavior.[19] Both volunteering for others and lower urinary cortisol levels have been associated with long-survival with HIV. Therefore, these factors could be considered as potential mediators of the relationship between the factors of spirituality/religiousness and long-survival.[19]

Depending on the length of observation, ethnic and gender distribution of the participants, and the tools used to measure the association between HIV disease progression and spirituality/religiousness, various potential pathways have been found to explain the connection between spirituality and health in people living with HIV.

Figure 12.1 illustrates hypothesized pathways between spirituality and health. While there is some evidence for links in the model, the model as a whole needs to be tested within a rigorous design, and in a large sample. As indicated in Figure 12.1, spirituality has been linked to both

Figure 12.1

Hypothesized Pathways from Spirituality to Health in People with HIV/AIDS: According to the literature, spirituality is more prominent in women, nonwhites, individuals who have at least a High School education, or are older than 45 years. Spirituality is linked to slower disease progression and better quality of life, directly and indirectly via finding meaning, benefit, and purpose in life, which is in turn linked to less depressive symptoms, and preserving an optimistic outlook. Beyond taking medication for HIV, less depressive symptoms and a disposition to optimism predict longevity and a better quality of life.

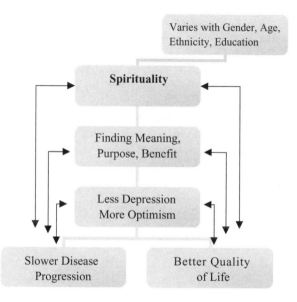

slower disease progression[19, 22, 26, 28] and better quality of life[6, 9, 22, 26] in people living with HIV. Spirituality can be an instrument for finding meaning and purpose[1, 4, 6-8] as well as a bridge to finding benefit in living with the illness. Attributing positive changes to the HIV diagnosis[1, 9, 18, 22-27, 29, 31] and finding new meaning and purpose in living with the illness may partially explain the connection between spirituality and health. In addition, increased spirituality, and perceiving meaning, purpose, and positive change due to the diagnosis are related to less depression,[11, 16, 18-20] more hope,[32, 33] and higher dispositional optimism.[24, 31] These factors are in turn related to improved quality of life and slower disease progression. Spirituality is more prominent in women,[21, 22] non-whites,[21, 22, 25] individuals with education at High School level or above, and an age over 45.[21] Spirituality can have both a negative and a positive impact on coping with HIV,[1,7,12,13,19,23,24,28,30,31] the readiness to take ART and the ability to adhere to ART,[1,12,13,23] the quality of dying[5] and the quality of living.[1,9,13,23,29] Spirituality can be tied to increased or decreased support from family, friends, and religious communities and institutions.[1,21,23] Patients feel that spirituality has helped them to live better[9,31] and longer lives.[24] There is biological evidence for this view, since higher levels of spirituality and spiritual growth were associated with less physiological signs of perceived stress (lower urinary cortisol levels) and slower disease progression (slower CD4 decline and less viral replication).[19,28] Thus, interventions that promote spiritual coping and positive reappraisal may enhance quality and quantity of life in many people living with HIV/AIDS.

Thus, spirituality and religion, at its best, can be very helpful for those who live with HIV/AIDS and likely contribute to better coping with the disease. Furthermore, spirituality can help minimize the risks of so many of the comorbid biopsychosocial problems that can emerge with this condition. Future research is much needed to better understand the relationship between spirituality and HIV/AIDS as well as to develop better interventions for this illness. There is much to learn and do to better help the numerous people who suffer from this challenging illness.

Acknowledgments

The authors wish to thank Lauren Kaplan for her useful comments and suggestions. We would also like to thank the Metanexus/Templeton Foundation for supporting our work on spirituality in people living with HIV.

References

1. Ironson, G., Kremer, H., & Ironson, D. (2006). Spirituality, spiritual experiences, and spiritual transformations in the face of HIV. In J. D. Koss, & P. Hefner (Eds.), *Spiritual transformation and healing: Anthropological, theological, neuroscientific, and clinical perspectives* (1st ed., pp. 241–262). Oxford: AltaMira Press.
2. World Health Organization (2006). *HIV treatment access reaches over 1 million in sub-Saharan Africa, WHO reports.* Retrieved on December 29, 2006, from http://www.who.int/mediacentre/news/releases/2006/pr38/en/index.html.
3. Braithwaite, R. S., Justice, A. C., Chang, C. C., Fusco, J. S., Raffanti, S. R., Wong, J. B., et al. (2005). Estimating the proportion of patients infected with HIV who will die of comorbid diseases. *The American Journal of Medicine, 118,* 890–898.
4. Hall, B. A. (1998). Patterns of spirituality in persons with advanced HIV disease. *Research in Nursing & Health, 21,* 143–153.

5. Pierson, C. M., Curtis, J. R., & Patrick, D. L. (2002). A good death: A qualitative study of patients with advanced AIDS. *AIDS Care, 14,* 587–598.

6. Fryback, P. B. & Reinert, B. R. (1999). Spirituality and people with potentially fatal diagnoses. *Nursing Forum, 34,* 13–22.

7. Barroso, J. & Powell-Cope, G. M. (2000). Metasynthesis of qualitative research on living with HIV infection. *Qualitative Health Research, 10,* 340–353.

8. Barroso, J. (1999). Long-term nonprogressors with HIV disease. *Nursing Research, 48,* 242–249.

9. Tsevat, J., Sherman, S. N., McElwee, J. A., Mandell, K. L., Simbartl, L. A., Sonnenberg, F. A., et al. (1999). The will to live among HIV-infected patients. *Annals of Internal Medicine, 131,* 194–198.

10. Holstad, M. K., Pace, J. C., De, A. K., & Ura, D. R. (2006). Factors associated with adherence to antiretroviral therapy. *The Journal of the Association of Nurses in AIDS Care, 17,* 4–15.

11. Simoni, J. M. & Ortiz, M. Z. (2003). Mediational models of spirituality and depressive symptomatology among HIV-positive Puerto Rican women. *Cultural Diversity & Ethnic Minority Psychology, 9,* 3–15.

12. Parsons, S. K., Cruise, P. L., Davenport, W. M., & Jones, V. (2006). Religious beliefs, practices and treatment adherence among individuals with HIV in the southern United States. *AIDS Patient Care and STDs, 20,* 97–111.

13. Kremer, H., Ironson, G., Schneiderman, N., & Hautzinger, M. (2006). To take or not to take: Decision-making about antiretroviral treatment in people living with HIV/AIDS. *AIDS Patient Care and STDs, 20,* 335–349.

14. Ironson, G., O'Cleirigh, C., Fletcher, M. A., Laurenceau, J. P., Balbin, E., Klimas, N., et al. (2005). Psychosocial factors predict CD4 and viral load change in men and women with human immunodeficiency virus in the era of highly active antiretroviral treatment. *Psychosomatic Medicine, 67,* 1013–1021.

15. Ironson, G., Balbin, E., Stuetzle, R., Fletcher, M. A., O'Cleirigh, C., Laurenceau, J. P., et al. (2005). Dispositional optimism and the mechanisms by which it predicts slower disease progression in HIV: Proactive behavior, avoidant coping, and depression. *International Journal of Behavioral Medicine, 12,* 86–97.

16. Yi, M. S., Mrus, J. M., Wade, T. J., Ho, M. L., Hornung, R. W., Cotton, S., et al. (2006). Religion, spirituality, and depressive symptoms in patients with HIV/AIDS. *Journal of General Internal Medicine, 21, Suppl. 5,* S21–7.

17. Simoni, J. M., Frick, P. A., & Huang, B. (2006). A longitudinal evaluation of a social support model of medication adherence among HIV-positive men and women on antiretroviral therapy. *Health Psychology, 25,* 74–81.

18. Carrico, A. W., Ironson, G., Antoni, M. H., Lechner, S. C., Duran, R. E., Kumar, M., et al. (2006). A path model of the effects of spirituality on depressive symptoms and 24-h urinary-free cortisol in HIV-positive persons. *Journal of Psychosomatic Research, 61,* 51–58.

19. Ironson, G., Solomon, G. F., Balbin, E. G., O'Cleirigh, C., George, A., Kumar, M., et al. (2002). The Ironson-Woods Spirituality/Religiousness Index is associated with long survival, health behaviors, less distress, and low cortisol in people with HIV/AIDS. *Annals of Behavioral Medicine, 24,* 34–48.
20. Coleman, C. L. & Holzemer, W. L. (1999). Spirituality, psychological well-being, and HIV symptoms for African Americans living with HIV disease. *The Journal of the Association of Nurses in AIDS Care, 10,* 42–50.
21. Lorenz, K. A., Hays, R. D., Shapiro, M. F., Cleary, P. D., Asch, S. M., & Wenger, N. S. (2005). Religiousness and spirituality among HIV-infected Americans. *Journal of Palliative Medicine, 8,* 774–781.
22. Milam, J. (2006). Positive changes attributed to the challenge of HIV/AIDS. In L. G. Calhoun & R. G. Tedeschi (Eds.), *Handbook of posttraumatic growth: Research & practice* (1st ed., pp. 214–224). Mahwah, NJ: Erlbaum.
23. Tarakeshwar, N., Khan, N., & Sikkema, K. J. (2006). A relationship-based framework of spirituality for individuals with HIV. *AIDS and Behavior, 10,* 59–70.
24. Cotton, S., Puchalski, C. M., Sherman, S. N., Mrus, J. M., Peterman, A. H., Feinberg, J., et al. (2006). Spirituality and religion in patients with HIV/AIDS. *Journal of General Internal Medicine, 21, Suppl. 5,* S5–S13.
25. Cotton, S., Tsevat, J., Szaflarski, M., Kudel, I., Sherman, S. N., Feinberg, J., et al. (2006). Changes in religiousness and spirituality attributed to HIV/AIDS: Are there sex and race differences? *Journal of General Internal Medicine, 21, Suppl. 5,* S14–S20.
26. Milam, J. (2006b). Posttraumatic growth and HIV disease progression. *Journal of Consulting and Clinical Psychology, 74,* 817–827.
27. Ramer, L., Johnson, D., Chan, L., & Barrett, M. T. (2006). The effect of HIV/AIDS disease progression on spirituality and self-transcendence in a multicultural population. *Journal of Transcultural Nursing, 17,* 280–289.
28. Ironson, G., Stuetzle, R., & Fletcher, M. A. (2006). An increase in Religiousness/Spirituality occurs after HIV diagnosis and predicts slower disease progression over 4 years in people with HIV. *Journal of General Internal Medicine, 21 Suppl. 5,* S62–S68.
29. Siegel, K. & Schrimshaw, E. W. (2000). Perceiving benefits in adversity: Stress-related growth in women living with HIV/AIDS. *Social Science & Medicine, 51,* 1543–1554.
30. Pargament, K. I., McCarthy, S., Shah, P., Ano, G., Tarakeshwar, N., Wachholtz, A., et al. (2004). Religion and HIV: A review of the literature and clinical implications. *Southern Medical Journal, 97,* 1201–1209.
31. Szaflarski, M., Neal Ritchey, P., Leonard, A. C., Mrus, J. M., Peterman, A. H., Ellison, C. G., et al. (2006). Modeling the effects of Spirituality/Religion on patients' perceptions of living with HIV/AIDS. *Journal of General Internal Medicine, 21 Suppl 5,* S28–S38.

32. Phillips, K. D. & Sowell, R. L. (2000). Hope and coping in HIV-infected African-American women of reproductive age. *Journal of National Black Nurses' Association*, *11*, 18–24.
33. Heinrich, C. R. (2003). Enhancing the perceived health of HIV seropositive men. *Western Journal of Nursing Research*, *25*, 367–382; discussion 383–387.

CHAPTER 13

Spirituality at the End of Life: Issues and Guidelines for Care

KATHRYN Z. McNICHOLS AND DAVID B. FELDMAN

Terminal illness challenges dying persons as well as their friends and family with pressing questions of ultimate concern. Confronted with the end of life and its associated experiences of loss, suffering, and human limitation, the dying face a range of issues far broader than their medical diagnoses. These questions of meaning and purpose are spiritual matters, and often are addressed from within a spiritual tradition.

In this chapter, we first define religion and spirituality, initially focusing on the Judeo-Christian traditions that have so shaped the West. These traditions, while still influential, are losing dominance in a postmodern, pluralistic society that values individualism and eclecticism. It is therefore more useful to speak of "spirituality" rather than a religious tradition when discussing people's quest for meaning and transcendence. At the end of life, we believe that this quest focuses primarily on three spiritual issues: suffering and wholeness, finitude and destiny, and hope and hopelessness. Because empirical research on such matters at the end of life is very limited, we focus primarily on theory and clinical observations as we discuss each of these issues and offer suggestions for how to relieve spiritual suffering as people approach death.

General Definitions of Spirituality at the End of Life

Spirituality is a term that has proven difficult to define. Despite this elusive quality, the notion resonates in our postmodern world, as past sources of authority such as religious traditions are called into question and individuals are left to construct meaning as best they can. The term "spirituality" in its very lack of specificity allows for the multiple constructions of meaning that ensue.

It was not always this way. In the West, a Judeo-Christian paradigm governed constructions of the meaning of life and death for the better part of two millennia. The monopoly of the Judeo-Christian worldview began to break down with the challenges of the Reformation and the rise of the scientific method in the Enlightenment.[1] Modern thought, characterized by the examination and revision of all knowledge, understanding, and practice, limits the primacy and privilege of tradition, and encourages the individual to assume responsibility for all choices and commitments.[2] Spirituality, formerly the preserve of religious traditions like Judaism and Christianity, became unmoored from the anchor of its original theological system. With this context lost, spirituality was now free to include elements uniquely attractive to the individual. Consumer culture, which grew out of this same matrix, reinforced this eclectic, individualistic approach to spiritual issues. Thus today, people have the opportunity and the responsibility to choose what is of ultimate significance for them from whatever cultural and religious resources they find compelling.[3]

James Nelson, in his book *The Intimate Connection*, offers a working definition of spirituality that respects this new cultural context, and that can be usefully applied to end-of-life concerns:

> [Spirituality] is simply our basic life orientations and the patterned ways in which we express them. It is the patterning of our thinking, feeling, experiencing, and nurturing of whatever we take to be fundamentally important.[4]

The anticipation of death, felt perhaps throughout life but most acutely at the diagnosis of a terminal illness, confronts people with matters of spirituality and brings them face-to-face with the mystery that is at the heart of human life. The experience of dying and the anticipation of death are events both fascinating and terrifying. Unfortunately, in a society where death is generally a taboo topic, this places one on sacred ground for which many of us are ill-prepared.[5] The impact of this encounter with mystery can be to throw one's life into relief, to reveal as superficial many of one's interests and pursuits and to sharpen one's focus on matters of ultimate significance.

While the individual is negotiating these tumultuous waters at the end of life, he or she is most likely also interacting with a medical profession that frequently views matters very differently.[6] Rather than exploring issues of ultimate concern and spiritual significance to the patient, the medical establishment approaches the patient's body as an object of study and his or her illness as a pathology, a disease to be cured. The model is generally that of the person as a biological entity, a body rather than a body/spirit.

Certainly there are people who face death sharing these medical assumptions. But there are many others who face death in the context of ultimate concerns that transcend their own bodies and their own selves. Their concerns are more complex than the medical model allows. The hospice and palliative care movements emerged partially as a reaction against the view that death was merely a medical event, and the chapters in this volume attest to a similar conviction that body and spirit work in tandem and so can be treated more effectively together than apart.[7]

The Meaning of Death in Western Tradition and Contemporary Practice

The perception that body and spirit are integrated in the human person is a hallmark of Judeo-Christian belief and has therefore informed Western views of the meaning of life and death. So profound was this belief in the sanctity of spirit *and* matter together that, when Jews and Christians imagined life beyond death, they believed that both spirit and body would live, not just the spirit alone. This view of the afterlife remains very important to many patients and families coping with the last chapter of life.

These beliefs built on an ethics drawn from Jewish tradition that deeply honored the care of others. Visiting the sick and burying the dead, for instance, were consistently important in both religions. These works of mercy were institutionalized among religious orders dedicated to the care of the sick and dying. Both the nursing profession and the hospice movement owe their foundations, in part, to such communities of care.

Religious traditions are characterized not only by their stories, beliefs, and social organizations, but also by ritual practices, artistic traditions, and emotional dimensions.[8] Judeo-Christian traditions are replete with examples of behavioral expressions that organize emotional responses to suffering, dying, and death. These include the rituals of anointing the sick, funeral and burial practices, recitation of prayers such as the "Kaddish" in Judaism, official and popular festivals and physical monuments constructed to remember the dead, as well as artistic exploration of religious themes of death and resurrection such as the *memento mori* motif in Western art. These traditions symbolize self-transcendence, a highly important theme in Western religions.[9] "The fundamental desire of the self," according to Walter E. Conn, "is to transcend itself in relationship: to the world, to others, to God."[10] This desire for union with the transcendent source of life—what Ronald Rolheiser calls the "holy longing"—can never be wholly satisfied in this world.[11] Thus death is seen not only as an end, but as a consummation of a desire expressed provisionally throughout one's life.

The cohesive Christian system no longer holds a monopoly on even the Western mindset, however. In fact, it is characteristic of the modern period that no one worldview holds sway. As Cobb points out, some may hold a theistic view, but others have different ways of making sense of human existence. It may be understood in nontheistic, atheistic, ascetic, moral, psychological, and scientific ways.[2] A second factor in the modern landscape is the pluralistic milieu of multiple ethnic communities, each with its own cultural and religious traditions that shape the experience of life and death.[12,13] As mentioned previously, a third factor characterizing the modern world is the syncretism characteristic of an open society, as individuals select compelling practices and beliefs from various traditions to create their own eclectic working mix. All of these factors now shape how an individual makes sense of life and death.

Specific Spiritual Issues at the End of Life

There is a tendency in our culture to view a terminal diagnosis as death itself, as the end of life. But, in fact, the dying process may offer opportunities for growth and reconciliation that bring peace to the dying person.[14] The finality of death can focus a person on matters of ultimate concern, such as issues of suffering and wholeness, human finitude and destiny, and hope and hopelessness. Caregivers have an obligation to address these spiritual matters if they arise, particularly as the dying person becomes more dependent upon them. Below, we address each of these issues in turn.

Suffering and Wholeness

The dying person experiences suffering and hopes for wholeness in myriad ways. Modern medicine largely views suffering in physical terms. Although the phenomenon of suffering certainly includes physical pain, it is a complex matter that also comprises psychosocial-spiritual dimensions. Dr. Eric Cassel was one of the first to explore the larger context of suffering:

> Suffering occurs when an impending destruction of the person is perceived; it continues until the threat of disintegration has passed or the integrity of the person can be restored in some other manner.[15]

He argues that medical providers can exacerbate the suffering of their patients by treating pain as a purely physical matter when it is experienced by the patient within a more complex web of beliefs and relationships. For instance, research shows connections between spirituality, quality of life, and reduced despair, even in the presence of intense physical pain.[16,17,18]

Suffering encompasses a wide array of issues. Physical suffering includes bodily pain along with the emotional distress this pain can provoke. For instance, the presence of pain frequently focuses patients' concerns on the meaning/meaninglessness of suffering and anxieties about the process of dying. This is often compounded by practical concerns, such as the cost of pain relief, the emotional and financial burden that one's illness causes to family and friends, and anxiety about who will be there to provide care as one becomes more dependent. Suffering can also include regret or guilt over choices and missed opportunities in the past or the future—for example, knowing that one will not be able to attend the wedding of one's child, or wishing that one had not chosen work before family. Such regrets are linked to the myriad losses one experiences, from future dreams that can no longer be realized to the gradual loss of physical control. At the end of life, life and health cannot be restored to the person. But, there are a host of ways that integrity and wholeness can be restored short of cure. The reconciliation of broken relationships, the completion of unfinished business, and a network of care that addresses the medical, financial, emotional, spiritual, and practical needs of dying persons and their loved ones all offer opportunities for decreased suffering.

Human Finitude and Destiny

Another cluster of issues that emerge acutely at the end of life deals head-on with death itself. These issues encompass concerns about the meaningfulness of death and therefore life, the value systems that one brings to bear to address that question, and for some persons, images of God and the afterlife that likewise inform their constructions of meaning.

The question of whether death and therefore life are meaningful is a central issue that many dying persons raise. According to a study by Tomer and Eliason, it is one of the three immediate determinants of death anxiety, along with past- and future-related regrets.[19] Whether and how the dying person answers this question depends on many variables, including the specific constellation of beliefs to which the individual subscribes. Cobb observes that this spiritual constellation ranges on a spectrum from highly regulated, patterned beliefs characteristic of a traditional institutional religion, to the fragmentary and disorganized eclecticism that characterizes the postmodern world.[2] Another significant variable affecting constructions of meaning is one's cultural context, which goes beyond particular spiritual beliefs to cultural worldviews, views of illness and death, and patterns of communication.[12,13] Add to these factors one's existing social networks, gender and age, and one begins to appreciate how complex the issue of meaning can be. An additional variable is one's past experience of suffering and loss. Further and perhaps less tangible variables include how important belief is to the person in the first place, and the capacity for and tolerance of faith, mystery, and ambiguity.

For those who place their sense of self within a theistic framework, their particular image of God may affect the meaning they make of their own destiny. Some of the more common images of God are at best benign and at worst malignant, and can contribute to rather than relieve distress. Research demonstrates that these images can even effect decision-making regarding medical care.[20] Examples of potentially malignant images include God as puppeteer or judge. The puppeteer God is one who pulls the human's strings and is revealed in phrases like "My cancer is God's will so I must accept it," or "Why fight it? God must have wanted this to happen to my baby." God as judge often appears when the individual believes that one or more of his or her life choices are irredeemable. Both of these images of God disable human agency by eclipsing human free will. A more neutral image of God is of the clockmaker who creates the entire universe, sets its laws in motion, but does not intervene in human life or death. Contrast this to a beneficent image of a God who is understood to intervene in one's life only for the good.[21] Each of these images has profound implications for one's emotional distress in the face of death. It is also worth remembering that many people do not operate within these theistic frameworks at all. This does not mean that they lack belief, but simply that theism is not part of it. The way they understand the universe and their place in it will color their own sense of limitation and destiny.

Over the course of terminal illness, and as one approaches the end of life, the answers to these questions of suffering and wholeness, finitude and destiny, often change. This is visible even in people's relationship to their diseases, as their goals shift from the search for a cure and ongoing treatments to acceptance that life is coming to an end. We know these stages from the pioneering work of Elizabeth Kübler-Ross who identified denial, anger, bargaining, depression and acceptance as the five stages of grief.[22] Subsequent theorists have supplemented Kübler-Ross's stages with the deeper experiences of surrender and transcendence that lead the individual from the dread of engulfment to the serenity of spiritual transformation.[23]

Hope and Hopelessness

A final spiritual concern for many patients facing terminal illness is the tension between hope and hopelessness. This issue frequently takes center stage when patients are first diagnosed. A diagnosis of cancer, for instance, may initially trigger utter hopelessness. For some, the word "cancer" is synonymous with suffering and death. Because many cancers are not ultimately terminal, however, such hopelessness may quickly give way to hopefulness should treatment begin to work. Unfortunately, hope becomes more complex when treatment fails; under such circumstances, patients are no longer able to maintain hope for a cure. What then occurs is an individual matter. Although some patients maintain hope, others lose it completely.

The *Merriam-Webster Dictionary* defines hope as "to desire with expectation of obtainment."[24] C. R. Snyder offers a similar, though slightly more detailed conceptualization of hope that has been written about extensively during the past two decades.[25] Through research, Snyder concluded that high-hope people tend to share three commonalities, which he termed goals, pathways, and agency.

In order to be hopeful, people first must have something to hope for—a goal. Goals are outcomes that are important to an individual, from academic and work-related concerns, to relational and spiritual outcomes. Goals are known by many names, including objectives, projects, desires, aspirations, and even dreams. Robert Emmons refers to goals of a spiritual nature as "ultimate concerns."[26] To be truly hopeful, however, two additional factors are necessary—pathways and agency. A pathway is a plan or route to a goal. Spiritual pathways differ depending on one's beliefs, but frequently consist of prayer, faith, meditation, and ritual.[27,28] Finally, agency refers to the motivation and confidence necessary to implement one's pathways. As in Watty Piper's *The Little Engine That Could*, agency constantly conjures the thought, "I think I can."[29] Religious Christians may use Bible verses such as "I can do all things through him who strengthens me" (Philippians 4:13 NRSV) and "...for God all things are possible" (Mark 10:27 NRSV) to inspire agency.

For patients with serious illness, the initial goal is usually cure. In our modern medical system, patients have numerous pathways available to them. Their agency is bolstered by the promise of these treatments along with the encouragement and support of their medical providers, friends, and family. Religion and spirituality also can strengthen hope early in the illness progression. Prayer, consultation with pastors, meditation, yoga, and healing rituals all are very important pathways toward cure. Spiritual teachings and convictions also often strengthen agency. In this vein, Kenneth Pargament and his colleagues provide research evidence that individuals who engage in "collaborative religious coping" are motivated to work actively (i.e., agentically) in partnership with God to solve their problems, believing that "God helps those who help themselves."[30]

Studies demonstrate that people with higher hope tend to experience less depression and anxiety, report higher levels of life meaning, and are more likely to accomplish their goals than low-hope individuals.[31,32] It may be that hope also has medically salutary effects. In one study, college-aged women were asked to write down what they would do should they be diagnosed with cancer.[33] High-hope women were able to generate more possible ways to combat their cancer than low-hope women. When quizzed about their cancer knowledge, hopeful people also were better informed. Should cancer actually arise, all this presumably would lead to a "fighting spirit," better utilization of care, and a greater likelihood of cure.

Of course, even with the most exemplary fighting spirit, cancer and other serious illnesses often are not curable. Snyder and Gum suggest what happens in this case.[34] In their experience, most people realize that their diseases are not curable as they watch every treatment pathway fail. As this occurs, their agency also falters and diminishes. Finally, feeling hopeless and demoralized, they may give up the goal of cure. At this point, some choose a care approach such as hospice, which focuses on comfort rather than cure.

It is a mistake to conclude that hope will not return, however. Although some patients remain hopeless, others perform the difficult task of "re-goaling." In other words, they find new goals for which to hope. Hospice providers and other health care professionals can be especially important in helping patients to make this shift. Hope can once again thrive as patients find pathways and agency for accomplishing these new goals. In the last chapter of their lives, patients may set goals of making amends with es-tranged loved ones, getting practical affairs in order, visiting the beach one last time, or sharing important stories and advice with others. As previously noted, terminal illness often sharpens one's focus on matters of ultimate significance. For this reason, these new goals are frequently spiritual in nature. In fact, many patients simply hope to be "okay with God" as their lives draw to a close.[35]

Best Practices: Suggestions for the Care of Dying People

Compassionate care of the dying includes attention to the person's spiritual frameworks and concerns. We would like to offer five suggestions for this care. The first is the caregiver's attention to his or her own spiritual practice. The second and third suggestions address the interactions between the caregiver and the person facing death, namely the careful assessment of spiritual needs and the employment of a life review to help the dying person tend to unfinished business. The fourth suggestion involves the nurturing of hope. And, the fifth suggestion concerns the importance of building inter-disciplinary teams to address the manifold needs of the dying individual as a whole person.

Perhaps the most fundamental thing a caregiver can do for others is to attend to his or her own spiritual beliefs. This reflective practice begins with simple, disciplined attention to one's own values, experiences of loss, and spiritual framework. As Cobb notes, facing death takes both the care-giver and patient to profoundly intimate places.[2] Without being reflective, caregivers run the risk of projecting their own religious beliefs, fears, and un-resolved issues onto the dying person, or worse, avoiding the spiritual needs of the patient entirely. A reflective inner disposition cultivates an openness to difference and ambiguity, inhibits projection, teaches the breadth and complexity of spiritual concerns, and confirms in the caregiver that spiritual matters are an integral aspect of the person under care.

The caregiver who cultivates this self-reflective openness is better posi-tioned to implement our second suggestion, namely the compassionate as-sessment of the dying person's spiritual needs. In a survey of hospitalized adult patients, 77 percent thought that physicians should consider patients' spiritual needs, and 37 percent wanted physicians to discuss religious beliefs more often.[36] L. H. Heyes-Moore describes the process of reverent listening that is so important in the assessment of these needs:

> Effective help implies that the carer is fully present in relationship to the sufferer, person to person, deep calling to deep. The process of helping is based on the ill person finding meaning, through this dialogue, in his or her life experiences. Words, touch, symbolic imagery and rituals may all be vehicles for this unfolding story, which is, in essence, a contemplative process. It may truly be said that a person is healed by this in becoming whole while at the same time dying, so that death itself is not seen as a disaster but part of life.[37]

This approach calls for a genuine human encounter.[38,39] It avoids the simplistic metrics often employed by healthcare providers to diagnose spiritual needs, and allows the dying person to express his or her own issues in familiar terms. This does not mean that time-tested models of spiritual assessment are to be discarded, but rather that they are always secondary to the direct human encounter.[40]

A third practice that can be offered to the dying person is the opportunity for a life review.[41] This helps a person at the end of life to identify those relationships and beliefs in need of attention while one still has time. Life reviews are simply conversations in which the dying person is invited to share his or her history and beliefs. It gives the individual a chance to express all of the aspects of spirituality discussed at the beginning of this chapter, including values, views of God, meanings of life, and beliefs about death and the afterlife. Such conversations have been shown to lessen emotional distress and depression in older adults.[42,43] Although questions used in such a review would address every phase of life, those related particularly to the end of life may include: When you were a child, how was death or dying talked about in your family? What does death mean to you? What about your own death concerns you most? What about the process of dying concerns you most? How large a role has religion played in your attitude toward death? How do you want to spend your time until you pass away? If you had a choice, what kind of death would you prefer? What is one thing you would want to say to someone special before you die? Of course the particular questions and how they are framed depend upon the culture, social network, and beliefs of the dying person, and so it is incumbent upon the caregiver to learn as much as possible about the person in order for the life review to be of most benefit.

As dying individuals review their lives and anticipate their deaths, they react in a variety of ways. Although some feel empowered and wish to fully embrace the time they have left, others fall into hopelessness. In fact, depression is estimated to occur in 25 to 75 percent of people at the end of life.[6] This highlights our fourth suggestion—that everyone caring for the dying person (including healthcare providers, friends, and family members) attempt to nurture the hope of that person. We are not advocating superficially encouraging patients to "look on the bright side," nor are we promoting Pollyanna-like positive thinking. As discussed earlier, hope arises when people have goals for which to hope, are able to generate pathways for accomplishing these goals, and can engender the confidence and agency to get there. Hope can be nurtured by gently encouraging patients to explore what is important to them *now*, in the last chapter of life, and helping them to find pathways for accomplishing these goals.

The complexity of issues at the end of life and their interrelation argue for our final suggestion—that healthcare agencies adopt an interdisciplinary team approach to the needs of the dying person.[44] As we have seen, these needs range from the physical to the spiritual, from the practical to the interpersonal, and they rarely fall into one discrete category. For example, physical pain often raises profound questions about the meaning of suffering, and so cannot be addressed with medication alone. Likewise, a dying person may seek to survive beyond his or her original prognosis because of a deep spiritual need to reconcile a relationship or attend an important family event. These cases cannot be understood through one model of care, nor can they be best addressed by one type of specialist.

The hospice and palliative care movement has recognized the limitations of a purely medical approach that reduces the human person to a disease to be cured. It offers a model that is interdisciplinary, involving medical doctors, nurses, medical social workers, mental health specialists, physical and speech therapists, chaplains, and home health aides. Together, this team is poised to offer comprehensive care of the whole person and to support family members and friends. It is desirable that each of these professionals— not only the chaplain—be open to spiritual aspects of care.[45] In patient-centered care, priority must be given to the messy problems of greatest human concern that present in manifold, interrelated dimensions rather than along our neatly separated disciplinary boundaries.

Conclusion

The care of the whole person at the end of life requires attention to spiritual as well as medical matters. This entails that we expand our traditional notions of spirituality, suffering, and hope. As individuals approach death, they draw on whatever spiritual resources they have cultivated in life as well as those offered to them by caregivers and loved ones. In the intimate human encounter with the dying, caregivers can work as a team to address the suffering of those in their care by tending to their own spiritual practice, carefully attending to patients' spiritual needs, and facilitating a life review. They can cultivate hope in the dying by recognizing that hope thrives when people have goals, pathways, and a sense of personal agency, and that all of these are perhaps being redefined—but are still possible—as the end of life approaches.

References

1. Dupré, L., Saliers, D.E., & Meyendorff, J. (1991). *Christian spirituality: Postreformation and modern, World spirituality: An encyclopedic history of the religious quest 18.* New York: Crossroad.
2. Cobb, M. (2001). *The dying soul: Spiritual care at the end of life, Facing death.* Philadelphia, PA: Open University Press.
3. Miller, V.J. (2004). *Consuming religion: Christian faith and practice in a consumer culture.* New York: Continuum.
4. Nelson, J.B. (1992). *The intimate connection: Male sexuality, masculine spirituality.* London: SPCK.
5. Mitterand, F. (1998). Foreword. In M. De Hennezel, *Intimate death: How the dying teach us how to live,* trans. C.B. Janeway. New York: Vintage.
6. Hallenbeck, J.L. (2003). *Palliative care perspectives.* New York: Oxford University Press.
7. Illich, I. (1976). *Limits to medicine.* London: Penguin.
8. Smart, N. (1996). *Dimensions of the Sacred.* London: HarperCollins.
9. McBrien, R.P. (1994). *Catholicism,* rev. ed. San Francisco, CA: HarperSanFrancisco.
10. Conn, W.E. (1998). *The desiring self: Rooting pastoral counseling and spiritual direction in self-transcendence.* New York: Paulist Press.
11. Rolheiser, R. (1999). *The holy longing: The search for a Christian spirituality.* New York: Doubleday.
12. Gunaratnam, Y. (1997). Culture is not enough. In D. Field, J. Hockey & N. Small (Eds.), *Death, gender and ethnicity* (pp. 166–186). London: Routledge.
13. McLean, M.R. & Graham, M.A. (2003). Reluctant realism. *Issues in Ethics, 14,* 6–9 (Markkula Center for Applied Ethics, Santa Clara University).
14. Byock, I. (1997). *Dying well: The prospect for growth at the end of life.* New York: Riverhead Books.
15. Cassel, E.J. (1982). The nature of suffering and the goals of medicine. *New England Journal of Medicine, 306,* 639–645.
16. McClain, C.S., Rosenfeld, B., & Breitbart, W. (2003). Effect of spiritual well-being on end-of-life despair in terminally-ill cancer patients. *The Lancet, 361,* 1603–1607.
17. McClain-Jacobson, C., Rosenfeld, B., Kosinski, A., Pessin, H., Cinino, J.F., & Breitbart, W. (2004). Belief in an afterlife, spiritual well-being and end-of-life despair in patients with advanced cancer. *General Hospital Psychiatry, 26,* 484–486.
18. Tarakeshwar, N., Vanderwerker, L.C., Paulk, E., Pearce, M.J., Stanislav, K.V., & Prigerson, H.G. (2006). Religious coping is associated with the quality of life

of patients with advanced cancer. *Journal of Palliative Medicine, 9*, 646–657.

19. Tomer, A. & Eliason, G. (1996). Toward a comprehensive model of death anxiety. *Death Studies, 20*, 343–365.

20. Kaldjian, L.C., Jekel, J.F., & Friedland, G. (1998). End-of-life decisions in HIV-positive patients: The role of spiritual beliefs. *AIDS, 12*, 103–107.

21. Ferrell, B. (2005). Ethical perspectives on pain and suffering. *Pain Management Nursing, 6*, 83–90.

22. Kübler-Ross, E. (1976). *On death and dying.* New York: Macmillan.

23. Singh, K.D. (1998). *The grace in dying: How we are transformed spiritually as we die.* San Francisco, CA: HarperSanFrancisco.

24. *Merriam-Webster online open dictionary* (2006). Retrieved on November 30, 2006, from Merriam-Webster Online on the World Wide Web: http://www.merriam-webster.com/dictionary/hope.

25. Snyder, C.R. (1994). *The psychology of hope.* New York: Free Press.

26. Emmons, R.A. (1999). *The psychology of ultimate concerns.* New York: Guilford Press.

27. Snyder, C.R., Sigmon, D.R., & Feldman, D.B. (2003). Hope for the sacred and vice versa: Positive goal-directed thinking and religion. *Psychological Inquiry, 13*, 234–238.

28. Tarakeshwar, N., Pargament, K.I., & Mahoney, A. (2003). Measures of Hindu pathways: Development and preliminary evidence of reliability and validity. *Cultural Diversity and Ethnic Minority Psychology, 9*, 316–332.

29. Piper, W. (1978). *The little engine that could.* New York: Grosset Dunlap.

30. Pargament, K.I., Kennell, J., Hathaway, W., Grevengoed, N., Newman, J., & Jones, W. (1988). Religion and the problem-solving process: Three styles of coping. *Journal for the Scientific Study of Religion, 27*, 90–104.

31. Feldman, D.B. & Snyder, C.R. (2005). Hope and the meaningful life: Theoretical and empirical associations between goal-directed thinking and life meaning. *Journal of Social and Clinical Psychology, 24*, 401–421.

32. Feldman, D.B., Rand, K.L., Wrobleski, K.K., & Snyder, C.R. (2006). Hope and goal attainment: Testing a basic assumption of hope theory. Unpublished manuscript.

33. Irving, L.M., Snyder, C.R., & Crowson, J.J., Jr. (1998). Hope and coping with cancer by college women. *Journal of Personality, 66*, 195–214.

34. Gum, A. & Snyder, C.R. (2002). Coping with terminal illness: The role of hopeful thinking. *Journal of Palliative Medicine, 5*, 883–894.

35. Sulmasy, D.P. (2006). Spiritual issues in the care of dying patients: "...It's okay between me and god." *Journal of the American Medical Association, 8*, 1385–1392.

36. King, D.E. & Bushwick, B. (1994). Beliefs and attitudes of hospital inpatients about faith healing and prayer. *Journal of Family Practice, 39*, 349–352.

37. Heyes-Moore, L.H. (1996). On spiritual pain in the dying. *Mortality, 1*, 297–315.

38. Harrington, A. (2006). The "connection" health care providers make with dying patients. In E. MacKinlay (Ed.), *Aging, spirituality and palliative care* (pp. 169–185). Binghamton, New York: The Haworth Pastoral Press. Published simultaneously in *Journal of Religion, Spirituality Aging, 18.*
39. Pulchalski, C.M. (2002). Spirituality and end of life care: A time for listening and caring. *Journal of Palliative Medicine, 5,* 289–294.
40. Fitchett, G. (1993). *Assessing spiritual needs: A guide for caregivers.* Minneapolis, MN: Augsburg Fortress.
41. Butler, R.N. (1963). The life review: An interpretation of reminiscence in the aged. *Psychiatry, 26,* 65–76.
42. Hanaoka, H. & Okamura, H. (2004). Study on effects of life review activities on the quality of life of the elderly: A randomized controlled trial. *Psychotherapy and Psychosomatics, 73,* 302–311.
43. Serrano, J.P., Latorre, J.M., & Gatz, M. (2004). Life review therapy using autobiographical retrieval practice for older adults with depressive symptomatology. *Psychology and Aging, 19,* 272–277.
44. Connor, S.R., Egan, K.A., Kwilosz, D.M., Larson, D.G., & Reese, D.J. (2002). Interdisciplinary approaches to assisting with end-of-life care and decision making. *American Behavioral Scientist, 46,* 340–356.
45. Hudson, R. (2006). Disembodied souls or soul-less bodies: Spirituality as fragmentation. In E. MacKinlay (Ed.), *Aging, spirituality and palliative care* (pp. 45–57). Binghamton, New York: The Haworth Pastoral Press. Published simultaneously in *Journal of Religion, Spirituality Aging, 18.*

PART 5

ETHICAL ISSUES

CHAPTER 14

Spirituality, Religion, and Health: Ethical Issues to Consider[1]

THOMAS G. PLANTE

While contemporary health care has enjoyed remarkable advances in scientific research and technological advances, it has also rediscovered the ancient wisdom traditions associated with spirituality and religious influences on health and health outcomes.[2–5] There have been a large number of conferences, seminars, workshops, books, and special issues in major professional journals on spirituality and health integration of late. Journals such as the *Journal of the American Medical Association* and *Annals of Behavioral Medicine*, among others, have recently dedicated special issues to this important topic. Furthermore, the new weeklies such as *Time*, *Newsweek*, and *US News and World Report* frequently publish cover stories on the relationship between science and faith with particular attention to the relationship between religious faith and health outcomes.

Taken together, most of the quality research in this area as discussed throughout this book and elsewhere supports the connection between faith and health.[2–5] Furthermore, since the vast majority of Americans (and most others around the globe) consider themselves to be spiritual and/or religious,[6–7] many have been wanting health care professionals to respect, acknowledge, and even integrate spirituality and religious principles into their professional work.[8] Psychology's new focus on "positive psychology" also underscores the desire for a more friendly relationship between religion and mental health services.[9] While research and practice both now support many benefits to the integration of science and religion, some critics have cautioned that this integration of religion and spirituality into health care practice is ethically dangerous.[10,11] They argue that the research support for integration is weak, problematic, ethical conflicts abound, and clergy, not health care professionals, are best suited to address spiritual and religious concerns.[11]

The purpose of this Chapter is to review some of the most compelling ethical issues and principles involved with the integration of spirituality and health and outline an ethics model for reflecting upon potential conflicts with this integration regarding both clinical practice and also research.

A careful review of over 2,500 years of moral philosophy suggests that there are about nine different ways to approach ethical issues and conflicts.[12] These include the justice, utilitarian, absolute moral rules, values, and cultural relativism, among other approaches. While it is beyond the scope of this chapter to review all of the various ethical approaches, I'll highlight the values approach that has been found to be useful in making ethical decisions in an easy-to-use and understandable manner.[13] This approach uses five commonly used values to process and consider all ethical conflicts and issues.

Five Ethical Values: Using the RRICC Approach to Ethical Decision Making

If medicine and related health care fields continue to integrate religious and spiritual matters into their professional work, a variety of important ethical issues must be considered in order to proceed with this integration in a thoughtful, careful, and ethically sound manner. The RRICC model was developed in order to highlight the primary and commonly used values supported in just about all of the ethics codes associated with various health care professions both in the United States and abroad.[13] RRICC stands for the values of respect, responsibility, integrity, competence, and concern. Each of the five values will be defined and then examples will be provided to better understand their use in ethical decision making.

Respect

Sadly, too often highly religious and spiritually minded persons have been either ignored, disrespected, or even pathologized by many healthcare professionals. Their beliefs and lifestyles were often considered uneducated, unscientific, and sometimes harmful. Their religious perspectives and practices were often not respected. The American Psychological Association's Ethics Code[14] and other professional healthcare ethics codes now better articulate the need to respect the beliefs and values associated with religion in the spirit of cultural diversity and to avoid pathologizing those who seek religious and spiritual integration in their healthcare services. While professionals are not required to agree with all faith beliefs and behaviors and even might find some religious beliefs and behaviors destructive to health and well-being, we must be respectful of the religious and spiritual beliefs, behaviors, and traditions of others being sensitive to this aspect of cultural diversity. We also must be respectful of the role of clergy and various spiritual models have in the lives of our religious and spiritual clients. Therefore, we must be sure that we are respectful to those from all religious and spiritual traditions and beliefs without discrimination or bias.

As researchers, we must be respectful of empirically based scientific findings that may seek to find answers to questions we may or may not respect. For example, some professionals are disrespectful toward others who conduct research that examines spiritual and religious questions. When one colleague asked me what I thought of his research on distance prayer that many others thought was "out there," I replied that no serious research question should be "off the table" as long as quality methodological and statistical procedures were followed and no harm was done to participants. Researchers who pride themselves on being empirical and objective can sometimes be anything but these qualities when confronted with research in spiritual and religious dimensions that they find to be unworthy of scientific investigation. This bias is certainly not respectful as well as not being in the best interest of scientific research and clinical applications.

Responsibility

Quality research and polling from multiple sources over many years clearly indicates that most Americans (as well as others from around the world) believe in God, are associated with some religious tradition and type of church, mosque, or temple, desire to be more spiritually fulfilled, and want their healthcare providers to be respectful of their religious and spiritual traditions, beliefs, and practices.[3, 7, 15, 16] Therefore, since religion and spirituality is such an important part of the lives of so many people, it is irresponsible to ignore this critical aspect of peoples' lives as we work with them in healthcare or in other professional services. We have a responsibility to be aware and thoughtful of how religion and spiritual matters impact those with whom we work. Furthermore, when desired by our clients, professionals should work collaboratively with clergy and other religious leaders involved with their pastoral care.[17, 18] Just as we have some responsibility to be aware of the importance and influence of biological, psychological, and social influences on health behavior and functioning, we must also manage the responsibility of being mindful of religious and spiritual influences. Furthermore, we have a responsibility to seek out appropriate consultation and referrals to religious and spiritual professionals such as clergy as needed, just as we do with other healthcare providers when our clients experience relevant medical or psychiatric concerns.

As researchers we must be responsible in the manner in which we conduct our studies. We must use state-of-the-art methodologies, statistics, theory, and conduct our work without an agenda that deviates from the best science and research has to offer. We must be responsible to go where the data leads even if the data supports theories and perspectives contrary to our beliefs and research desires.

Integrity

We are required to act with integrity in being honest, just, and fair with all those with whom we work. Integrity calls us to be sure that we are honest and open about our skills and limitations as professionals and to avoid deception. We should not be dishonest in any way. Integrity asks us to be sure we carefully monitor professional and personal boundaries, which can be easily blurred with healthcare and religion integration. For example, we must remember that we are healthcare professionals and not members of the clergy (assuming this is true for most readers). Even if we are members of a particular religious faith tradition, it does not make us experts in religious areas that were not part of our professional training, development, and licensure process.

Integrity calls us to be honest in our research as well. We must avoid all deception, lying or deception with statistical procedures, and both conduct and publish research findings in an honest, fair, and complete manner. We cannot allow our personal beliefs or research agendas to get in the way of presenting research findings in an honest manner.

Competence

Since the vast majority of graduate and postgraduate training programs in various health care disciplines currently ignore spirituality and religious integration within professional training, how can professionals competently provide the much needed services of integration? Currently, professionals are pretty much on their own to get adequate training and supervision to ensure that they provide state-of-the-art and competent professional services if they plan to integrate spirituality and religion into their professional health care work. Richards and Bergin[5] offer several specific recommendations about training to better ensure competence in spirituality and health care integration among professionals. They suggest that professionals read the quality books and other publications now available on this topic, attend appropriate workshops and seminars, seek out supervision and consultation from appropriate colleagues, and to learn more about the religious and spiritual traditions of the clients they typically encounter in their professional activities. Luckily, there are many quality workshops, conferences, seminars, books, articles, and even special series of professional journals dedicated to religion and spirituality integration in healthcare today. Furthermore, securing ongoing professional consultation with experts in integration is now possible in most locations due to the popularity of this topic. It is important for professionals to be keenly aware of their areas of competence in order to not overstep their limits and skills.

Being attentive to our competence is also important in research. We must carefully select research studies that we are competent to conduct and seek guidance from others who may have the competencies we need but lack. Just being interested in the topic does not make us competent to conduct high quality research in the area. Luckily, there are now many researchers skilled and interested in this area of inquiry who are happily willing to consult and collaborate with others. For example, the spirituality and health special interest group of the Society of Behavioral Medicine has quickly become the largest special interest group of this prestigious national organization and includes numerous willing collaborators and consultants.

Concern

At the heart of the healthcare profession is concern for the well-being and welfare of others. This concern must be nurtured and expressed among those working in the integration of health care and religion area. Unfortunately, many people have suffered a great deal due to religious conflicts and beliefs over the centuries and still do so today. There are too many examples of people being abused, neglected, victimized, and even killed for religious beliefs and behaviors. Sadly, religion and spiritual tensions can be very harmful to others. Our concern for the welfare of people must be paramount in our work in health care and especially with those whose religious beliefs create harm to self or others. Thus, while we are asked to be respectful to those from various religious traditions, this respectfulness has limitations when religious beliefs and behaviors turn violent and destructive. Concern for the welfare of others always trumps other ethical values.[13] Thus, when someone seeks to "kill infidels," support terrorism, or abuse others in the name of their religious beliefs, our concern for others must force us to act to prevent harm. This concern might propel us to report child abuse, to involuntary commit someone to a psychiatric or health care facility, or engage law enforcement to avoid serious harm to self and others.

Concern for others must be reflected in our research activities as well. Giving research participants full and informed consent, being thoughtful of how we conduct our research to ensure the safety and well-being of others is paramount.

By carefully reflecting upon ethical principles that best guide our professional behavior, we are better able to integrate healthcare and religion in ways that can enhance our work. We next turn to several common ethical pitfalls in the religion and health care integration area.

Four Ethical Pitfalls

There are several important ethical pitfalls that can likely emerge among professionals seeking to integrate healthcare and religion. While this list of four pitfalls is certainly not an exhaustive one, they do provide guidance for common ethical dilemmas. Case examples will be provided as well for each pitfall.

1. *Respect issues: Spiritual and religious bias.* As mentioned, most professionals interested in spiritual and religious integration with health care likely come from an active and involved religious tradition. They may feel very comfortable and knowledgeable about their own tradition yet rather uninformed about issues related to other faith traditions. For example, a Christian doctor may know a great deal about the Christian tradition from their denominational perspective (e.g., Catholic, Methodist, Seven Day Adventist) but very little about the non-Christian traditions or even other Christian denominations different from their own. A Jewish professional may know a great deal about the Jewish cultural and religious tradition from within their particular branch of Judaism (e.g., Reform) but may not know very much about other branches (e.g., Orthodox, Reconstructionist) or much about non-Jewish religious traditions. Thus, it becomes important for the professionals to keep their own potential biases in check, most especially when they know little or perhaps are even antagonistic toward particular religious traditions and denominations.

   This may be one of the most critical ethical issues in the spirituality and health integration area. One's religious beliefs, perspectives, and biases can be very strong and may easily seep into professional work in an inappropriate and unethical manner. The following example is somewhat typical of this type of bias.

   > *Case Example: Dr. Z*
   > *Dr. Z. is an evangelical Protestant neurologist who is highly active in his church and faith community. He also serves as a deacon in his church and participates in missionary activities overseas each summer. He enjoys working with patients and bringing spiritual and religious issues into his sessions. However, he believes that unless you accept Jesus as your personal savior, you are doomed to hell. Patients who are either from a different religious group or not interested in religion at all get referred to him since he is well known for his skills in pain control. In a conversation with an agnostic patient who suffers from chronic headaches, he suggests that the patient accepts Jesus*

as his personal savior and further implies that by doing so the
headaches would greatly improve or stop.

Dr. Z has clearly overstepped his professional bounds and has allowed his bias to infringe on his professional work. Regardless of Dr.
Z's religious beliefs, he must keep his bias in check in order to provide professional, ethical, and state-of-the-art services to his clients.
Furthermore, his professional license to practice medicine demands
that he provide competent professional services in a respectful manner
and does not give him license to preach about his religious views. Ongoing consultation or supervision may help him better manage these
potential conflicts.

2. *Integrity issues: Blurred boundaries and dual relationships.* In another
common ethical dilemma, many health care professionals who are
active members of a religious tradition may secure ongoing referrals
from their clergy or church community group. This creates boundary
conflicts when the professionals now treat or evaluate many members
of their own faith or church community. Many religious and spiritual
people desire to work with professionals who share their faith tradition and interests. Therefore, it would be common for church members
to refer to a member of their own group. There are rarely hard and
fast rules about these potential boundary conflicts other than avoiding possible exploitation of others and confused roles. Taking into
consideration the nature of the professional work, the size of the religious congregation, the type of possible dual relationships that might
emerge, and the need for clarity of roles and responsibilities all need
to be carefully considered.

Furthermore, professionals who integrate spirituality and health
care usually are active in some faith tradition. But being an active
and involved member of a church or religious group doesn't make
someone an expert in that area of theology and pastoral care. Thus,
if clients are well aware of the professional's religious affiliation, they
may seek spiritual, theological, or pastoral guidance, which may not
be in the area of professional competence of the provider. Healthcare
professionals may inappropriately and unethically usurp the role of
the clergy in these situations. Thus, keeping these boundaries clear
and knowing when to consult with and refer to others is vitally
important.

Case Example: Dr. F
Dr. F is active in her reform Jewish temple, serving on various
committees and attending both regular religious services and var-
ious ongoing study groups. Since she is well known to her faith

community, she regularly gets referrals from the rabbi, cantor, and fellow congregants to provide internal medicine services to members of the Jewish community in the area. Dr. F welcomes these referrals and very much enjoys working with others who share her faith and cultural tradition. However, several challenging ethical dilemmas emerge quickly. One of her patients is HIV positive from an extramarital affair where the spouse and family are unaware of both the affair and medical condition. Since the family are members of the same faith community, Dr. F. interacts with them regularly at temple events.

Dr. F could have avoided this ethical dilemma by being more thoughtful about who to accept as patients and who to refer to other professionals. Dr. F may have developed a plan that would have minimized ethical binds by being very selective in the cases she takes on (if any) from her own temple. Perhaps she could accept referrals from congregants from another temple while referring members of her own temple to another appropriate professional located nearby.

It is reasonable and understandable that Dr. F would get referrals from her religious community who get to know and trust her over time as a member of a shared faith tradition and community. She must thoughtfully consider potential dual relationships and the many potential unforeseen consequences of blending her spiritual and professional life. While she may choose not to rigidly refuse to professionally treat or collaborate with any members of her temple, she must at least carefully consider how to interact with them during any possible professional interaction and carefully weigh the pros and cons of all of these collaborations.

3. *Competence issues: A member of a faith tradition doesn't make one an expert.* Just because a healthcare professional is a member of a particular faith tradition doesn't mean that he/she is either an expert in that tradition or can integrate spirituality and religion into his/her professional work. Members of faith traditions vary greatly in their knowledge and comfort level and thus professionals must be cautious in using their spiritual and religious knowledge with their clients in a manner that appears that they are experts in their faith tradition. Furthermore, they must be sure that they do not usurp the role of clergy in their work. They must avoid falling into pastoral care, spiritual direction, or theological consultation if they are not competent to do so or if their professional role does not include these areas of competence or expertise.

Case Example: Ms. O
Ms. O is a Catholic hospice nurse who is well known for her work

with the Catholic Church. Her patient experiences a great deal of guilt that she attributes to her strict Irish Catholic background. She has cancer and worried about how her thoughts, behaviors, and impulses might be sinful. She knows that Ms. O is a Catholic and asks if some of her most embarrassing thoughts and feelings, which she is too uncomfortable discussing with her priest, might be sins. She asks questions about life after death and about Church teaching on a variety of topics. While Ms. O has thoughts on these matters as a Catholic, she informs her that these types of questions are best addressed in spiritual direction with a clergy person or church professional but that others can help with the feelings and coping strategies associated with her beliefs.

Ms. O has carefully articulated her area of competence and tries to provide her with appropriate referrals to help address her religious questions. Ms. O may certainly be tempted to express her views on religious matters but must be mindful of her professional obligations to practice her services within the boundaries of her training and licensure. She also must be careful to refer to other professionals (including members of the clergy) to help her client better understand religious teachings and theological understandings of sin and other religious concepts within her faith tradition.

4. *Concern issues: Destructive religious beliefs and behaviors.* Tragically, religious beliefs can lead people to engage in highly destructive and lethal behaviors. While terrorism and suicide bombing in the name of religion are extreme examples, less fatal yet still destructive behaviors occur in the name of religion. For example, parents of particular religious traditions refuse medical treatment for sick children or believe that physical punishment of children and spouses is acceptable. Some believe that circumcision should be conducted on adolescent girls. Others believe denying females medical services is the right thing to do. We certainly cannot be complacent or condone destructive thoughts, feelings, and behaviors most especially when they result in significant physical or mental harm, abuse, or neglect as defined by both legal and ethical definitions. Our concern for the welfare of others, as well as both the legal and ethical mandates to protect others from harm, force us to act when religious and spiritual beliefs put our clients or others at risk.

Case Example: Dr. S
Dr. S treats a family who maintain very conservative religious beliefs in the Scientology Church. The parents refuse to engage medical professionals to treat their child suffering from cancer. Doctors believe that the child can easily live a normal lifespan

with medical intervention but will likely die rather soon without it.

While Dr. S may be respectful of the parent's religious tradition and beliefs, he cannot condone the disregard for the medical well-being of the child. Dr. S would likely need to make a child protective services report to increase the chances of medical attention for the child. In most jurisdictions, Dr. S would be a mandated reporter of child abuse and neglect and is legally required to report any reasonable suspicion of abuse or neglect to civil authorities for further investigation. Even if abuse and neglect is justified by the client based on religious reasons, the professional is still mandated to break the confidentiality arrangement and report the abuse or neglect.

Conclusion

Medicine and spiritual integration is likely to continue to evolve and develop in ways that will hopefully benefit patients and others.[19, 20] Americans as well as most of the world's population tend to be religious and spiritual[6] and thus those highly engaged and involved with spiritual and religious issues are likely to find their way to healthcare professionals. Ongoing quality research has begun and will likely continue to apply state-of-the-art research methodologies to spiritual and medical integration topics that will provide a more solid scientific foundation for this integration.[2, 3, 21] Spiritual and healthcare integration is unlikely to be a trendy fad.[8] People have been interested in spiritual and religious matters for thousands of years. It is only more recently that modern medicine and healthcare as professions and as disciplines has evolved to better accommodate and accept these interests and perspectives into their professional work.[8, 9, 19]

Thus, it appears clear that healthcare and spiritual integration is here to stay and likely has many benefits for both professionals and the public.[8, 15] Closely monitoring ethical issues that emerge or are likely to emerge during the course of our professional work is critical. Being thoughtful of ethical principles such as respect, responsibility, integrity, competence, and concern for others (RRICC) as well as possible ethical dilemmas and getting appropriate training and ongoing consultation can greatly help the professional navigating these often very challenging waters.

References

1. Parts of this Chapter have been presented elsewhere and most especially in T.G. Plante, Integrating spirituality and psychotherapy: Ethical issues and principles to consider. *Journal of Clinical Psychology*, in press.

2. Plante, T.G. & Sherman, A.S. (Eds.) (2001). *Faith and health: Psychological perspectives*. New York: Guilford.

3. Koenig, H.G., McCullough, M.E., & Larson, D.B. (2001). *Handbook of religion and health*. New York: Oxford.

4. Pargament, K.I. (1997). *The psychology of religious coping: Theory, research, practice*. New York: Guilford.

5. Richards, P.S. & Bergin, A.E. (1997). *A spiritual strategy for counseling and psychotherapy*. Washington, DC: American Psychological Association.

6. Gallup, G. (2006). *The Gallup Poll: Public opinion 2006*. Wilmington, DE: Scholarly Resources.

7. Myers, D. (2000). *The American paradox: Spiritual hunger in a land of plenty*. New Haven, CT: Yale University Press.

8. Miller, W.R. (Ed.) (1999). *Integrating spirituality into treatment*. Washington, DC: American Psychological Association.

9. Lopez, S.J. & Snyder, C.R. (Eds.), (2003). *Positive psychological assessment: A handbook of models and measures*. Washington, DC: American Psychological Association.

10. Sloan, R.P., Bagiella, E., & Powell, T. (1999). Religion, spirituality, and medicine. *Lancet, 353*, 664–667.

11. Sloan, R.P., Bagiella, E., & Powell, T. (2001). Without a prayer: Methodological problems, ethical challenges, and misrepresentations in the study of religion, spirituality, and medicine. In T.G. Plante & A.C. Sherman (Eds.), *Faith and health: Psychological perspectives* (pp. 339–354). New York: Guilford.

12. Rachels, J. (2003). *The elements of moral philosophy* (4th ed.). New York: McGraw-Hill.

13. Plante, T.G. (2004). *Do the right thing: Living ethically in an unethical world*. Oakland, CA: New Harbinger.

14. American Psychological Association (2002). Ethical principles of psychologists and code of conduct. *American Psychologist, 57*, 1060–1073.

15. Hartz, G.W. (2005). *Spirituality and mental health: Clinical applications*. Binghamton, New York: Haworth Pastoral Press.

16. Koenig, H. G. (1997). *Is religion good for your health? The effects of religion on physical and mental health*. Binghamton, New York: Haworth Pastoral Press.

17. McMinn, M.R. & Dominquez, A.W. (2005). *Psychology and the church*. Hauppauge, New York: Nova Science.

18. Plante, T.G. (1999). A collaborative relationship between professional psychology and the Roman Catholic Church: A case example and suggested principles for success. *Professional Psychology: Research and Practice, 30*, 541–546.

19. Miller, W.R. & Thoresen, C.E. (2003). Spirituality, religion, and health: An emerging research field. *American Psychologist, 58*, 24–35.

20. Sperry, L. & Shafranske, E.P. (Eds.), (2005). *Spiritually oriented psychotherapy*. Washington, DC: American Psychological Association.

21. Hill, P. & Pargament, K.I. (2003). Advances in the conceptualization and measurement of religion and spirituality: Implications for physical and mental health research. *American Psychologist, 58*, 64–74.

About the Editors and Contributors

Editors

THOMAS G. PLANTE, PhD, ABPP, is professor and chair of psychology at Santa Clara University and adjunct clinical associate professor of psychiatry and behavioral sciences at Stanford University School of Medicine. He also founded and directs the Spirituality and Health Institute at Santa Clara University. He has authored, coauthored, edited, or coedited ten books including *Sin against the Innocents: Sexual Abuse by Priests and the Role of the Catholic Church* (Greenwood, 2004); *Bless Me Father for I Have Sinned: Perspectives on Sexual Abuse Committed by Roman Catholic Priests* (Greenwood, 1999); *Faith and Health: Psychological Perspectives* (2001, Guilford); *Do the Right Thing: Living Ethically in an Unethical World* (2004, New Harbinger); *Contemporary Clinical Psychology* (1999, 2005, Wiley); and *Mental Disorders of the New Millennium* (Vols. I, II, III, 2006, Greenwood). He has also published well over 100 professional journal articles and book chapters. He is a fellow of the American Psychological Association, the American Academy of Clinical Psychology, and the Society of Behavioral Medicine. He maintains a private practice in Menlo Park, CA.

CARL E. THORESEN, PhD, is professor emeritus of education and, by courtesy, psychology, and psychiatry/behavioral science at Stanford University. He is also a senior fellow in the Spirituality and Health Institute at Santa Clara University. He was a founding fellow in the Society of Behavioral Medicine in the late 1970s. In the late 1980s he began examining the role of spiritual factors in health. He established and continues to chair a Special Interest Group within Behavioral Medicine on spirituality. He also served on the expert panel of Office of Behavioral and Social Sciences at the National Institutes of Health, coediting articles on spirituality, religion, and health published in a special section of the *American Psychologist* in 2003. Author of over 175 articles and book chapters and eight books [most recently *Forgiveness: Theory, Research and Practice* (2000)] he continues to lead groups and conduct research on spiritual practices and health.

Contributors

ALBERT BANDURA, PhD, is David Starr professor of social sciences in psychology at Stanford University.

RICHARD A. BOLLINGER is a graduate student in clinical psychology at Biola University.

JILL E. BORMANN, PhD, RN, is a research nurse scientist at the VA San Diego Healthcare System.

SIAN COTTON, PhD, is an assistant professor at the University of Cincinnati and a research scientist at the VA Medical Center in Cincinnati.

DIANE E. DREHER, PhD, is a professor of English and director of faculty formation at Santa Clara University.

DAVID B. FELDMAN, PhD, is an assistant professor of counseling psychology at Santa Clara University.

CAROL LEE FLINDERS, PhD, has taught courses on mysticism at the University of California, Berkeley, and the Graduate Theological Union, Berkeley. Her most recent book is *Enduring Lives: Portraits of Women of Faith and Action* (Tarcher/Putnam).

TIM FLINDERS studied English and Sanskrit literature at the University of California, Berkeley, and is coauthor of *The Making of a Teacher* (Nilgiri) and *The RISE Response: Illness, Wellness, & Spirituality* (Crossroad).

DANIEL H. GROSSOEHME, DMin, BCC, serves as a staff chaplain at Cincinnati Children's Hospital Medical Center. He is an Episcopal priest and a board-certified chaplain.

PETER C. HILL, PhD, is a professor of psychology at Biola University.

GAIL IRONSON, MD, PhD, is a psychiatry and psychology professor at the University of Miami, Florida.

KATIE J. KOPP is a graduate student in clinical psychology at Biola University.

HEIDEMARIE KREMER MD, PhD, is a psychiatry and psychology professor at the University of Miami, Florida.

KEVIN S. MASTERS, PhD, is an associate professor of psychology and director of clinical training at Syracuse University.

KATHRYN Z. McNICHOLS, MEd, MDiv, is a former community liaison manager at Hospice of the Valley, San Jose, CA.

DOUG OMAN, PhD, is an adjunct assistant professor at the school of public health, University of California, Berkeley.

MICHELLE PEARCE, MA, is currently a medical psychology intern at Duke University Medical Center completing her doctoral degree in clinical psychology at Yale University.

SHAUNA L. SHAPIRO, PhD, is an assistant professor of counseling psychology at Santa Clara University and adjunct clinical faculty of medicine and behavioral sciences at the University of Arizona School of Medicine, Integrative Medicine Program.

ALLEN C. SHERMAN, PhD, is director of behavioral medicine and associate professor in the department of otolaryngology at Arkansas Cancer Research Center and the University of Arkansas for Medical Sciences.

STEPHANIE SIMONTON, PhD, is director of program development in behavioral medicine and associate professor in the department of otolaryngology at Arkansas Cancer Research Center and the University of Arkansas for Medical Sciences.

JOEL TSEVAT, MD, MPH, is a professor of medicine at the University of Cincinnati and the director of health services research and development at the VA Medical Center in Cincinnati.

AMY B. WACHHOLTZ, PhD, MDiv, is a clinical associate faculty member at the Duke University Medical Center in the division of medical psychology.

ROGER WALSH MD, PhD, is professor of psychiatry, philosophy, and anthropology, and adjunct professor of religious studies at the University of California at Irvine. His publications include the books *Paths Beyond Ego: The Transpersonal Vision*, *Essential Spirituality: The Seven Central Practices*, and *The World of Shamanism*.

Index